WHY ABM?

WHY ABM?

Policy Issues in the Missile Defense Controversy

Edited by

Johan J. Holst & William Schneider, Jr.

With Contributions from:

Frank E. Armbruster
Donald G. Brennan
Raymond D. Gastil
Charles M. Herzfeld
Johan J. Holst
Herman Kahn
William Schneider, Jr.
Michael E. Sherman
Albert Wohlstetter

A Collection of Papers by
Staff and Fellow Members of Hudson Institute

PERGAMON PRESS
New York • Toronto • Oxford • London • Mexico City
Edinburgh • Sydney • Paris • Braunschweig • Tokyo • Buenos Aires

PERGAMON PRESS INC.
Maxwell House, Fairview Park, Elmsford, N.Y. 10523

PERGAMON OF CANADA LTD.
207 Queen's Quay West, Toronto 117, Ontario

PERGAMON PRESS LTD.
Headington Hill Hall, Oxford;
4 & 5 Fitzroy Square, London W. 1

PERGAMON PRESS S.A.
Villalongin 32, Mexico 5, D.F.

PERGAMON PRESS (SCOTLAND) LTD.
2 & 3 Teviot Place, Edinburgh 1

PERGAMON PRESS (AUST.) PTY. LTD.
Rushcutters Bay, Sydney, N.S.W.

PERGAMON PRESS S.A.R.L.
24 rue des Ecoles, Paris 5e

VIEWEG & SOHN GmbH
Burgplatz 1, Braunschweig

PERGAMON PRESS DIVISION
Barton Trading K.K.
French Bank Building,
1-1-2 Akasaka, Minato-ku, Tokyo

Printed in the United States of America

08 015625 8

CONTENTS

CONTENTS

Part II: Alternative BMD Deployments and Rationales

Part III: Interactions with Other Policy Areas

CONTENTS

Part IV: Some Other Perspectives

ACKNOWLEDGMENTS

THIS VOLUME could never have been completed without the wholehearted support and cheerful cooperation of all the contributors. We had many long debates about the contents of particular sentences, paragraphs, and sections of the various chapters as well as the structure of the arguments. We hope and believe that this process did not result in any lasting animosity towards the editors. The editors owe a particular debt of gratitude to the President of Hudson Institute, Max Singer, and its Director, Herman Kahn, for their advice and encouragement. Through the successive drafts of this volume, other members of the professional staff, especially Edward S. Boylan and Andrew J. Pierre, furnished helpful criticism and assistance. Nancy M. Kavenagh applied skill and tolerant patience to the preparation of the index.

A special expression of appreciation is required for those of the Hudson Institute support staff who labored above and beyond the call of duty to meet the impossible and erratic demands of the editors. We want to thank, in particular, Helen Iadanza, Anne Marsek and Mary Mitchell, and also Cecelia Deighton, Rosa Dogan, Nance Glass, Ann Marie Hampson, Brenda Horton, Jean Robinson, Lucille Schwartz and Lucy Stephenson. Sylvia M. Halpern of Pergamon Press was an exceptionally helpful and patient copy editor.

Some portions of three of the chapters in this volume have appeared elsewhere (parts of Chapter 4 in *Fortune,* June 1969, of Chapter 5 in *Adelphi Papers* #43, 1967 and *Foreign Affairs,* April 1969, and of Chapter 8 in *Adelphi Papers* #43, 1967). We are grateful to The Council on Foreign Relations, *Fortune* and the Institute for Strategic Studies for permission to incorporate the material into the expanded essays included in this volume.

J.J.H. & W.S.

INTRODUCTION

THE PROBLEM of devising and deploying defenses against ballistic missiles has confronted policy-makers for almost a decade. The debate over such deployment has at various times emphasized the technical aspects, and,at other times, the political aspects have been in the forefront. At no time has either component been absent. With the September 1967 decision of the Johnson Administration (ratified later, although in modified form by the Nixon Administration) to deploy an operational system to defend the U.S. against at least some types of nuclear attack, the issues, once almost the exclusive domain of national security specialists, have now received widespread public attention. In this process, however, many of the important (even crucial) issues involved have become obscured by a bewildering barrage of conflicting statements by scientists, political figures, and other opinion leaders.

The present volume does not purport to be balanced in the sense of containing the views of both fervent advocates and impassioned opponents of ballistic missile defense. All of the contributors are either friendly to some form of missile defense or feel that the issue remains open. We do feel, however, that the volume as a whole is balanced in the sense of presenting an analytical and, given the assumptions laid down by the authors, fair evaluation of the various issues. Clearly some chapters are more polemical than others. To some extent this is a matter of style as much as of conviction. There is no chapter outlining the case against any missile defense deployment, although the reader will find most of the arguments against ABM mentioned in various contexts. The opponent of ABM will find most of the facts which are relevant to his argument in the present volume. Those who are interested in studying the case against ABM may be referred to the bibliography for specific references.

In particular, we want to emphasize that the present volume is not focused on any particular deployment decision of present or past Administrations. The analyses address issues which are associated with missile defenses in general and with a wide spectrum of potential deployment configurations.

All of the contributors to the present volume are staff members of the Hudson Institute, except Dr. Herzfeld and Professor Wohlstetter who are both Fellow Members of the Institute. We should emphasize that the points of view expressed by the contributors to this volume do not reflect the general political position of the Hudson Institute staff, or more important, the position of the organization or its Board and Members. A cursory examination of the list of Fellow and Public Members suggests that there is probably something like an even split on the ABM issue. The analyses contained in this book should illustrate, moreover, that the issues involved are much more complex than what is suggested by a simple pro-con dichotomy.

We have found it useful to consider the problem of missile defenses in three broad categories. The first of these concerns the background and context of missile defense deployment (Part I). This area is the only one where the technical and political issues overlap—the essence of the missile defense problem is political, not technical. To introduce the reader to the jargon of missile defense and place the recent debate over the deployment of the Safeguard system in perspective, William Schneider, Jr. ("Missile Defense Systems: Past, Present, and Future") discusses early attempts at the resolution of the technical difficulties as well as the representatives of the current state-of-the-art, the Sentinel-Safeguard systems. Some future concepts of ballistic missile defense are also discussed in this connection.

Charles M. Herzfeld discusses in considerable detail ("Missile Defense: Can It Work?") some issues concerning the efficacy of currently programmed missile defense systems with respect to the range of potential threats posed by adversaries. This chapter aims first of all at identifying and asking the relevant questions.

Given a workable missile defense system, Raymond D. Gastil ("Missile Defense and Strategic Doctrine") considers the role of doctrine in our evaluation of ballistic missile defenses. This essay serves as a useful introduction to the political discussion in the remaining sections of the book which consider alternative deployments and some of the most relevant policy considerations.

In Part II, Herman Kahn presents the case for the immediate deployment of a "thin" defense—approximately represented by the proposed Safeguard program recently announced by the Nixon Administration ("The Case for A Thin System"). The two major alternative missile defense deployments seriously considered—the defense of population centers and the exclusive defense of strategic forces—are presented respectively by Donald G. Brennan ("The Case for Population Defense") and Albert Wohlstetter ("The Case for Strategic Force Defense").

Part III analyzes some of the most important policy issues involved in any deployment decision. The reaction of the Soviet Union has become a crucial issue in the debate over the arms race implications of the U.S. deployment of ballistic missile defenses. Johan J. Holst examines Soviet attitudes and behavior in regard to active defense in general and missile defense in particular ("Missile Defense, The Soviet Union and The Arms Race").

Any significant change in U.S. strategic weapon procurement policy has implications for America's alliance relationships, especially as they affect the credibility of the American commitment. The issue has been raised most urgently with respect to U.S. relations with our NATO allies. Some of the important issues in this connection are weighed by Johan J. Holst in "Missile Defense: Implications for Europe."

Another question frequently raised during the debate over missile defense is its impact on the future process of nuclear proliferation. Michael E. Sherman ("Missile Defense and Nuclear Proliferation: Friends or Enemies?") explores the interactions between Superpower BMD systems and the incentives and interests of the non-nuclear powers.

The possibility of an "irrational China" has been one of the principal official justifications offered by both the Johnson and Nixon Administrations for their respective Sentinel and Safeguard systems. Frank E. Armbruster considers this and alternative scenarios of Chinese behavior in "The Problem of China."

Although the once-vociferous debate in the early 1960's over passive (i.e. civil) defense has become of interest only to professional analysts, the relationships between active defense, passive defense, and offensive forces remain important if missile defense is to be seriously considered as a national policy option. Raymond D. Gastil ("Civil Defense and Missile Defense") weighs the issues involved.

Part IV contains some further perspectives which are relevant to an examination of the issues involved. It is now almost certain that the United States and the Soviet Union will enter into a series of talks aimed at a limitation, reduction or regulation of strategic weapons, including ABM. In "Strategic Arms Control and Stability: A Retrospective Look" Johan J. Holst considers the last attempt by the superpowers at serious discussions of strategic force issues, the 1958 surprise attack conference, and asks what lessons can be drawn from it. Finally, Herman Kahn ("The Missile Defense Debate in Perspective") offers his analysis of the debate over the ballistic missile defense issue and tries to place the present volume within the context of that debate.

JOHAN J. HOLST
and
WILLIAM SCHNEIDER, JR.

Croton-on-Hudson, N. Y.
May 28, 1969

Part I

BACKGROUND AND CONTEXT

Chapter 1

MISSILE DEFENSE SYSTEMS: PAST, PRESENT, AND FUTURE

by William Schneider, Jr.

FEW TASKS ever assigned to the defense research community have been as difficult to fulfill technically as the problem of devising defenses against ballistic missiles. The development of ballistic missile defense (BMD)[1] systems has undergone considerable evolution since the major research and development effort was begun in 1956. The evolution of BMD systems has, however, primarily been a refinement of the basic concept of ballistic missile interception defined at the outset of the BMD research program. The incoming warhead is detected and tracked by some combination of radars. The information obtained by the radars is interpreted and processed by sophisticated computer facilities. The destruction of the incoming warhead is accomplished by an interceptor (missile) warhead exploding in the vicinity. of the incoming warhead. The sheer magnitude of the task, intercepting an enemy warhead traveling at four miles per second with an interceptor traveling much more slowly, seemed to give meaning to the metaphor of "hitting a bullet with a bullet."

[1]Ballistic missile defense (BMD) is used frequently in this volume rather than ABM (anti-ballistic missile) on the grounds that the former is a more generic expression not specifically tied to any given solution to the problem of providing defenses against ballistic missiles.

3

EARLY MISSILE DEFENSE CONCEPTS

Despite the discouraging prognosis for the successful resolution of the problem of devising defenses against ballistic missiles, research work began in 1956 on the Nike Zeus ballistic missile defense system.

As the Nike Zeus system developed, it became necessary to design and build separate radars for each of the functions necessary to eventually intercept the incoming ballistic missile warhead. These functions include:

acquisition:	the detection of the incoming enemy warhead
target track:	the tracking of the incoming enemy warhead with sufficient precision to permit a successful intercept
discrimination:	to distinguish between the true warhead and decoys or other objects
missile track:	to track the interceptor missile so that it can accurately complete the intercept.

Moreover, since Nike Zeus was a terminal/late mid-course defense[2] system, these facilities would have to be duplicated for each city which required protection.

By 1962, the Nike Zeus system had successfully intercepted its first inter-continental ballistic missile (ICBM) on a test firing from the Pacific test range at Kwajalein Atoll. Further tests conducted on ICBM's fired from Vandenberg Air Force Base (California) demonstrated the feasibility of the technique of interception, but it also became clear that the Nike Zeus system had limitations which would make deployment of the system undesirable.

[2]All ballistic missile defense systems ever seriously considered for deployment have been either "area" or "terminal" defense or some combination thereof. An area defense permits coverage for thousands of square miles (e.g. about 12 area defense missile batteries can provide protection for the entire continental U.S.). Terminal defense on the other hand, can only afford protection for a few hundred square miles—typically the size of a city. Thus many terminal defense batteries would be required for complete protection of the U.S. population.

Perhaps the most significant limitation with respect to the Nike Zeus interceptor itself was its slow speed (about one-fourth the speed of an ICBM warhead). This limitation required the interceptor to be fired while the ICBM warhead was at a considerable distance from the point of impact. Under these circumstances, interception had to be carried out above the atmosphere so the defense could not take advantage of the ability of the atmosphere to filter out decoys. Thus the use of decoys of a relatively simple variety would be an attractive option for the attacking forces. The fact that the radars used in the Nike Zeus were mechanically rather than electronically steerable (i.e. changes in the direction of the radar beam were carried out by mechanically rotating the radar antenna rather than having the beam directed electronically from a fixed radar face) made it possible for the system to be overwhelmed by relatively simple offensive tactics. Despite the fact that the system was not effective enough to be deployed (although some advocated deployment), Defense Department officials associated with the project considered the program successful because of the information it provided for future missile defense development.[3]

Early in 1963, research was initiated on a new ballistic missile defense system, designated Nike X. There appeared to be no small amount of optimism that a truly effective operational ballistic missile defense system could be developed because of favorable changes in technology associated with missile defense. Perhaps the most significant development was the availability of operational phased-array radar. This development made heavy missile defense feasible by making it possible to overcome a major weakness of the earlier Nike Zeus: the susceptibility of its radars to being overwhelmed by a heavy attack. To overcome the obvious vulnerability of Nike Zeus resulting in its inability to complete intercepts in the atmosphere (where chaff, decoys, and other light objects would be filtered out), the high acceleration Sprint missile was developed.

[3]Testimony of Daniel J. Fink (Former Deputy Director of Defense Research and Engineering for Strategic and Space Systems), *Strategic and Foreign Policy Implications of ABM Systems,* Hearings Before the Subcommittee on International Organization and Disarmament Affairs of the Committee on Foreign Relations, U.S. Senate, Part 1, March 6, 1969, p. 22.

WHY ABM?

The mechanically steerable radars used in Nike Zeus were replaced by several types of phased-array radars.[4] These radars make the "traffic handling" capability of the system much greater because the radar signal can be steered electronically across the horizon in microseconds tracking many objects simultaneously. The Nike X system later included the *area* defense concept (to be utilized in the Sentinel-Safeguard systems) by incorporating the Spartan missile. Unlike the Sprint, the Spartan missile performed the intercept of the enemy warhead above the atmosphere by the detonation of a high yield (in the megaton range) nuclear warhead which destroys the ICBM by the release of X-rays. This system was designed primarily against a massive Soviet attack. The Nike X system was explicitly considered for both "light" and "heavy" deployments by the Johnson Administration. The anticipated costs of both postures (the "A" posture having perhaps two thousand interceptors, and the "B" posture having perhaps four thousand interceptors) is shown below.

TABLE I

TWO U.S. NIKE X DEPLOYMENTS

	Posture A $ billion	Posture B $ billion
Radars [TACMAR, PAR, MSR] Invest. Cost	6.5	12.6
Interceptors [Spartan, Sprint] Invest. Cost	2.4	4.8
DoD Invest. Cost	8.9	17.4
AEC Invest. Cost	1.0	2.0
Total Invest. Cost (ex. R&D)	9.9	19.4
Annual Operating Cost	0.38	0.78

[4]These radars included a powerful, long-range Multifunction Array Radar (MAR), a smaller version of MAR, called TACMAR. Other radars, also used in the Sentinel-Safeguard systems are the Perimeter Acquisition Radar (PAR) for long-range detection, and Missile Site Radar (MSR) for the control of Spartan-Sprint interceptors from launch. The MAR, because of its high cost (about $400 million) was not included in later Nike X deployment schemes.

The Nike X system was not, however, approved for deployment. One former senior Department of Defense official has noted that:

> The reasons were severalfold, but at least included the following: It was a very expensive terminal defense system which for a given amount of money could provide protection to some number of cities, but leaving many totally unprotected, and it suffered the flaw of any terminal defense system—namely, that every piece contributes to the cost but the enemy can choose where to attack and only a small part of the system can be brought to bear to counter such an attack.[5]

Despite the fact that the Nike X system was not deployed, the hardware and concepts developed served as important components of the Sentinel-Safeguard BMD systems considered later for deployment to meet threats whose character was substantially different from the assumptions under which the Nike X developers operated.

CURRENT MISSILE DEFENSE CONCEPTS

The official (i.e. Department of Defense) perception of the nature of the threat posed to U.S. cities and strategic forces changed in 1967. Prior to that date, it was assumed that the major threat to the U.S. came from the possibility of a Soviet attack on U.S. cities. The possibility of a Communist Chinese attack began to appear following their successful testing of a thermonuclear device in May 1966. Moreover, the Soviet trend toward larger and higher quality strategic forces seemed to pose a threat to the survivability of our strategic forces—particularly our land-based ICBM's and manned bombers.[6] On September 18, 1967, the Johnson Administration announced

[5]Testimony of Daniel J. Fink, *op.cit.*

[6]The threat to the U.S. strategic forces comes from both the increases in numbers and improvements in the quality of Soviet strategic forces. Soviet ICBM CEP (Circular Error Probability, i.e. the radius within which 50% of the warheads can be expected to impact) is believed to be improving substantially. Yet our land-based ICBM's are housed in silos designed to withstand static blast overpressures of not more than 300 pounds per square inch

plans to deploy the Sentinel system.[7] The system was explicitly "anti-Chinese" in that the configuration of radars and missiles was related to the expected Chinese ICBM threat in the mid-1970's.[8] The Sentinel system, basically a modified Nike X, employs two radars—the Perimeter Acquisition Radar (PAR) would be deployed along the northern rim of the continental United States. The less expensive Missile Site Radars (MSR) would continue to be located around the cities to be protected by the Sentinel system[9] to control the firing of the Spartan-Sprint Interceptors. The Spartan would be used (as in Nike X) for long-range intercepts above the atmosphere (up to twelve hundred miles) and the Sprint would be used for local defense of cities. The Sentinel system was considered to be a relatively low-cost (about five billion dollars over five years) means of providing "light" protection of U.S. cities when compared to the Nike X alternatives.

Because Sentinel was optimized to meet only the expected Chinese ICBM threat in the mid-1970's, it possessed obvious vulnerabilities to even a modest Soviet attack. For example, there were no southward looking faces on the radars. Thus the system was vulnerable to a Soviet Submarine Launched Ballistic Missile (SLBM) attack or a Fractional Orbiting Bombardment System (FOBS) attack from the south. In short, the system was configured in a way which would emphasize its exclusively

---

(to gain a sense of scale, a brick house would be demolished at about six psi). The size (i.e. weapon yield—up to 25 megatons) and accuracy (CEP) of Soviet weapons makes missiles in these silos vulnerable. It has been estimated that placing ICBM's in "superhard" 3,000 psi silos would cost almost as much as a missile defense system— $5 billion with no guarantee that such protection would not disappear with further improvements in Soviet CEP.

[7]Speech of Secretary of Defense Robert S. McNamara before the United Press International Editors and Publishers, San Francisco, September 18, 1967.

[8]Daniel J. Fink, Strategic Warfare, *Science and Technology,* October 1968, p. 67.

[9]These cities included such major population centers as Boston, Chicago, New York, Los Angeles, San Francisco, and Seattle. Although Secretary McNamara noted the potential danger to our strategic forces in his September, 1967 speech, this rationale was heavily deemphasized in favor of the anti-Chinese rationale in most later statements.

anti-Chinese character, and minimize the possibility of the Soviet Union misconstruing U.S. intentions to the effect that the system was intended to alter the U.S.-Soviet strategic balance (see Chapter 7 for an extended discussion of this issue).

The incoming Nixon Administration authorized a complete review of the objectives and configuration of the Sentinel deployment. The result was to redefine the objectives of the Sentinel program, altering both the name and character of the system without any technical changes in the component parts (i.e. radars, computers, or interceptors) utilized.

The result of the Nixon Administration review of the Sentinel system was Safeguard announced on March 14, 1969. The redefinition of the objectives took account of the rapid rate of Soviet ICBM deployment, noting that "a continuation of these trends could constitute a threat to our strategic forces."[10] Although the rapid rate of deployment had been going on since 1966, it was no longer believed to be a safe assumption that the Soviet Union intended to merely gain strategic parity with the U.S. The problem of defending the U.S. against an irrational or unauthorized attack from China has been advanced as a justification for Safeguard deployment, but the focus is on the protection of U.S. strategic forces.[11] The Safeguard deployment of PAR and MSR and their associated Spartan/Sprint interceptors emphasizes the effort to protect U.S. land based ICBM's and manned bombers. With the exception of Washington, D.C. (a military command and control center) none of the U.S. cities have MSR/Sprint terminal defenses—these defenses are allocated to defend ICBM and bomber bases as well as the PAR sites. Some city protection is afforded by the area defense capability of the Spartan interceptor and the Perimeter Acquisition Radars.

The Safeguard system will be deployed in two phases. The first phase will include the deployment of PAR and MSR radars as well as Spartan and Sprint interceptors around Minuteman sites at Grand Forks (North Dakota) and Malstram (Montana) Air Force Bases. The purpose of this deployment is to give limited protection to a part of our deterrent, and to provide the

[10]Address of Dr. John S. Foster, Jr., Director of Defense Research and Engineering before the Aviation/Space Writers' Association, Dayton, Ohio, May 12, 1969.

[11]Address of Dr. John S. Foster, Jr., *ibid.*

operational experience that will be beneficial to the second deployment phase.

The character of the second phase of the Safeguard deployment is to be dependent on the nature of the threat perceived after the initial phase of the deployment is completed. Three options are considered. The first phase 2 option is designed to increase the survivability of the U.S. ICBM force if the Soviet ICBM threat increases. This option would deploy two additional PAR/MSR and Spartan/Sprint sites at two other Minuteman wings in addition to adding a heavier complement of Sprint missiles at the existing batteries. Washington, D.C. would also receive protection if this option were exercised. The second option of providing heavier protection to the U.S. bomber force would be exercised if the Soviets increased their submarine force to the point where our bomber bases would be seriously threatened. To counter this threat, additional radar and missile sites (a total of twelve) would be deployed near bomber bases. The third option would be exercised if the Chinese ICBM threat increased to the point where U.S. cities would be severely threatened. Under this option, the area rather than point defense aspects of Safeguard would be emphasized by the procurement of additional Spartan missiles.

The Safeguard deployment DoD costs [not including AEC ($1.1 billion) and R&D ($2.5 billion) costs] exceed Sentinel by $1.1 billion ($6.6 vs. $5.5 billion respectively). This additional cost is the effect of adding two more PAR sites (five for Sentinel, seven for Safeguard) and a total of eleven rather than five radar faces. Similarly, the number of MSR faces has been increased from thirty-four to forty-eight to improve the system coverage, and the number of Sprint missiles (to protect radar sites) has been increased accordingly. This system could be made "thicker" if the deployment were extended to cities.

Alternatively, different types of missile defense systems could be deployed which would complement the existing Safeguard system. Some of the candidates for this sort of deployment are discussed below.

FUTURE MISSILE DEFENSE CONCEPTS

In recent years when the philosophy of "Assured Destruction"[12] has been the dominant element of U.S. strategic doctrine, U.S. forces have been structured in a way as to have significant redundancy. That is, we have deployed different strategic weapon systems to do essentially the same task— maintain the U.S. assured destruction capability. This practice not only gives us a higher level of confidence that the mission of the strategic forces will be accomplished, but also inflicts a substantial cost upon a potential aggressor to provide defenses against redundant offensive weapon systems.

If strategic doctrine shifts to the point where (as some have suggested) defense will be emphasized, and the offense will be deemphasized or even limited by treaty, then the notion of redundant types of defensive systems might be of considerable interest. Below are discussed a number of alternative concepts of missile defense which appear to be technically feasible during the next ten to twenty years, at least in some form.

One possibility is a Seaborne Anti-Ballistic Missile Intercept System (SABMIS). This system is envisioned with radars and interceptors mounted on surface vessels (although the interceptors could also be mounted on submarines). These vessels could be deployed in the Northwestern Pacific and the North Atlantic to protect the continental U.S. from Soviet or Chinese attack. Some believe that since SABMIS interceptors would intercept ICBM's in mid-trajectory, the problem of discrimin-

---

[12]Former Secretary of Defense Robert S. McNamara has defined assured destruction as the ability of the U.S. "to deter deliberate nuclear attack upon the United States and its allies by maintaining, continuously, a highly reliable ability to inflict an unacceptable degree of damage upon any single aggressor, or combination of aggressors at any time during the course of a strategic nuclear exchange, even after absorbing a surprise first strike." To this end, U.S. strategic forces have been designed to minimize their vulnerability to destruction during an attack. Intercontinental bomber bases are dispersed. Land-based ICBM's are in blast-resistant underground silos, while nuclear submarines are continuously on station. All of our strategic forces are tightly linked to the President by a secure command and control system.

ating between decoys and the true warhead would be reduced.[13] Moreover, with the development of MIRV (Multiple Independently Targetable Reentry Vehicles) technology, a mid-trajectory intercept may be substantially more effective than terminal defenses of the Nike X-Sentinel-Safeguard variety.

Furthermore, SABMIS may be a useful means of strengthening U.S. nuclear guarantees to allies since a mobile SABMIS installation could be deployed in an area which is threatened by Chinese or Soviet nuclear blackmail.[14]

A similar concept proposed by the Air Force, known as Airborne Ballistic Missile Intercept System (ABMIS) might be able to accomplish objectives similar to SABMIS and in addition, be especially effective against low trajectory attacks from submarine launched ballistic missiles, but would require different countermeasures by an enemy. This system envisions radars and interceptors fitted on specially equipped aircraft of the C-5A variety on around-the-clock patrol over open seas adjacent to major cities.[15] These mobile missile defense systems could, of course, be deployed in areas outside of the U.S. in a manner similar to the role suggested earlier for SABMIS.

A suggested alternative concept has recently been proposed which would enable the Minuteman 3 ICBM to perform a dual role—performing both offensive and defensive missions.[16] By fitting the missile with a maneuverable post-boost vehicle, which would be mounted atop the missile's third stage, the missile could either intercept incoming warheads (conventional ICBM's or FOBS), or operate offensively as a FOBS vehicle or in a MIRV-ICBM role.

Space-based concepts of missile defense have also been proposed. These concepts generally consider the use of orbiting satellites for the detection and interception of enemy ballistic missiles.

[13]Proposals Due on Seaborne ABM System, *Aviation Week and Space Technology,* July 17, 1967, p. 43.

[14]Colonel Paul C. Davis, Sentinel and the Future of SABMIS, *Military Review,* March 1968, p. 62.

[15]Air Force Eyes Dual Role for Minuteman, *Aviation Week and Space Technology,* March 31, 1969, p. 45

[16]Air Force Eyes Dual Role for Minuteman, *ibid,*., p. 44.

An example of this type of concept would be the Ballistic Missile Boost Intercept System.[17] This system anticipates the use of satellites deployed in 250-300 mile high circular orbits. These would be deployed randomly and not be maintained in a specific pattern, but any one satellite would be within range of the potential target area for about ten to fifteen minutes. Each satellite would be equipped with a surveillance sensor and a computer as well as six to eight interceptors to attack the enemy ICBM in its launch phase. An alternative intercept scheme suggests having an interceptor release several thousand steel pellets at extremely high velocities to destroy the enemy warhead. The space-based defense systems are, perhaps, the most expensive and visionary missile defense concepts, but they cannot be conceptually excluded from a thorough analysis of future possibilities.

The aforementioned concepts of missile defense represent possible additions to U.S. defensive capabilities should the U.S. decide to emphasize the defense over the offense. Each, of course, requires advances in technology, but none appear to be remote possibilities, given a relatively high level of enthusiasm for defense.

[17]USAF, Industry Studying ABM Concepts, *Aviation Week and Space Technology,* May 15, 1967, pp. 84-5.

Chapter 2

MISSILE DEFENSE: CAN IT WORK?

by Charles M. Herzfeld

INTRODUCTION

A comparison of offense and defense effectiveness involves facts, judgments, and (very importantly) the logical structure of the arguments used. For the last ten years or so, there have been public and private disagreements about the facts. Though there are now far fewer such disagreements, some remain. Differences in judgments have existed and some persist. But perhaps most importantly, some flaws in the logical structure of the arguments seem to have gone largely unnoticed. These flaws are basic. They involve the use of grossly asymmetric logic, which largely begs the questions supposed to be resolved. The use of asymmetric logic has been aggravated by the fact that the majority of Defense technologists and analysts have concentrated professionally on either the offense or on the defense alone.

In this chapter we try to sort out the issues in ABM effectiveness by trying to clarify the facts, by isolating the crucial judgments, and by resolving the logical asymmetries.

Much of the discussion is relevant to general offense-defense interactions, and the analysis of logical asymmetries should be a useful tool for the construction or critique of a wide class of arguments in the field. The main thrust of the chapter is devoted to the examination of ABM systems in general, and of the Safeguard system in particular. Portions of this analysis have appeared elsewhere.[1]

WHAT IS THE JOB OF ABM?

Some General Reflections on Offense and Defense

To understand clearly the role of ABM, a short discussion of the general role of defense in warfare is perhaps indicated. There are basically two missions for any defense.

First, the defense should exact a price from the offense of the other side, and

Second, it should complicate the attacker's job, and deny him a "free ride."

Only very rarely in history can a defense provide real security, or immunity. It can do so only when the defense is far ahead of the offense technologically, as the English defense was at the battle of Crecy and as the technology of castle-building was "ahead" before the systematic use of gunpowder.

In the field of air defense and offense, the offense has been said to be ahead of the defense technologically for a long time. Attrition rates of attacking aircraft of three to five percent have been quoted widely as being representative of the relative state of the art of air defense and offense. This argument is often used to depreciate the value of any kind of defense, especially ABM.

The numbers are correct, but *only* on the *average*. What really happens is more complicated, and also more significant: The defense can and should defend some targets, those of higher value, more heavily than the rest of the targets. When the offense attacks these well defended targets it loses quite heavily, losses of twenty-five to thirty percent of attacking aircraft are possible, together with only moderate damage to their target. But the offense cannot sustain such losses for long, goes off after less well defended (and less important) targets, and in these attacks loses

[1]C.M. Herzfeld, Ballistic Missile Defence—This Time for Real, *Nature*. Vol. 219, 1315-17, September 28, 1969; Ballistic Missile Defense, Center for the Study of Democratic Institutions, 1968, unpublished; Hearings before the Subcommittee on National Security Policy and Scientific Developments, Committee on Foreign Affairs, House of Representatives, April 1969.

much less. This occurred in World War II, and in the North Vietnam bombing campaign. Thus, in any analysis of the relative effectiveness of offense and defense, one must know the defensive goals and strategy, the offensive goals and strategy, and assess the actual damage involved. Gross averages can divert too easily from the mainpoint.

We conclude: A defense which frightens the attacker away from heavily defended targets has done the first part of its job, and is a major military asset.

Another often-used argument against ABM is also fallacious. It runs like this: Because any defense can be countered by some reaction to it which can be imagined, no defense should be built at all. The argument is irrelevant and it misleads. All defense systems of whatever kind can eventually be countered, but this, by itself, does not reduce the value of the defense system to zero. To argue against anti-tank systems by saying that tanks can be built to supersede a given anti-tank technology is about as sensible an argument against anti-tank systems as saying that because safes can be cracked there is no point to having safes.

Any defensive system that diverts resources of the offense, either by forcing a building up of the offense qualitatively or quantitatively, or by "absorbing" part of the offense in an attack has done a major portion of its second task stated above.

The real issues of offense vs. defense are different. They have to do with two questions:

1.   does having the defense solve problems worth solving?
2.   what other consequences (good or bad) does installing the defense have?

Both questions will be discussed below in some detail.

The Technical Functions and the Jobs ABM Could Do.

The technical functions of an ABM system are these: The target, that is, the attacking missile, has to be acquired. This is customarily done with a radar, and can usually be done at very great distances, though at these distances the defense may not know the details of what is coming, because the attacker can deny this detailed information by hiding the attacking objects in chaff. Next, the defense must discriminate the real targets, the re-entry vehicles carrying nuclear warheads, from false ones, i.e., the decoys, the chaff, and others. Discrimination is the most difficult part of the defense problem, and hundreds of millions of dollars of R&D have been expended towards its solution. No easy foolproof discrimination methods have been found so far, but much has been learned, especially about what *cannot* be done to decoy the threat, a most important thing to understand well.[2] Finally, interceptors must be launched against the threatening objects. The interceptors are likely to be large and fast rockets, carrying nuclear warheads.

The choice of interceptor warheads is a subtle matter. Nuclear warheads are the most effective, because they have the largest lethal radius. But when they explode, they also create interference for the defense's radars, the so-called "radar black-out," which is a serious problem for the defense.[3] (It is not true, by the way, that the explosion of a defensive warhead, when used according to plan, produces damage in the defended area. Nor would such an explosion produce radioactive fall-out locally.) Non-nuclear warheads for interceptors produce no black-out, but because of their much smaller lethal radius they would require vastly better (and much more complicated and costly) guidance for the interceptor. As a consequence, nuclear warheads are preferred at this time.

Ballistic missile defense systems can be characterized by the portion of the missile trajectory in which intercept is to take place and by the military problem to be solved by the defense. It is possible to contemplate a defense system which attacks enemy ICBM's during their launch phase. The principal advantage of such a defensive system, should it be feasible, would be to catch the enemy over his own territory, to fight "over there," rather than closer to home. Another advantage would lie in the fact that a real defense in depth would become feasible, by combining a launch defense system with other systems described below. The BAMBI system was a launch defense system where all functions such as detection of launches, discrimination of real from false targets, and launching interceptors, were to be carried out from satellites. A reasonably effective system would have involved thousands of satellites. After several years of intensive studies, it was concluded that such a system would cost between ten and a hundred billion dollars per year to maintain.

[2] It turns out that there are no *foolproof, cheap, simple* and *high confidence* ways to decoy the threat. The best *high confidence* methods are not cheap, nor are they simple to execute. These methods are however quite feasible, but at a considerable price in the effort required to install them and, particularly, to verify their effectiveness.

[3] This blackout is taken into account when calculating the expected effectiveness of a missile defense. See note at end of the present chapter.

Further work on the system was, therefore, abandoned. (In the event of future radical improvements in reliability and reductions in launch cost, such a system may become reasonable from a purely technical point of view.) Other launch defense systems can perhaps be built, but this is not certain.

Other defensive systems attack the enemy missiles in the mid-course phase of flight, while the enemy missiles float through space on a ballistic trajectory. (Such a defensive system would be similar technically to an anti-satellite defense system.) The chief advantage of such a system would be its long reach, again providing the possibility of defense in depth. Its chief problem would be discrimination of the warhead from chaff and balloon decoys. It is possible to design a defense system for "late mid-course" interception, when the effects of the atmosphere on the reentry vehicle are still slight, while retaining the advantageous long reach of the mid-course system. The proposed Safeguard system includes such a defense. It is discussed again below.

The U.S. Navy has been studying a shipborne ABM system called SABMIS. This would involve putting radars and interceptors on ships. It would be basically a mid-course defense. Because it would be movable it could be used to defend allies from off-shore positions. This system is still in the paper-study phase.

The terminal defense system is designed to intercept in the atmosphere. Its chief advantage is the feature that much of the air battle occurs in the atmosphere, which makes certain kinds of discrimination methods feasible.

Another way to categorize ABM systems is by the military problem to be solved by the defense. One type of system is geared to defend cities which are targets of moderate size (two to ten miles in diameter) and which are rather soft, i.e., vulnerable to attack. Cities must be defensible for a long time, and casualties should be held to low levels. Airfields and major troop concentrations are also soft targets. Airfields need to be protected only long enough for the aircraft required to retaliate to take off. To protect these soft targets requires that attacking warheads of large yield be intercepted at large distances. This is difficult for a terminal defense, and one of the arguments for a late mid-course defense.

A still different type of defense is designed for the protection of "hard points," such as hardened missile silos, hardened command posts, and the like. These targets are small, and

highly resistant to the effects of nuclear explosions. As a consequence, the defense can let the attacker come close, and be
satisfied with a very late terminal interception system. This in
turn makes atmospheric discrimination more effective, and,
hence, the defense relatively more effective. It is sufficient that
some fraction of these targets survives for retaliation purposes.

Another system which needs some protection is the National
Command and Control System. It consists of command posts
(some of which are hardened) and an elaborate warning and
communications network. This latter is not particularly hard
but survives through much redundancy. This Command and
Control system must be defended long enough for the President
to authorize retaliation.

Finally, there is the area defense. Here, using mid-course or
late mid-course defense methods, large areas are defended. This
is made possible by the use of powerful long-range radars,
together with large interceptor missiles carrying large warheads
and having a long reach. Such a system can be easily supple-
mented by terminal defense. In fact, it is wise to defend the
principal radars of an area defense system by a special terminal
defense, because these radars (usually fairly few in numbers)
make attractive targets for the offense, since their destruction
would eliminate the fighting capability of the defense. The Safeguard system is a combination of a thin area defense, together
with some terminal defense for the added protection of particularly important targets.[4]

As is indicated in our last example, defensive capability
is to some degree an additive matter. The defense can be designed for a certain "thickness," which requires the offense to
pay a certain "entrance price" in missiles to overwhelm the
defense. The cost of a defense increases with the entrance price
it wishes to exact from the offense.

[4]Thin area defenses have been studied for some time, though this is
not appreciated outside of the ABM field. Early studies by the Rand
Corporation on this subject were carried out for ARPA in 1962 and
1963. At the direction of the Secretary of Defense, a number of
detailed, parallel studies of such systems were carried out from
1963 to 1966. The tentative results of these studies were reported by
this writer to the New York Academy of Sciences in 1965, 119, Vol.
34, 1965; reprinted in *Survival*, March 1966.

The Tasks of Sentinel and Safeguard

Both Sentinel and Safeguard were designed to cope with only some of the problems discussed above. Both are basically an area defense, augmented by a terminal defense. The purpose of the Safeguard System was defined by President Nixon as follows:[5]

1. Protection of our land-based retaliatory forces against a direct attack by the Soviet Union.

2. Defense of the American people against the kind of nuclear attack which Communist China is likely to be able to mount within the decade.

3. Protection against the possibility of accidental attacks from any source.

The emphasis is different from the original Sentinel purpose, but only by modifying the relative priorities of the tasks.

The Safeguard system is to consist of large PAR's, perimeter acquisition radars, of smaller MSR's, missile site radars, of large Spartan missiles, and smaller Sprint missiles.

The "phase I deployment" will be designed to provide some protection for Minuteman; the later phases will address tasks 2 and 3, and strengthen the protection for Minuteman, if this becomes desirable.

In addition, Safeguard will provide for some protection from sea-launched ballistic missiles, and also includes some other improvements.

It is important to be quite explicit about what Safeguard does not intend to provide. It does not intend to provide significant protection against a large, all-out first strike of Soviet ICBM's against U.S. cities. It does not intend to provide fool-proof protection against a future large Soviet attack launched from submarines against U.S. cities. Nor does it intend to provide full protection against a *large* and *sophisticated* attack such as Communist China might be able to launch in the 1980's. Its goals are quite modest, relatively speaking, and I believe it can meet these goals.

Let me address briefly here the question whether ABM is needed for the goals cited, or whether alternative methods might be preferable.

[5]March 14, 1969.

Task 1—protection of our land-based retaliatory forces. At this time (May 1969) I believe that our Minuteman force could not be easily wiped out by a surprise attack from the Soviet Union, and that, should such an attack occur, a substantial portion of Minuteman would be available for a retaliatory strike, together with a significant portion of the SAC bomber force and of the Navy Polaris force.

There are some disturbing signs on the horizon, however, that this will not always be so, and that in a relatively few years, perhaps three to five, the Soviet Union may have the capability to destroy essentially all of the Minuteman force in a first-strike. These new developments are chiefly the rapid buildup in the Soviet missile inventory and Soviet experiments in multiple warhead technology.

In the light of these developments, the U.S. must respond. It does not seem wise to rely in the future only on bombers and Polaris/Poseidon for deterrence. Soviet activity in submarine-launched ballistic missiles will degrade the effectiveness of bombers, and Soviet ABM could degrade the effectiveness of Polaris/Poseidon, as could improvements in Soviet ASW.

A proper U.S. response must, it seems to me, cover several approaches simultaneously. First, and in my view most importantly, we must try to negotiate with the Soviet Union a leveling off of strategic arms. Such discussions may achieve important results. On the other hand such talks may fail, and fail after prolonged negotiations. Therefore, some additional steps should be taken now. These should include R&D on harder missile silos (such a program is under way) and also some protection of Minuteman by deployment of some form of hard point ABM such as Phase I of Safeguard. Past ARPA R&D programs have shown how to build an optimal hard point defense, using many small radars and many short range interceptors. Sprint is quite a good hard point defense interceptor, but smaller radars than the MSR may be desirable. However, *Safeguard technology* is the *only technology which is ready for deployment now,* and hence can reach operational status roughly at the same time at which the threat becomes most serious.

Some opponents of the Safeguard System now go so far as to urge a national policy of launching Minuteman on early warning of a Soviet attack on the U.S. Quite apart from the considerable technical problems involved in achieving such a posture, it seems that such a posture would represent the ultimate in world-wide *in*stability, and that such a posture would make accidental and undesired war much more likely than it is now. The many implications of such a drastic proposal should be studied carefully, but until such studies are completed, it does not seem wise to actively pursue this policy.

Task 2—protection of the population against Chinese Communist and other "Third Country" attacks. Sometime in the 70's Communist China (CPR) is very likely to have a capability to launch small ICBM and submarine-launched ballistic missile (SLBM) attacks against the U.S., as well as against the USSR and other countries. I believe that it is a sensible precaution for the U.S. (and also for the USSR) to deploy a thin area ABM system of such size that it would reduce greatly the damage which the Chinese could do with such an attack.

Let me be very clear here. I do not desire or expect war with the CPR. I think it is highly desirable, and possibly even feasible, for the U.S. to establish meaningful relations with the Communist Chinese in the future. But should such moves fail, crises more serious than any we have known can arise, during which threats and counter threats may be common occurrences. It is not at all clear that the CPR can be deterred by U.S. missiles and bombers alone. Relatively few of their population live in cities (a much smaller percentage than in the U.S. and the USSR), where they would be threatened by retaliation. Further, so called "irrational" attacks occur all the time; ships are hijacked on the open sea, aircraft shot down over international waters, countries are suddenly invaded, and so on. It is not far-fetched to suppose that such provocations as recently carried out by North Korea and others could reach nuclear proportions, given the means.

It is my conviction that a system like Safeguard could defend the population of the U.S. against attacks from the CPR for many years. Critics of Safeguard claim that countermeasures can be cheaply and quickly devised which would largely negate the effectiveness of such a system. It is not correct that a well designed thin area defense can be easily countered by a third country such as Communist China. This matter will be discussed in more detail below.

Another problem which Safeguard could solve is countering the following threat. In the not-too-distant future, several technologically sophisticated "third powers" may have submarine-launched ballistic missiles. Britain and France already are procuring such forces, and others may follow. This means that there may arise the danger of small attacks, *whose country of origin is unknown*, carried out, perhaps, for catalytic purposes, to stimulate war between various nuclear powers. A thin defense would deny such attacks any large measure of confidence, hence reduce tension levels in large, thinly defended countries such as the U.S. and the Soviet Union during intense crises involving such "third countries."

Safeguard, together with improved Early Warning of SLBM attacks will go far to reduce the importance of such threats.

Task 3—protection against accidental attacks, and the ability to manage intense crises. We must begin this discussion by considering how war between the U.S. and the USSR might break out. Most people talk and worry about an all-out surprise attack by either the USSR or the U.S. on the other. This surprise attack is said to occur without any warning, without a crisis, without any hint. While this is certainly a conceivable event, it seems a very unlikely way for major war to start. Rather, several of the following ways seem more plausible:

1. An accidental or unauthorized launch of a few ICBM's by one country, which is interpreted as an all out attack by the other country. Then the other country tries to pre-empt with an all out strike against the first.

2. In a very serious crisis between the USSR and the U.S., the USSR threatens to attack a few targets in the U.S. to demonstrate its seriousness.

3. A nuclear attack by a third country on either the U.S. or the USSR, in the hope of catalyzing war between the U.S. and the USSR.

A thin ABM defense system can be extremely useful in the above types of crises, and would enable the U.S. to view such events with a measure of confidence and restraint.

PENETRATION AIDS AND TACTICS

The Magnitude of the Penetration Task.

A variety of penetration aids and tactics are available for the offense. In fact the profusion of *possible* penetration aids clouds the present ABM debate. Various myths have arisen in the public discussions of penetration aids (pen aids) and ABM. Among these myths are these: any pen aid will work, pen aids are cheap, they are quickly procured and easily installed, a few pounds of decoys uses up a multimillion dollar interceptor, and so on.

The real story is more complex, more interesting, and more relevant.

The facts are that *real* pen aids (as opposed to pen aids on paper) are not cheap, are not easily developed, are not quickly procured and installed. Most importantly, not all pen aids work.

The U.S. has been fortunate in its approach to ABM and pen aids. It has had large R&D programs working on both sides of this question: the Army Nike program on ABM, the Air Force and Navy programs on pen aids, and ARPA's Defender program (until recently) working on both ABM and pen aids. As a consequence of the size and kind of these programs, a degree of knowledge, valid competition and cross fertilization exist in these two fields which are unequalled in recent Defense R&D history.

It is perhaps of interest to summarize the sheer magnitude of the U.S. R&D effort which has been carried on over the last ten years in this area. The grand total of R&D expended on ABM so far is approximately four billion dollars. This includes about ten years of Sentinel, Nike X and Nike Zeus funding, and about nine years of Project Defender effort. This is a larger, and more thorough, R&D effort than has been expended on any other single military problem. The magnitude of the U.S. effort on penetration is comparable and ranges, depending on how one allocates costs, from one to two billion dollars. Also, a large fraction of the information obtained from ABM R&D has contributed directly to improving U.S. penetration capability and, in fact, was required for pen aids research and development.

These costs have gone to support relevant laboratory work, very extensive flight programs and field measurement programs, as well as radar and missile development. Also, a comparatively

very large effort has gone into detailed system studies. It is hard
for the outsider to imagine how detailed these system studies
were, and how many of them were carried out and indeed still
are carried out. The total effort has been large. More importantly,
the effort has been of very high quality. Some of the best technical
talents of universities, of industry, and the government were devoted to this effort.

Several important insights have come out of all this effort.
The most important one is, perhaps, that there is a *relatively
wide gap between being conservative in designing a defense,
and being conservative in designing an attack.* Let me explain.
When designing a defense one must take into account the number of attackers and their technological sophistication, the
quality of their pen aids and tactics. The number of attackers
comes either from intelligence projections, or from assumptions
designed to be reasonable or interesting. The estimate of the
attacker's pen aids technology, and also of one's defense technology, comes from estimates of what will be in operation on both
sides at the time the study applies to, say X years from now.

When making this technology estimate in designing a
defense, it is proper and wise to be "defense conservative." This
means that one takes all the known or possible ways for the offense to penetrate the defense and estimates how many enemy
missiles it will take to penetrate the defense. While doing this,
one tries to make the *defense* "look bad," that is, one shades
the technological uncertainties (and there are always some) in the
direction that favors the offense, and counts heavily those
things that may go poorly for the defense and well for the
offense. In this way one arrives at an estimate of the *minimum*
effectiveness of the defense, one gets a *minimum* price that the
defense can exact from the offense. Being "offense-conservative" when designing the offense, means, on the other hand, that
one shades all the technological uncertainties (just as many)
against the offense. In this way one gets the maximum penetration price, the *maximum* price the defense can exact from the
offense. Each conservatism is appropriate for its task, and
most people who look at only offense or only defense are not
confused by this. But if one wishes to strike a net balance between offense and defense, the matter becomes more subtle.
Then one must be consistent, and one must take into account
a balanced estimate for the attackers and defenders of *both*
sides. It is, of course, true that propagandists for weapons

systems rarely make or use conservative estimates, but I am talking here of serious analysis, not propaganda.

Net Comparison of Offense and Defense.

Three basic logical errors must be avoided in making net comparisons of offense and defense. These are: comparing effectiveness of technologies of different vintage (errors of type I), ascribing grossly different technological sophistication to offense and defense of one country at one time (errors of type II), and using only offense-conservative or defense-conservative estimates for the net comparison (errors of type III). The errors are obvious, and they vitiate any argument in which they occur.

Let me explain in more detail what these errors are, and how they compound confusion in complicated analyses.

The first (type I) error is to set up a straw man by pitting a technologically old system against a technologically new system when both sides have comparable technical capabilities and comparable resources. Of course, such an asymmetric situation could develop (by good luck or bad, as the case may be) but no one should count on it, nor is there anything inexorable about such an asymmetry developing, or remaining.

Examples of such errors are:

1. Old Soviet ICBM's vs. new U.S. ABM. Clearly the U.S. defense wins. This was a popular fallacy in the early 60's.

2. New Soviet ICBM's vs. old U.S. ABM. This is the argument often used to prove that "no" U.S. defense can cope with "any" Soviet attack.

3. Old Soviet ABM vs. new U.S. ICBM's. This is the proper argument to prove that the U.S. has "gone too far," has "over-reacted," in improving its missile force.

Such arguments are actually used by some advocates. Clearly more logical symmetry is required.

When comparing net offense-defense effectiveness of countries that have greatly different technical resources such asymmetries can occur, and can to some extent be relied on existing. Thus, the CPR is not likely to *overtake* U.S. ABM discrimination know-how, and it is unlikely that it will match it.

Another error (type II) occasionally committed is to suppose that a country would let a great imbalance in sophistication between different important military systems technologies happen in similar time frames. Yet, some opponents of ABM are logically comfortable predicting a Soviet defense posture that has:

1.   Soviet ICBM's modern, hence U.S. ABM is useless, and
2.   Soviet ABM outmoded, hence U.S. ICBM assured penetration techniques (MIRV's) not needed.
(And all this for the Soviets, who are well-known to believe in having strong defensive systems!)

The third, and most serious error of logic (type III) is to consider only the defense-conservative calculations for both sides, which results in the answer that all defense is useless, or else to consider only the offense-conservative calculations for both sides, which yields the answer that defense is "very good." Clearly both approaches are wrong. The problem is exhibited in Table I. (All entries are calculated in a conservative way,

TABLE I

U.S. Estimate	Soviet Estimate
U.S. offense technology is weak (offense-conservative)	U.S. offense technology is strong (defense-conservative)
U.S. defense technology is weak (defense-conservative)	U.S. defense technology is strong (offense-conservative)
Soviet offense technology is strong (defense-conservative)	Soviet offense technology is weak (offense-conservative)
Soviet defense technology is strong (offense-conservative)	Soviet defense technology is weak (defense-conservative)

thus the U.S. estimate of U.S. offensive technology from the offense's point of view, done in an offense-conservative way says: U.S. offensive technology is weak; the Soviet estimate of U.S. offensive technology, done in a defense-conservative way says: U.S. offensive technology is strong.) The solution to the problem is this: Each technology is in fact either weak or strong, or in between, no matter that each side assesses it differently. What has to be done is to look at a balance between offense-conservative and defense-conservative estimates. The defense is not likely to be as bad as the defense-conservative calculation indicates, nor as good as the offense-conservative calculation indicates. Conversely, the offense is never as bad as the offense-conservative calculation indicates, nor as good as the defense-conservative calculation indicates. This is summarized in Table II. The point is basic and simple, but is often lost sight of, when

TABLE II

Defense-Conservative Calculation:	Offense-Conservative Calculation:
overestimates offense capability	underestimates offense capability
underestimates defense capabilities	overestimates defense capability

advocacy rather than analysis is the objective. Most arguments about ABM involve some degree of violation of this logical point.

In addition to logic, facts are needed for the comparison. It is possible that gaps in technology do exist. Some are obvious, such as the gap in ICBM technology between the CPR and the U.S. Others may be less obvious. When real technology gaps exist, they are important, at least for a time. Technology comparisons are important for estimating capabilities in the future, because the technology of today fundamentally determines the quality of the forces in being five to ten years from now. In the short run, however, forces in being (which were determined by the technology and the deployment decisions of five years or more ago) determine net comparisons.

Offense Conservative (High Confidence) Penetration Methods.

The methods most certain to penetrate a defense are two: interceptor exhaustion, and leakage. Interceptor exhaustion is simply the tactic of attacking with more warheads than the defense has interceptors, and to do this in such a way that the defense must expend at least one interceptor per warhead, that is, to deny the defense multiple kill of warheads. This is, on principle, an absolutely sure method, and it is the most expensive method. It is absolutely sure (at least on principle) because once the defense has run out of interceptors, the defense is finished, and the offense can attack where it will. It is the most expensive, because it matches offense warheads with interceptor warheads and, roughly, offense payload with defense payload. The most serious difficulty with the method is that the number of interceptors available to the defense is not known with certainty.

Leakage works differently. It counts on the fact that the defense is not perfect at any time of the engagement, but can only intercept and kill some fraction of attacking warheads. What this fraction is, whether twenty or ninety-five percent, or in between, is an important question. It will be discussed below. But whatever it is (unless it be one hundred percent which no one believes to be correct) there will be some level of attack which will let a certain number of attacking warheads slip through. Those that slip through hit targets. *How much this matters depends on the job of the defense.* If the job is defense of cities, then this slipping through is serious. If the job is to defend missile silos it is serious only if the warheads that slip through damage or destroy the radars of the hardpoint defense.

One way to reduce the effectiveness of leakage penetration is to put in several layers of defense, as in Safeguard. Here, those warheads which leaked through the first layer are attacked by the second layer of defense.

A disadvantage (or confidence reducing factor) of a leakage attack is the fact that the attacker must estimate the kill probability of the defense. It makes an enormous difference to the leakage rate whether the kill probability is twenty or ninety-five percent. There is not much likelihood that the Soviets, or Chinese Communists, will find it easy to measure the kill probability of Safeguard. They will have to estimate it.

Another high confidence penetration method against an area defense is the FOBS (fractional orbital bombardment system). Because it comes over the horizon in a very shallow trajectory, it reduces the area which can be covered by the area defense. Again the importance of this effect depends on the job of the defense. If the job is to protect hard points, or a few large population centers, a protection against FOBS is feasible.

Penetration Methods of Low Confidence.

There exists a whole host of penetration methods of lesser confidence than those discussed above. They include decoys, chaff, jammers, nuclear black-out, and others. These methods must be considered seriously when making the defense-conservative estimate. These methods *might* work, and so the *defense calculation must* take them into account. On the other hand, they *might not* work, and so an offense-conservative *offense calculation* must *not* take them into account.

The effectiveness of these types of methods can be estimated only if certain crucial properties of the defense are known, particularly how much knowledge the defense has of discrimination technology, and the extent to which this discrimination technology is implemented in the defense system. The offense can make some estimate of the defense's *knowledge* of discrimination technology, by estimating the capability of the ABM research radars of the defense, but the offense does *not* know with *high reliability* how much of this discrimination knowledge has been *implemented*. The effectiveness of the "low confidence" pen aids depends crucially on the quality of discrimination technology implemented by the defense, and may range from total and complete effectiveness to total lack of effectiveness. In fact, the chief purpose of low confidence pen aids is to force the defense to become more sophisticated, to deny *it* a "free ride."

The pen aids of lower confidence listed above have always been favorites of opponents of ABM. Such pen aids are always easily invented, usually "on the back of an envelope," and they "always work." As part of the large U.S. Pen Aids R&D effort mentioned above, an enormous variety of decoys, chaff and of other pen aids has been built and flown for years against an extremely well instrumented R&D facility in the Kwajalein Atoll. The overwhelming majority of these pen aids tested have been ineffective. The few that have survived this screening and that can be usefully introduced into the inventory have taken many years (and the expensive Kwajalein facility) to develop. It was neither cheap nor simple nor fast. In addition, this research has provided an impressive catalog of discrimination methods effective against many of these penetration aids.

Low confidence penetration methods are only useful if they are the outcome of a large R&D effort. The purchase price of these items finally put on missiles may be low, but the R&D price to get them was very high, and so was the time it took to get them.

One of the arguments much heard against Safeguard deployment is that the CPR could easily and quickly provide its missiles with pen aids which would make Safeguard useless. This argument completely ignores the difficulties of getting such pen aids, and of getting them to be effective. Any country that wishes to design and build high confidence penetration aids must have research radars of sophistication and complexity comparable to the radars of the defense which the missile with its penetration aids is supposed to go against. If the defense radars are sufficiently sophisticated and complex, then the penetration aid research radars must be of comparable sophistication and complexity to yield a penetration aid of reasonable performance. It is absurd to suppose that Communist China or any other third country can quickly or cheaply develop a radar capability comparable to that of the U.S. in this field. On the other hand, if this type of pen aids R&D effort has not gone on, the penetration aids cannot be of a high quality, and *we* and *everyone else would know* this fact. Therefore, such penetration aids would not provide a credible threat.

Possible Catastrophic Failures.

It is perhaps useful to make a few remarks about possible catastrophic failure modes of the defense. These are things that might happen and that would make the defense totally ineffective. A significant catastrophic failure mode might be that the authorization to fire "never comes." Others can be imagined. They all have several things in common. First of all, they are real threats, and a conscientious defense builder will examine each of them and will "fix" them as well as possible. Second, the attacker cannot count on any of them. While they have the highest effect when they work, they are also the least reliable.

THE CAPABILITIES OF SAFEGUARD

Some "Ground Rules".

Let us limit our attention to hard point defense, to area defense against attacks of moderate size and sophistication, and to defense against an attack of very few (accidental) launches of high sophistication. I believe that the defense of cities against a large, sophisticated, well-designed and executed attack is not really worthwhile. (For a different estimate, see Chapter 5). Another "ground rule" that we have invoked is to insist on logical symmetry in our viewpoint, and to avoid basing our final conclusions only on one-sidedly conservative estimates.

Whenever anyone assesses the probable performance of any complex type of hardware, he needs to know three things:

1.   How similar is the hardware to its predecessors, that is, how big a step was taken in developing the hardware to be evaluated;

2.   What do test data show so far, and how far "up the learning curve" are they, that is, how much improvement can be expected; and

3.   What technological growth is possible for the hardware, to overcome difficulties encountered during its service life, or to counter enemy counters to the equipment.

The risk in developing a complex hardware item for actual deployment depends greatly on the first and last of the three factors just mentioned. If the new hardware is too similar to its predecessor, then the risk is low, to be sure, but then there is also no point in developing the new hardware. If the new hardware is too far ahead of its predecessor, if the step to be taken is too great, then the risk is too high. The wise choice lies in between. The new hardware to be deployed should be an improvement over existing types, but should not go all the way to the most advanced concepts and techniques which are being studied.

New hardware should, at the time of a deployment decision, have some growth potential, so that the new system can evolve to keep pace with a changing threat, and does not get frozen into an ineffective posture.

A comment is required here about the usefulness of test data. It is often alleged that an ABM system is, by its very nature, untestable, and can therefore be expected to fail catastrophically from any one of many causes. This argument is basically incorrect (type III error) and is fundamentally irrelevant. *No strategic weapon system can be tested realistically in a nuclear war environment whether the system is defensive or offensive. Just as the ABM cannot be tested with full realism, so neither can the offense which must penetrate the ABM be tested with full realism.* It may be said that ABM is peculiarly vulnerable, much more so than the offense. Those who have to concern themselves professionally with the hardness of the offense against attack would probably not agree. We have here another example of the unbalanced judgment which can be obtained by looking only at a defense-conservative estimate. In fact, there are serious uncertainties on both sides, and both sides must constantly concern themselves with reducing the gap of uncertainty in the performance of their systems.

In what follows below we will examine each subsystem of Safeguard with respect to its technological ancestors, its test status, and its growth potential. In addition, we will examine very briefly some of the arguments that have been made throwing doubt on the ability of the subsystems to function properly. We will close with an equivalent discussion of the system as a whole.

The PAR.

At present the PAR is being brass boarded, that is, a fully functioning model is being built that will, however, not use the final packaging of the parts. Components have been tested. The technological ancestors are many and illustrious: Phased array radars have been studied in the U.S. in detail since the work at Lincoln Laboratory, MIT, (approximately 1958 onward), and several advanced types have been built, e.g., ESAR, Typhon, ADAR, the now operational FPS-85 (which is in important ways similar to the PAR), and the Nike X MAR radar. The degree of risk in building PAR is very slight. The radar has considerable growth potential. Its power can be increased, and more sophisticated ways to transmit and process radar signals (now in R&D) can be installed.

Critics have claimed that some penetration aids are easily employed to make the PAR useless. They overestimate the ease with which such pen aids are developed and deployed, and give the PAR no growth potential at all (Type III error). Others have estimated that the average availability of PAR would be poor. Yet experience has shown that a system as complex as the DEW line had 99.8 percent of its equipment available between 1959 and 1964, except for a few months, when overall equipment availability was lower, but never below 99.6 percent.[6] Present performance is comparable.

The MSR.

Because its functions are more complex than the PAR, to reduce risk, an early MSR was tested in White Sands. Another is being tested in Kwajalein. Otherwise, the MSR has the same general ancestry as PAR, and similar growth potential.

[6]W.G. Donaldson, 8th MIL E Con., Washington, D.C. Sept. 14 1964. Publ. in *Electrical Communications,* 40, 369, 1965.

Spartan

The Spartan missile is a moderately scaled-up version of the Nike Zeus missile, but improved in several ways. A successful test-firing program has been going on for over a year, which will be continued. A number of growth-directions are available for Spartan, especially a longer range. Development risk is small. Some critics have claimed availability factors of thirty-five to sixty percent, and on this basis have assumed that three to ten interceptors have to be allocated per attacking warhead to have a high probability of interception. These assumptions are wrong in two important ways. First of all, interceptor availability can be counted on to be higher than what they assume. Second, most failures of interceptors occur at launch or in the early parts of the trajectory. Therefore, should an interceptor fail at launch or early in flight, another interceptor can be launched to take its place. Hence, in normal operation, between one and two interceptors per warhead are required. This makes a dramatic difference in the defense of hard points against large attacks, or in the area defense against unsophisticated attacks.

Sprint.

Sprint has been in a very good test program since 1965. These tests will continue at Kwajalein. Growth potential is excellent. A "hotter" interceptor technology, Hibex, is now available, should it become required. The risk of development is minimal.

The Computer, Command and Control System

This is the heart of the whole system which integrates all the rest. Much has been made by ABM opponents of the difficulties of making this part of the system work effectively. But Safeguard does not start from scratch. The Kwajalein complex once had a completely integrated piece of Nike Zeus, which was functionally practically equivalent to a Nike Zeus battery, complete with Zeus missiles, with four types of radars, one ZAR (Zeus acquisition radar), two TTR's (target track radars), one DR (discrimination radar) and several MTR's (missile track radars), all tied together by a computer, which did all the things such computers need to do. The U.S. will have a similarly complete complex at Kwajalein for checking out any bugs in the computer which is now being built. Opponents of ABM seem to confuse the problem of building an ABM battery with its com-

puting center, which is not so terribly hard but is essential, with
the problem of netting all the batteries together, which is harder,
but not essential. This degree of netting is, in fact, one of the important possible growth areas for the system. Another confusion
about risks concerns the use of time-sharing in the ABM computers. There is a wide range of possible degrees of time-sharing
and while it is true that some of the extreme forms of time-sharing
are still research problems, other, lesser forms of time sharing
are commercially available now, earlier difficulties notwithstand-
ing. The early forms of ABM computing will, no doubt, be comparatively simple. But as time goes on, better and more sophisticated computing will become feasible, and could be installed if
required. This form of soft-ware growth of an ABM system
implies considerable growth potential in performance, and is
one of the most important advantages of the defense.

The Over-all System and its Capabilities.

As the component subsystems discussed above go through
their test phases, more attention will properly focus on overall
system integration and its many problems. The Phase I deployment will offer an excellent opportunity to work out the various
problems which will arise. There is no real reason to suppose that
a system will be fielded that will not be effective in doing the
jobs assigned to it. Virtually all objections of informed critics
seem to have erred either in fact or in logic or both. I believe that
the verdict on their charges must be "not proven".

DOES SAFEGUARD SOLVE PROBLEMS
WORTH SOLVING?

In the section above entitled What Is the Job of ABM?, we
posed the real issue of defense deployment as:
1.   does having the defense solve problems that are worth
solving?, and
2.   what other consequences (good or bad) does installing
the defense have?
We now return briefly to these two most important questions.
It is clear that any serious approach to the issues of national
security is one in which arms control must play a large role. We
have all learned in the recent past the need to control, limit and,

if possible, reduce the burdens which an arms race would put on the peoples of the world. We need to reduce the likelihood of war, and we need to try to reduce the destructiveness of war if it should break out. At the same time we must preserve U.S. military strength commensurate with the requirements of U.S. foreign policy.

Therefore, weapons systems should be designed to avoid accelerating the arms race, to avoid increasing the fears of war, and to reduce the likelihood of war.

Beginning in the late 50's and early 60's we learned that in a bipolar nuclear world, a secure deterrent was the key factor providing stability. We learned that offensive weapons systems should be able to survive a surprise attack by an enemy, and that therefore ICBM's should be in hard silos, that bombers should have the ability to take off in time to avoid being hit on the ground, and that submarines with ballistic missiles should be able to hide in the oceans of the world. This approach has worked well so far.

We are now, however, moving into an era which differs from the early and middle 60's in several important ways. First of all, there has been an unfortunate diffusion of nuclear weapons. Second, the Soviet Union has begun to deploy ballistic missile defense, and the U.S. has decided to do so also. Third, the Soviet Union has approached parity with the U.S. in the number of ICBM's, and has probably more payload in these ICBM's than the U.S. Fourth, the U.S. has begun development of the MIRV, and will probably deploy this.

These and other changes affect in a significant way the national security problem and hence the problem of defense and of arms control.

Many arms controllers still say that "the only good ABM is no ABM". This was probably true in the early 60's when there were only two large nuclear missile powers, the U.S. and the Soviet Union. At that time a posture without missile defense deployed by either had some advantages. But this seems no longer correct. In fact, I am convinced that the most weighty reasons in favor of the deployment of an ABM of a certain type are arms control reasons.

To keep the tone of the discussion neutral, I propose to talk about two countries, A and B, with large missile forces and several countries, C, D, etc., with small missiles forces. What are some of the large concerns country A, say, should have?

Country A would surely be concerned about some of the following dangers:

    1.   An accidental or unauthorized launch of a few ICBM's by country A, which is interpreted as an all-out attack by country B. Then country B tries to pre-empt with an all-out strike against A; or,

    2.   In a very serious crisis between A and B, B threatens to attack a few targets in A, to demonstrate B's seriousness, or, finally,

    3.   A third nuclear power, C, threatens either A or B, to force A or B to comply with some desire of C.

Any posture designed to handle the above three threat situations should also have the feature that it not accelerate the arms race between A and B, and in particular that it give neither A nor B a credible first-strike capability against the other.

One should therefore devise a defense system which has the following properties:

    1.   The defense should be good enough to take care of a few attacking missiles from anywhere. This would take care of an accidental or unauthorized launch, and would thus reduce the danger of an accidental war very substantially. *Both* A and B would find such a system useful to have.

    2.   The defense should be good enough to make incredible a threat by A to attack B in a small way, as a "demonstration of seriousness." Such a defense would have the effect of raising the stakes in such a situation. The "demonstration" would either fail or would have to be a large attack. Therefore such a defense system would act as a "fire break" in an extremely serious crisis, and would give both sides a chance to cool off, and to negotiate their way out of the crisis. *Both* A and B would find such a defense useful to have.

    3.   The system should be good enough to reduce the credibility of a nuclear threat by a third party C against A or B. *Both* A and B should find such a defense useful to have.

    4.   The system should not be good enough to stop a second strike by either A or B, hence it would not imperil mutual deterrence. *Neither* A nor B should feel threatened by such a system, and hence the system should not accelerate the arms race.

It seems that a thin area defense like Safeguard would satisfy these requirements, and thus help solve some significant problems of national security.

Let me recapitulate here briefly why a "thick city" defense is not attractive compared to the "thin area" defense.

The "thin area" defense, such as Safeguard and the "thick city" defense are really limiting cases of ABM. They provide significant benchmarks of real systems. Each of these systems is rated in Table III in terms of several sets of standards. Consider some of the entries of Table III briefly. The thin system is *no* help in confrontation with a large sophisticated attack, and the thick system, *not much* help. The thin system is quite

TABLE III

EFFECTIVENESS OF THIN AREA DEFENSE (TAD)
AND THICK CITY DEFENSE (TCD)

	TAD	TCD
Against Sophisticated Attack (by Soviet Union)		
effect on Soviet war planning	small effect.	increases Soviet planning problem.
effect on deterrence of Soviets	no effect.	some effect.
effect on war outcome	no effect.	small to medium effect
Against Unsophisticated Attack (e.g., CPR)		
effect on war planning by CPR	strong effect.	very strong effect.
effect on deterrence of CPR by U.S.	makes threats by CPR not credible.	unnecessarily good.
effect on war fighting by CPR	very good defense	unnecessarily good.
Other Aspects		
effect on large irrational attacks	provides poor defense.	provides good defense.
effect on small irrational attacks	provides good defense.	provides too good defense.
effect on accidents	provides good defense.	provides too good defense.
stimulation of arms race with Soviet Union	small or zero.	large.
fire break in large crises	yes.	yes.
danger of miscalculation by U.S.	small.	large.

effective against an unsophisticated attack, the thick system is more effective than is necessary. Both systems provide marginal, though possibly important, advantages in times of serious crisis, accident, etc. Both systems provide fire breaks in very serious crises, because they make small token attacks, made for bargaining purposes, ineffective and not credible. Finally, the thin system is much less likely than the thick system to exacerbate the arms race with the Soviet Union, or to induce miscalculations in the U.S. or the Soviet Union concerning its effectiveness. A "thick" defense buys too little for the probable cost, and would exacerbate the arms race with the Soviet Union. A thick system also could mislead a future U.S. leadership into thinking that the defense system was really better than was supposed, and hence encourage more risk-taking than is desirable.

Finally a remark about other consequences of deployment of a thin area defense. These are treated extensively in other chapters of this volume. I would like to comment only on one aspect. One of the standard arguments against a thin defense system is that deployment of the system will ruin the chances of serious arms limitation discussions with the Soviet Union. There is no evidence available that such a deployment would jeopardize these talks. Furthermore, Soviet military thought and Soviet weapon system implementation are well known to be heavily oriented in favor of defense systems. There seems to be no reason to suppose that the Soviets would consider a thin ABM system as any kind of threat to them. In fact, I think it is likely that they will consider a thin ABM system desirable for them for the reasons mentioned above, and that they would find it possible to understand our reasons for deploying Safeguard.

NOTE ON "BLACKOUT"

It may be useful to say a word about "blackout." A nuclear explosion above the ground produces a "cloud" consisting of fragments of the nuclear weapon and ionized air. This cloud may absorb, reflect, or deflect radar waves, making it difficult or impossible for the radar to see behind the cloud. The area coverage and duration of the cloud depends on the altitude of the nuclear burst, its yield, the radar operating frequency (and related technical characteristics), and the object observed.

How much these clouds interfere with the defense depends on their timing and spacing in relation to the location of the defense, and the timing and spacing of the attack. The attack levels at which blackout is a problem can be estimated reasonably well (based on pre-1963 atmosphere tests and later related experiments) to assess the minimum defense capability. A blackout penetration is, however, fraught with major uncertainties about both the timing of the attack, and defense radar design and tactics.

Chapter 3

MISSILE DEFENSE AND STRATEGIC DOCTRINE

by *Raymond D. Gastil*

INTRODUCTION

Whether ballistic missile defense for civilian protection[1] seems desirable or not depends upon the explicit or implicit strategic assumptions that one holds. In its simplest form the BMD controversy is merely another chapter in the continuing opposition of "hard-line" and "soft-line" positions. Those who more strongly fear the intentions of the communists or believe that some day we are likely to have to defend Europe, or even America, with nuclear weapons, ·make up an important part of the backing for the deployment of missile defense systems. Those who believe that most communist aggressiveness and weapon development stems from reasonable fear of American (or German) intentions, or who believe that nuclear war is simply not going to occur, probably make up the majority of those actively opposing ballistic missile defense. Although reasons of economy or ineffectiveness are often added by current critics of BMD, positions on nuclear strategy or Soviet intentions seem fundamental to much of the opposition. (Which is not to say that there are not people genuinely concerned about technical or economic questions. Such questions need to be seriously considered and are discussed in subsequent chapters.

After describing the standard theoretical positions of these two groups as they are generally expressed in nuclear strategy,

[1]For discussion of the role of BMD in force protection see Chapter 6.

we will propose an *anti-nuclear* strategy in terms of which BMD plays a rather different role than it does in the thinking of the majority of opponents or proponents of BMD today. The discussion of this policy is appropriate here because to a greater or lesser extent several of the contributors to this volume believe that BMD should be discussed more in terms of its possible contribution to such a strategy than is general in the public discussion. Those of us who take this position hope to use the current BMD debate as a platform from which to attack the general view that we must choose between the assured destruction, doomsday approach that has recently characterized strategic policy and reliance on nuclear superiority and first-strike capabilities.

The United States and the Soviet Union spend billions of dollars every year on nuclear weapons, their means of delivery, the coordination of the systems that surround them, and on research and development leading to even more effective weapons and systems. Britain, France and China have spent more billions trying to achieve or maintain an effective nuclear force. If a nuclear war occurred, and these weapons were put to use on a general scale, destruction would occur such as the world has not known since the Mongol conquests. There is a small chance that the results could be considerably worse. On the surface the whole business would seem to be a particularly horrifying misallocation of attention; almost any way out of this game would seem preferable. Although the situation is analogous to the Vietnam war, and just as difficult, decisions here are many times more serious in their implications.

Changing Strategic Approaches

Today nuclear weapons are seen by most analysts as useful only if they are not used. They were not always so regarded. In World War II the allies developed nuclear weapons because of fear that the Germans would develop them first. After their development, they were used directly against population centers because by the end of the war massive bombing of cities (Hamburg, Dresden, Tokyo) had become accepted policy. It is important to note that the original atomic bombs were not used as a deterrent—of course, they were experimental and threats to use a new weapon might not have been effective. When the Korean war broke out nuclear weapons were not used in Korea because the military command wished to save our small supply for a possible war in Europe. At about this same time Bertrand Russell was suggesting that a preventive war might be begun with the Soviet Union in order to avoid the destruction of the world in a later cataclysm once Russia had developed a stockpile of weapons. After 1950 attitudes began to change, and the more destructive fusion weapon added to the change. By the mid-fifties Churchill was talking of making war impossible through the possession of nuclear weapons, and Dulles was talking brinkmanship with no intention of going over the brink. Strategic nuclear weapons seemed to have become unusable except as a threat. Since it was generally assumed that any major war would necessarily involve nuclear weapons, many saw our century as that of all-or-nothing war; a major non-nuclear war was thought to have become impossible.

About this time there developed a new and much more complicated attitude toward the use of nuclear weapons. It was generally felt that we had superior technology and they (primarily Russia; now one would add China) had more manpower and massed force. Against this threat it might be possible to make small nuclear weapons and adapt them to battlefield requirements. These "tactical nuclear weapons" could even the balance without necessarily escalating to a strategic nuclear exchange between Russia and the United States, although Germans or other peoples caught on such a tactical battlefield might not enjoy the result.

Once it was generally agreed that strategic nuclear use was not a foregone conclusion in a large war, some analysts went further and suggested the possibility of fighting a fairly large conventional war, even in Europe, without nuclear weapons at all. It was argued that tactical and strategic nuclear use might be hard to keep distinct in the fog of war. If an opponent fought without the use of nuclear weapons NATO nations might well wish that they had the capability to also remain non-nuclear. This argument suggested that America's decline in non-nuclear power relative to the Soviet Union must be arrested if we were to be secure against the full range of threats. Would it not be better to concentrate on developing conventional, non-nuclear armies to defend our interests?

In the late fifties it was also proposed that we might be able to fight *limited* intercontinental nuclear wars of two types. One approach was the use of a few weapons for demonstration without going all the way. The other approach would be to target only the opponent's forces in the first stages of a strategic war, with the hope that the war could be ended without widespread urban destruction on either side. Nuclear attacks were distinguished as countervalue or counterforce, with only the former involving attacks on urban targets *per se*.

The Kennedy Administration brought into positions of responsibility a larger number of defense intellectuals deeply concerned with these issues. They pushed improvements in the relative invulnerability of our forces, in warning systems, and in command and control. They emphasized a wide spectrum of forces, and, in particular, built up our conventional capabilities, from counter-guerrilla forces on up. Instead of relying on the big threat we were going to have the capability to match communist forces at any level. Budgets were raised considerably at the same time as careful cost-effectiveness analysis was supposed to provide more defense per dollar. We were to have good air defenses, civil defenses, a counterforce capability to destroy the enemy's forces before they were launched, and an invulnerable second-strike force. Leading Defense Department intellectuals pointed out that counterforce was the only moral form of fighting nuclear war.

As the Kennedy-Johnson Administration grew older, the approach changed, until by late 1968 only the invulnerability and cost-effectiveness were left. Civil defense was first to be abandoned. Rightly or wrongly, to many, especially on the intellectual left, civil defense as proposed in 1961-62 became an issue of war or peace, while it seemed a cowardly, too defensive approach to some on the militant right. The temporary civil defense measures initially suggested for family protection also led to controversy over unrelated issues. Civil defense was quietly and slowly dropped as a central aspect of our posture. A decision to go ahead with BMD deployment was deferred repeatedly and on a variety of grounds. The competition of other programs, and the relative uncertainty as to effectiveness against rapidly evolving missile technology raised persistent objections. We were left with expensive air defense and anti-submarine systems, but long range bombers were coming to be regarded as obsolescent and anti-submarine systems are probably not highly effective on a nuclear war time-scale.

Strategic forces came to be seen as performing two functions: damage limitation and basic deterrence (later "assured destruction"). Forces for "damage limitation" included both offenses and defenses, but increasingly for the missile age they were considered to be offensive forces for the counterforce mission. Although United States officials almost never talked about first strikes, in fact counterforce for damage limitation seemed necessary to make credible our implicit threat to defend Europe with a nuclear first use if there seemed no other way to defend it against a full-scale Soviet attack. Conventional capabilities were not growing in Europe as we had hoped. Soviet initiation of nuclear warfare confined to Europe also had to seem deterable if were going to hold NATO together. Assured destruction "forces" were identified with basic deterrent countervalue capabilities, but were not necessarily more than theoretically distinct from the general strategic force. For example, if the Soviets tried to destroy our forces in a first strike, we would have enough forces to destroy the Soviet and Chinese societies in a second strike.

The Soviets built up their nuclear forces in the late 1960's, both offenses and defenses, while the United States had heavy budgetary demands for more pressing issues in the cities and Vietnam. The Chinese began to build a strategic force, but with unknown rate and direction. American reaction to a potential Chinese threat appears to be an attempt to maintain in relation to China that force balance which earlier characterized the U.S.-Soviet relationship—including a full spectrum of forces for offense and defense and the maintenance of superiority. On the other hand, official reaction to the evidence of the buildup of Soviet forces in the late 1960's has emphasized the unthinkableness of war, and the maintenance of assured destruction forces, and the irrelevance of superiority. Our forces were to be developed to *get through* any defensive screen the Soviets put up, to convince them of the fallacy of defense, and thus to hold down the strategic budgets on both sides. The current administration may change this course, but one suspects it will be under many of the same pressures that moved the last administration. Indeed, the approach of 1967-68 was rather closer in spirit to that of the Eisenhower years than to the early Kennedy years. The Nixon period is apt to carry this return even further by going back to the nuclear rather than conventional emphasis.[2]

---

[2]The author is aware that the history of strategic thinking and administrative policy is more complicated than this outline, but from the present vantage point these seem the important movements.

Current Issues

   U.S. leaders are now seriously considering a range of reactions to the Soviet offensive and, perhaps, defensive buildup. It is in the framework of this appraisal that most are reconsidering BMD. If assured destruction is all we need, then BMD is seen primarily as a supplement to force mobility, force hardening, or the increase and proliferation of strategic delivery systems through such devices as turning present missiles into buses carrying many warheads (e.g., MIRV). If we maintain an assured destruction capability, is there any distinction between parity and superiority? Did past U.S. numerical superiority give us any advantage in past crisis bargaining such as Cuba? If we had a strategic advantage in 1962, did it help to resolve the crisis, to prevent escalation to war? Instead of introducing our BMD, and, thus, another round in the arms race, shouldn't we move in the direction of really serious arms limitation or arms reduction agreements? And, finally, what should be the place of nuclear deterrence and defense in our overall national defense posture?

   Most people would agree that the primary purpose of nuclear forces must be to prevent nuclear war, and if some nuclear weapons are used, to prevent more nuclear weapons from being used. Many would add that we should also strive to reduce or limit the number of nuclear weapons in the world, so that nuclear war will be less intense if it does occur, as long as initiating this process of reduction does not increase the chance of nuclear war. It is not at all clear what policies lead most surely toward these objectives, or to what extent other and secondary objectives should be attained by strategic force development, or whether these latter objectives have any weight if they compete with the first two.

   In which situations are our leaders likely to consider that they should initiate nuclear war? For which situations should we procure our forces and plan to use them? It can be argued that if it appears that the United States is prepared to fight in many ways other than nuclear war, then countries may be more willing to risk becoming involved in war with the United States in those situations that seem peripheral to our interests. And since the greater danger of nuclear war derives from situations in which a fairly large non-nuclear war has been allowed to develop, it would follow that a Dulles style massive deterrent policy may be more apt to prevent nuclear war than the more sophisticated policy of graduated deterrence which appeared at first glance to be both more humane and more careful.

However, how can our leaders credibly imply that they would initiate nuclear war in a wide range of situations? If our nation is to appear as though it will initiate nuclear war rather than lose even minor points such as Quemoy or Matsu, then it must appear to have "reliable superiority." Reliable superiority would mean that an opponent would gain very little by attacking first, and would lose nearly all of his deterrent capability if we struck first. It would mean that in either case there could be a fair degree of confidence that no more than a conceivably "acceptable" level of damage would be done to the United States in an all-out war. Against the Soviet Union it would be very expensive to win back this kind of superiority, even if it were technically feasible. Our nuclear threat, therefore, may well come down to being a threat of committing something close to suicide. The credibility of this threat seems low. While the posture may be strong and deterring in ordinary crises, perhaps against most communist "fishing expeditions," if we were pushed very hard in a crisis, opponents might calculate we would have to back down. If they were right and we back down too often, the deterrent becomes both seriously weakened and dangerously erratic. For backing down in the face of threat could enflame ambition and overconfidence in opponents, and give birth to bitterness and irrational stubborness in our own leadership.

Some suggest that we could use strategic forces in a limited demonstration mode to strengthen the look of determination. But the use of a few strategic weapons, or even just one, in a deep crisis may be interpreted by opponents as anything from the beginning of general war to a sign of weakness. Even with written messages it is hard to know what an opponent would make of such an employment of nuclear weapons. Little prevents him from responding with a somewhat larger demonstration, and so on.

The tactical nuclear alternative has some of the same defects of the threat of strategic retaliation. Once the nuclear "threshold" is crossed, further escalation is likely to be hard to control. Of course, further escalation is not automatic. In some scenarios a few tactical weapons could be used without going further, but the probability of escalation to general nuclear war after nuclear use is generally much greater than before.

While the conventional approach to most defense and even deterrent situations is expensive in men and materiel, and does make war more thinkable, its credibility is higher than any other approach. The United States has shown repeatedly that we will engage in at least some large conventional actions even though the Soviets have nuclear weapons; we have not shown that we would go to nuclear weapons to attain limited objectives. (We have been careful to suggest that in Europe even our conventional actions will be completely defensive.) The conventional approach is particularly believable and safe if we make it clear that we are not going to cross the nuclear threshold, no matter what the non-nuclear provocation; and *if* we have conventional forces of such quality and quantity that it looks like it would be sensible for us to try to use them.

In the nuclear age conventional wars are apt to be stalemates, or fought to stalemates. We cannot bring conventional wars to an end in World War II fashion by landing and threatening Peking or Moscow—maybe not even by taking Hanoi. There is an interminable character to conventional approaches in the nuclear world that is extremely frustrating, but, as this kind of war becomes "institutionalized," there is more and more confidence that aggressions and other dangers can be met without involving the danger of nuclear war—if we have sufficient conventional forces.

THREE ALTERNATIVE STRATEGIES

Finite Deterrence

In addition to deterring an opponent, to what extent should we be concerned with reducing destruction in the United States should war occur? Those who advocate concentration on the "assured destruction" mission, on offensive forces directed ultimately against cities, believe that through simplifying the equation of nuclear war in this way, they have directly reduced the chance of war, and increased the chance of cooperation between the United States and the Soviet Union. They see this as the only ultimate guarantee of world peace. They do not worry about the fact that the Soviet Union has the capability of destroying the United States, for as long as the Soviets have this invulnerable capability, Soviet leaders will not be nervous about our actions. They can rest assured that we will never attack them. As the Soviets become assured of our intentions, they will come to de-emphasize the further development of their own strategic capabilities. This will provide the context for future agreements to limit arms. Even if important agreements are not signed, there will then develop a tacit arms limitation relationship between the superpowers.

Those who would advocate de-emphasizing efforts to reduce casualties from Soviet attack, or continued de-emphasis in this area, believe that the alternative to the assured destruction focus is a continued arms race. They reason as follows: Neither side knows the capabilities of the other in detail. If the Soviets develop what might be an effective defense against missiles, we will feel we must maintain our destructive capability. Using conservative calculations we are then likely to develop a much larger and more complex offensive delivery capability than we have today. If we build ballistic missile or other defenses at the same time, the Soviets may well decide that to maintain their deterrent they must also upgrade their forces both quantitatively and qualitatively more than they would otherwise. The building up of forces rapidly on both sides will necessarily leave recurrent gaps or opportunities for one or the other side, and will raise questions about the intentions of both parties. The end result may well be that the offensive forces developed by both sides would in fact be at least as destructive in an actual war as today's forces would be, for both countries would tend to overestimate their competitor's defenses in making offensive calculations.

The foregoing is one vision of a world without nuclear war, and how to get there. Emphasizing assured destruction, this position is often called basic deterrence or *finite deterrence*. (The required finite size of the deterrent has been officially seen as quite large—theoretically, under some conditions it could be much smaller than the current force.)

Balanced Deterrence

Many believe that a more complex or balanced nuclear force than that for finite deterrence should be developed for both offense and defense, for both counterforce and counter-value missions. Offensively this force would strive for largely invulnerable forces, with a capability for careful and detailed targeting. Such a force might be either "superior" or "equal" to

Soviet forces, depending on judgments of what these terms mean and judgments of strategic requirements. This approach might be referred to as a *balanced deterrence* strategy emphasizing damage limitation. In view of the destructiveness of nuclear weapons and the reluctance of any nation to strike first, a balanced deterrence posture may well be one of *defensive emphasis* in which superiority or parity is achieved through defensive systems rather than offenses. This is particularly true if BMD technology makes this seem feasible in the future.

If we look at Soviet weapons procurement since the early 1950's, it would appear that the Soviets have either not reacted to our policies in a direct manner or have reacted in a way that did not mirror-image the assured destruction vision. In the 1950's we built a large defensive system against planes, but the Soviets did not go on to build up their bomber fleet. In fact, they developed few offensive forces in the early 1960's. Then in the mid-sixties they started to rapidly build up both offensive and defensive forces. This emplacement was at a time when our budgets were in a trough (although it is not inconsistent with a decision made in response to the McNamara increase in U.S. strategic force budget and the Cuban crisis). Threats to use incomparably smaller forces, such as the Chinese will probably have in the 1970's, will be felt to be quite deterring in the absence of U.S. and Soviet BMD. This raises the question as to whether the defenses the Soviets have built or may built actually threaten our deterrence capabilities in the near future. If they really do not, then if we build BMD defenses would the Soviets necessarily feel threatened? Or wouldn't it be possible for both sides to let the level of potential destruction go down as defenses were built?

Deterrence can be measured in terms of many capabilities other than the capability to reliably destroy a society. Historically, leaders of nations have been deterred from inaugurating war primarily because they thought that their opponents were stronger in forces or will or both. They did not need to feel that their women and children were at risk. Indeed, it would appear that they have often felt that it was worthwhile losing civilian "values" if victory were possible—without victory there can be little worthwhile in a war. Churchill writes:

> Far more important to us than the protection of London from terror bombing was the functioning and articulation of these airfields and the squadrons working from them. In the life and death struggle of the two forces, this ,was the decisive phase. We never thought of the struggle in terms of the defence of London or any other place, but only who won in the air . . .
>
> It was therefore with a sense of relief that Fighter Command felt the German attack turn on to London Sept. 7, and concluded that the enemy had changed his plan.[3]

This does not mean that leaders cannot be deterred from beginning wars in the nuclear age by the massive destructive capabilities of a potential opponent. It does suggest that there is an alternative basis for deterrence. Reducing the expectations of Soviet or Chinese leaders that they might achieve political or military victories through either nuclear blackmail or nuclear war is probably as important in preventing war as proving to them the certainty of widespread destruction. It would appear from the record of World War II that Hitler and many Japanese leaders would at the end have sacrificed half of the population of their nations for a good chance at victory. Even the Japanese people were briefly encouraged after Hiroshima by the rumor that the Japanese had used a similar device on Los Angeles.[4] The war ended because from a military point of view the losers did not have any capability to fight. Deterrence that emphasizes preventing an opponent from hoping to win a nuclear war also has the further advantage that deterrence based on this approach is credible. It would seem reasonable to friend and foe that our leaders would be much more likely to actually stand up to an opponent in a crisis if they appear to have prepared for America's survival, and are interested in relative outcome, rather than only in our absolute ability to destroy an opponent's society.

[3]*The Second World War*, Vol. II, pp. 330-31, quoted in George Quester, Bargaining and Bombing During World War II in Europe, *World Politics*, April 1963, XV, pp. 417-37 (428).

[4]In source quoted by Fred C. Iklé, *The Social Impact of Bomb Destruction*, Univ. of Oklahoma Press, 1958, p. 180.

If we accept balanced deterrence, then we will look on Soviet defensive capabilities as being matched at least as well by U.S. defenses as by ensuring our capability to negate what the Soviets might do to defend themselves. Today, a full-scale nuclear war might mean one hundred million fatalities on each side. This looks like a good deterrent balance, but is it? Would we use it to defend Taiwan? Or Berlin? Or West Germany? Would we use it even if the Soviets initiated nuclear use and as a result conquered Western Europe, or helped the Arabs defeat Israel? On the other hand, if we had offensive *and* defensive forces that looked equal or superior to the Soviet forces, and if expected fatalities on both sides were more like twenty to forty million instead of one hundred million, would not the Soviets be just as deterred? Many would judge deterrence would be stronger. In crises a simple capability to kill one hundred million would appear superficially to be more terrifying to the Soviets. But since it would obviously also terrify us, it might suggest to them that it might pay to press, to threaten, to talk a tough line. An American policy oriented to competitive American advantage or at least survival would be more likely to discourage crisis generation and nuclear blackmail by, instead of against, an aggressor.[5]

The main argument against a more complex or balanced deterrent is that it will encourage continuation of the arms race. The case for this view has been sketched above, but the case against it is at least equally convincing. Political conflicts lead to both wars and arms races. It is hard to show cases in which arms races have themselves made wars more likely, although certain ways of structuring forces may, e.g., accident-prone forces, or the inflexibility of German plans before World War I. Arms races are undesirable primarily because weapons are expensive, and in the nuclear age increase the potential destruction of society. Those arms races of the past that did not precede a war ended because neither side saw much point in them, and both eventually reduced their efforts. A reduction may come about either because two states have no further cause of conflict or because neither state gains a useful advantage. This is particularly true when a challenging state that is trying to catch up or go ahead cannot see any chance of surpassing the wealthier or more technologically advanced state. In the nineteenth century France

[5]Thus, while deterrence is usually considered as defensive, there is also "offensive deterrence," the deterrence of a response to a provocation; in the jargon this is now often called nuclear compellence.

tried several times to race British naval procurement, but each time it quit when its efforts merely encouraged the British to greater efforts. Thus, not procuring weapons at a level consistently higher than a poorer opponent may encourage that opponent to an effort it would not otherwise make. It may be that our declining strategic budgets in the mid-1960's have incited the Russians to try harder. It may be that if in the future we show willingness to allow the Soviets to build defenses without competing with them, we may inspire the Russians to procure more rather than less in the strategic area.

Two questions stand in the way of most potential disarmament agreements: what to do about states that do not come in, and how to provide inspection adequate enough that the parties can trust the agreements. These questions are particularly important if weapons levels are to be reduced to ten to twenty percent of what is now programmed, and only such reductions would achieve large reductions in potential destruction. At these weapons levels and without complex defenses protecting the superpowers, much less wealthy states can rapidly become the nuclear equals of the United States and the Soviet Union. Thus, with primarily offensive weapons for the urban destruction mission, it is unlikely that the superpowers can, or should, agree to significant arms reductions. Turning to the second question, if the inspection arrangements are not what we would hope for, and they are not likely to be, at low weapons levels each hidden weapon would be of considerable significance without defenses. On the other hand, with defenses on both sides a small amount of hiding of offensive weapons would be of much less significance, for most would be negated in any case. These arguments suggest the theoretical contribution BMD could make to arms reduction. Past Soviet interest in arms limitations on offensive and not defensive systems suggests that reducing ICBM's in the presence of maintained or enhanced BMD is a feasible form of agreement.

Several objections to balanced deterrence were suggested by the arguments in favor of a policy emphasizing assured destruction discussed above. We might add here only the objection that balanced deterrence seems capable of bringing back the option to initiate first strikes by the United States, and therefore may give an opponent a motive in a deep crisis to strike first. Implicitly, we have argued the pros and cons of this position. There seems to be no realistic hope of making sense of the first

strike for either party in the next decade. While an estimated
outcome of twenty to forty million dead is very different from
one hundred million, our leaders could never be sure they
could reduce fatalities to the former level. Even if they were
sure, an expected result in this range would look so horrendous
that it is not likely to give us a realistic first-strike force in the
thinking of the leaders of either party. At any rate, from the
point of view of war prevention, eliminating the hope of
"winning" from future opponent calculations, and giving them
less reason to believe we will back down under pressure should
more than balance the slight increase this picture might give to
the likelihood of American leaders initiating nuclear use in a
severe crisis. It should also be remembered that we are a status
quo power, and peace is most assured when the status quo power
is least afraid and others have greatest regard for its strength and
will.

Finite Deterrence and Balanced Deterrence

We have now distinguished two approaches to nuclear
strategy. Finite deterrence is based on preserving an offensive
nuclear deterrent, currently at quite high levels, and threatening
mutual suicide if war occurs.[6] The balanced deterrence policy
would emphasize defenses in the current context in which offensive weapons are overbuilt. It would hope to provide America
with a "theory of survival," including a hope for fewer casualties
if war occurs. The second approach is not preferable because of
the strength of the rather sophistic argument on both sides as
to the influence of policy on the likelihood of war. These arguments have been developed on a subject with which there is too
little directly applicable human experience to be of much use.
The testing of the "soft arguments" for both positions suggests
only that balanced deterrence offers about as good a chance for
nuclear peace and arms reductions as other approaches. The
edge that balanced deterrence has is that it may reduce the effects
of nuclear war if it occurs.

Analysts often get carried away, and come to put more
faith in their argument than it will bear. It does not appear that

----

[6]This is the current contrast of positions. Of course, many of those
who want only offensive systems would be willing to go down to a
much lower level at which nuclear war would not be suicide. This
has other problems as discussed under arms control above, although
it may be preferable to our present course.

anyone can guarantee that nuclear weapons will not be used in war, or that any particular policy will lead to this result. The movement of Bertrand Russell's suggestions from preventive war to unilateral disarmament was a kind of hysterical affirmation of this view. Thus, those who are most interested in arms control often want simple deterrence without defenses—yet their further suggestions clearly imply that they do not trust the strategic system they support; their real goal is arms reduction.

Anti-Nuclear Policy

Admittedly, however, the balanced deterrent posture is by no means reassuring. It may be wrongheaded. There are, however, certain ways to improve the policy by making it more explicit. I would suggest that the United States adopt a third alternative, *the anti-nuclear* policy. In this strategy, nuclear war is treated as a dangerous phenomenon that we may or may not be able to prevent. American leaders would explicitly state that they would never initiate the use of nuclear weapons—i.e., American weapons would only be used to deter the use of nuclear weapons. In addition, U.S. leaders would explicitly renounce the goal of being able to hold opponent populations or other civil works hostage to the good behavior of opponent leaders. (At present U.S. leaders proudly proclaim that we have a second-strike capability to wipe out other societies. There must be a moral catch here somewhere. At the very least such public calculations do little to inspire restraint in any possible first-strikes that might be made against the United States.) Finally, U.S. leaders might add that they expect and hope that cities will be evacuated in nuclear wars. We would intend to evacuate our cities in deep crisis, and we would not attack opponent cities without warning them to evacuate first.[7]

Of course, verbal statements and plans cannot guarantee civilized policy in an actual nuclear war. They do fit the old "rules of war" and some of the limitations we have officially put on our forces in Vietnam. While limitations have often not been successful in either case, they have tempered a great deal the behavior of forces (e.g., deliberate attack on population was only slowly and reluctantly developed by both sides in World War II; prisoners have generally not been shot or tortured in modern war). At a minimum, statements of our intentions could

[7]For further discussion of the evacuation alternative in civil defense see Chapter 11.

be made in a context that would somewhat reassure the world of our intentions. If our allies have relied on us to continue to threaten to initiate nuclear use in their defense, they will be dissatisfied—but they are already coming to doubt our will in this regard. Alliance problems can be reduced by emphasizing that our anti-nuclear posture gives us the will to respond against those nuclear forces that are used to attack any state. In particular, we would be able, and committed, to respond to any nuclear attack against any non-communist state that does not possess nuclear weapons. So while one kind of guarantee is weakened, another could be considerably strengthened by the anti-nuclear approach.

The idea that it is better to have a big and bloody threat than to try to regulate the forms of war is by no means new. About 1900, Britain's Admiral Fisher summed up the position of many who would prevent war by a policy of assured destruction:

> I am not for war. I am for peace. If you rub it in, both at home and abroad, that you are ready for instant war with every unit of your strength in the front line, and intend to be first in, and hit your enemy in the belly, and kick him when he is down, and boil your prisoners in oil if you take any, and torture his women and children, then people will keep clear of you.[8]

However, those who have actually had to fight wars among civilian populations have often looked for limits. The traditional, legalistic military attitude toward attacking civilians is far different from Fisher's and from the assumption of assured destruction advocates. According to the law of war as understood by a recent U.S. government army manual: "Devastation as an end in itself or as a separate measure of war is not sanctioned by the law of war."[9] This would imply "countervalue" targeting as usually understood is not acceptable.

The manual goes on to say that if a law of war is broken by another state, then there are several remedies of which reprisals is the last. If reprisals are necessary, then it must be remembered that reprisals:

[8]Admiral Sir R. H. Bacon, *The Life of Lord Fisher of Kilverstone,* Vol. I, London, Hodder and Stoughton, p. 121.

[9]FM 27-10, Paragraph 56, U.S. Army, *The Law of Land Warfare,* Washington, D.C., 1956.

1. are only used "as an unavoidable last resort to induce the enemy to desist from unlawful practices."

2. are used after the exhaustion of other remedies. Even then, one should consider "whether the opposing forces are not more likely to be influenced by a steady adherence to the law of war on the part of their adversary."

3. are not necessarily in kind.

4. should not be excessive or exceed the degree of violence committed by the enemy.[10]

Although the context is different, there are obvious analogies to nuclear war. The attitude and spirit of the declarations are quite opposite to those of Admiral Fisher, and they represent the inevitable result of thinking seriously about situations in which people are really going to get hurt on both sides.

Since, as suggested above, there is no guarantee that nuclear war can be prevented by whatever policy, it would seem that it is in the long-term interest of the world to think out and cling to limits of some kind rather than take the Fisher approach. For with the Fisher approach actual war would leave us all naked to the worst that current technology might devise. Of course, we must be well aware that the manual's approach could be used to justify considering careful nuclear war as a future instrument of policy. It is to be hoped that we can accept this danger and ward it off.

The anti-nuclear policy borrows the use of defenses and counterforce from the balanced deterrence approach but also the depth of abhorrence of nuclear destruction that characterizes most of the advocates of finite deterrence. I feel that the anti-nuclear policy goes as far in the direction of controlling U.S. violence in nuclear strategy as is politically feasible. Reward and punishment are basic to the mangement of all human affairs; in international relations this might be called the orchestration of relaxation and tension. Both friends and enemies have been heard to publicly call upon us to scale down our emphasis upon force, to be content with simple forces. They hold out the promise that arms reductions and general reduction in opponent pressures will follow. Historically, however, lack of capability has often not been rewarded. In crises our allies would be worried if we seemed less powerful than the Soviets in nuclear forces, if the Soviets had a ballistic missile defense and we did not. The Soviets might well react to our finite deterrence posture with a

[10]*Ibid,* Paragraph 497.

new belligerence at Berlin or in the Middle East. In fact, by softening or simplifying our nuclear posture we give those in the Kremlin who believe in the necessity for accommodation less of an argument for that accommodation. Of course, certain men in the Kremlin probably do believe in detente, and we do need to have certain types of at least tacit agreements with the Soviets, for between us we must prevent world war. But we must also realize that the shortest distance between two points is sometimes not the way to cover the ground most quickly.

Those who advocate a simple, assured destruction approach because of their interest in arms reduction, tension reduction and accommodation are gambling too much on a mechanism of un-coerced accommodation, of pure, reciprocal tension reduction. Some place along the line they are too likely to be disappointed, and when they are they will face a more hostile world and maybe more potential casualties than other approaches can offer. In its general form the balanced deterrence approach also offers little advantage and some dangers. However, we have suggested that it is possible to build on the balanced deterrence format another alternative, an anti-nuclear policy, that makes more realizable the goals of the first approach by using the methods of the second. If sincerely followed, it is along this route that we can most closely approach the goal of a non-nuclear world.

One can decide to reject this argument on several bases. If the rejection is not total, if it is conceivable that the anti-nuclear approach might turn out to be better in certain contexts, then this has implications for the advocates of simple deterrence and arms control. For if the simple deterrent approach can fail at high weapons levels, then it is even more important that these weapons levels start declining, that the vision of the arms controller be made into reality. *But if the vision fails to material-ize after many more years of effort, it should perhaps be abandoned by its present advocates, and more indirect approaches to the same goal be followed.*

Let us then turn to some subsidiary questions in regard to the anti-nuclear approach.

Either through an anti-nuclear policy, arms reduction or some combination of these we may return toward a world without any nuclear weapons. It has been argued above that those who believe that nuclear deterrence is essential to "the security of the West" need not fear that nuclear deterrence will be shaken in the foreseeable future by defensive emphasis or arms control. But if it were, then the advocate of the anti-nuclear policy would welcome this outcome. Nuclear weapons are good neither for American nor world defense interests. With our all-around defense capabilities and mobilization potential, it seems reasonable to argue that it has been primarily U.S. power and the bilateral U.S.-Soviet balance that has prevented those entanglements and misestimations of power and will that could have led to World War III. The existence of nuclear weapons is not the most likely cause of the relative peace we have had since World War II.

It is true that if the superpowers were able to achieve exceptional defensive forces through a combination of offensive arms limitations and defensive emphasis, there might develop special instabilities that would be different from a simple return to the pre-nuclear war era. The Soviets could, for example, achieve both a relatively better counter-force capability and a relatively better defensive system than the United States, and at this level superiority would be more meaningful than it would be today. However, the question is not whether there is danger here, but rather what is the better alternative. If we concentrate on preserving only an offensive capability, and we fail in this regard, then there is both the instability of terror and potential catastrophe.

Although the discussion emphasizes defenses after the many years in which the United States has emphasized offenses, this does not mean that there are not technological problems with current and proposed defensive systems. What is the best expenditure will change with estimates of future offensive threats and our capability to meet them. Counterforce is the most effective means to counter opponent weapons under some conditions, but against a hardened force, and when our firm intention is never to go first, these conditions become less probable. Against smaller powers counterforce would be a highly effective deterrent as a second-strike. Air defense is important as long as planes are a threat, but much harder to do well than is often imagined. In fact, because of the range of tactics available to planes, air defense may remain as hard to do well for the foreseeable future as ballistic missile defense. A large ballistic missile defense system would take as great a toll of missiles in the 1970's as our air defense system would have taken of Soviet planes in the early 1960's.

A case can be also made for spending a good deal more of the defense budget on civil defense.[11]

SUMMARY

This analysis has attempted to place BMD in the context of two or three visions of the future. The *assured destruction or finite deterrence* policy seems to be current U.S. policy as far as the Soviet Union is concerned. It would concentrate on maintaining only a capacity to destroy the opponent's society. Advocates of this policy hope to discourage the development of population defenses and of subsequent action-reaction procurement. This choice is believed, then, to tone down the arms race and reduce hostilities. There is little place for BMD directed against Soviet counter-city attacks in such a strategy, except as an alternative way of protecting missile sites. An alternative *balanced deterrence* approach would hope by emphasizing defenses and counterforce to reduce casualties significantly in a war between the superpowers, and to greatly reduce casualties in contests with other powers. It was suggested that this approach would give the Soviets less reason to hope they could attain superiority and make less sense of their threatening nuclear use in crises. A ballistic missile defense of civilian values is essential for this strategy. Advocates of both approaches may hope to make possible offensive weapons reductions, although through different political mechanisms. An *anti-nuclear policy* was then proposed as preferable to either of the previous approaches. In this policy BMD is only another way of reducing the role that nuclear terror will play in future international relations. In this strategy American leaders would renounce first use, even for the defense of Europe, and pledge never to directly attack civilians. On the other hand, the United States would agree to respond to nuclear use almost anywhere in the world.

The threat of nuclear war will never disappear entirely, but we can start now to develop policies, attitudes, and capabilities that will control its terrible potentialities for this and future generations.

[11]For the comparison of civil defense and BMD, see Chapter 11.

Part II

ALTERNATIVE BMD DEPLOYMENTS AND RATIONALES

Chapter 4

THE CASE FOR A THIN SYSTEM

by Herman Kahn

IN THE CURRENT debate on ABM there appears to be a growing tendency in the press and the other media to attribute all the intellectually sound and morally tenable arguments to those who oppose such a defensive system. The arguments put forward by ABM proponents are increasingly treated as callous, short-sighted, at times downright foolish; inspired by the most obvious political considerations or designed to further the ends of the military/industrial complex. It may well be true that the balance between a thick ABM and no ABM at all, struck by both Secretary McNamara (when he proposed the Sentinel system) and President Nixon (when he proposed the modification known as the Safeguard system), resulted from competing political pressures. But I also believe it no accident that the balance was struck where it was. I am myself on record, since 1964, as favoring deployment of a thin ABM system.[1] At the time when I and some of my colleagues at Hudson first put forward the arguments for a thin ABM defense, we met virtually unqualified hostility on both sides of the debate. But we had not intended our case as a political compromise position but simply as the one which seemed to us the most desirable course to follow. A number of technological developments since that time have made the argument for the thin system, as far as I am concerned, even more persuasive. And I rather suspect that, as is often the case in political discussion, the political compromise actually reached reflects the intrinsic

[1]These arguments are presented in Herman Kahn, *On Escalation: Metaphors and Scenarios*, Frederick A. Praeger, New York, 1965, pp. 157-9.

substantive reasonableness of the so-called "compromise position" rather than a sheer and fortuitous balance of political forces. Nor is it an accident that two successive administrations have come out for similar deployments—and both of them rather reluctantly and after much internal debate.

There are, of course, a number of commonly-noted advantages and disadvantages to deploying a thin ABM system of either the Sentinel (Johnson Administration) or Safeguard (Nixon Administration) variety. Before considering specific issues let me try to set the discussion in context by considering some of the general reactions people usually have against almost any defense deployment. The following three are often expressed:

1.   The suggested measures are *completely ineffective* and will accomplish nothing useful if a thermonuclear war breaks out.

2.   The suggested measures are *much too effective* and will either give the government inordinate confidence and thus encourage risk-taking behavior, or will stimulate an arms race between the U.S. and the U.S.S.R.

3.   Both 1 and 2 above—i.e., both completely ineffective and too effective.

Most discussion of course stops here, but sometimes it continues, and somewhat more coherently, as follows:

4.   While the deployment is not effective enough to furnish a useful degree of protection if war breaks out, it provides a facade of protection, stimulating both the arms race and risk-taking.

The advocate of any particular defense measure will usually argue that it is somewhere between "completely ineffective" and "too effective," perhaps formulating his position as follows:

> "The deployment, while of limited effectiveness, is effective enough (at least by reasonable criteria) in certain circumstances to warrant its various economic and other costs, but is not so effective as to increase dangerously the tolerance for risk-taking policies or to stimulate significantly an acceleration of the arms race."

Finally, let me give my own position with regard to either the Sentinel or Safeguard systems. The proposed deployment is effective enough—in many possible circumstances—to increase deterrence against attack. More important, there are many situations and attacks in which it will decrease casualties markedly, particularly if a little more cover (about one or two billion dollars' worth to cover some gaps in the proposed system) is added, but even if such cover is not added. There are some conceivable scenarios in which the deployment might increase the tolerance for risk-taking; it might also constitute or cause a minor stimulation of the arms race; but neither of these two possibilities would seem to loom large enough to balance the benefits. (This is not because I do not take very seriously any increased tolerance for risk-taking, or am indifferent even to a small augmentation of the arms race, but because the first effect is most likely to be felt only in situations where one might actually want an increased "tolerance for risk-taking" and the second effect seems so small as to be in fact negligible.) Additionally, all of the above discussion, while it addresses important issues—and the issues most usually addressed—tends to overlook or ignore a number of equally (or more) important issues. Many of these neglected issues seem to me largely to support a decision to deploy a thin ABM system of either the Sentinel or Safeguard type. However, attempting to strike a balance of gains and losses is really quite complex, often involves subtle but important effects, and is likely to be heavily dependent upon the exact context and perspective of the analysis and on the ways in which the Soviets and the Americans actually carry through their respective policies.

The idea of having an ABM, of course, came as a direct result of the development of the intercontinental ballistic missile and, to a lesser extent, of the submarine-launched ballistic missile. These devices conjured up a now-familiar image of a surprise attack launched out of the blue, directed at American cities. It was also assumed that such an attack would be coordinated, intelligent, well-designed, and probably designed to maximize civilian casualties. We wanted to be able, in the face of such an attack, to protect very close to one hundred percent of American civilians and their property.

While this perhaps is to some extent an exaggeration of what people believed, to some important degree it is not, and this view of the threat resulted in much distortion and misemphasis in the studies, development effort, and finally the public discussion which followed. Actually, the question the country faces is not whether ABM will give complete and reliable protection but, rather, what can ABM do, if anything, that is worth doing and how do these potential benefits balance the potential costs. (One does not refuse to go to a doctor when one has pneumonia just because the doctor cannot cure cancer. It would be good if the doctor could cure cancer, but if you have pneumonia it is worth going to the doctor to have something done about pneumonia. This may also be true even if one has both cancer and pneumonia, but the cancer is not at a crisis stage and the pneumonia is.)

There are at least ten relatively persuasive missions which a country such as the United States might wish to pursue by procuring a "thin" ballistic missile defense system. Including only serious reasons, and in order (as I would judge it) of decreasing importance, these could be:

1. *ABM systems may play an important, perhaps central, role in controlling and stabilizing the arms race.* Thus one important, and relatively feasible and stable long-run possibility is that the United States and the Soviets agree to procure extensive and elaborate defenses, but to limit sharply the number of offensive missiles. Such a concept goes counter to current fashion and argument among most arms controllers, who have tended to believe that arms control is best served if nations such as the United States or the Soviet Union do almost the exact opposite of the suggestion and procure a number of invulnerable missiles and no defenses at all. Of course, a simple balance of terror does indeed have a number of great virtues. If neither side procures any defense, then even if only a small number of missiles survived an attack by the other side, these would presumably be sufficient to create such retaliatory damage that the first side would not have risked the attack. It is clear that if one is unwilling to use offensive missiles for a first-strike, they are not really aggressive, but are so-called second-strike weapons and are designed for the purpose of deterring a first strike rather than for aggression against a potential enemy. Such a simple balance of terror seems to many to both limit the arms race and to make war completely unthinkable. It also eliminates the necessity to worry about details, or at least seems to. Finally, it is relatively inexpensive.

However, a number of military strategists have in the past five or six years developed a different point of view. We argue first of all that if the two superpowers are completely naked, other countries can buy relatively simple weapons systems and using relatively simple (though sometimes dangerous) techniques for getting invulnerability (such as hiding missiles at the bottom of the ocean, putting them into certain kinds of parking orbits in outer space, or otherwise concealing them) can then claim to also be great powers. There would then be an almost overwhelming temptation to either gain or improve a nuclear capability so that one could also have enough (say, ten to twenty) invulnerable missiles to threaten big powers—either in the first-strike or in re-taliation—thus converting both deterrence and the possibility for nuclear threats into a two-way street. If, however, the mark of great power status is not the procurement of some inexpensive offense missiles but an ability to protect one's country from missiles then in fact there will be only two super-powers—the United States and the Soviet Union—for a long time to come. Unlike offense, defense systems are complicated and relatively expensive. Therefore I argue that, for many reasons, the following long-term prospects are desirable: Rather than have, say, two countries such as the Soviet Union and the United States with a thousand missiles pointed at each other and all ready to go at a moment's notice so that any accident, misunderstanding, or other triggering event could cause an immediate and total cataclysm, it seems to us to be much better to have both countries very strongly defended but with only a limited number of offense missiles. Of course, on paper at least, this Arms Control Through Defense Emphasis looks like it has destroyed the balance of terror. However, even one hundred missiles can probably do a great deal of damage even against a country with a very large defense system; or at least there will be enough uncertainty in physics, in engineering, in tactics, in weapons effects and in failure mechanisms, so that no one would lightly test the performance of the system. However, because the defense is large, even if one side or another cheated by a factor of two in, say, the number of missiles, it would not necessarily make a great deal of difference. Thus while deterrence is no longer a matter of a stark and naked balance of terror, there is probably enough deterrence through both fear of immediate or later damage and risks.

Thus the Arms Control Through Defense Emphasis position is one which tries to make clear that defense is not necessarily antithetical to arms control. It further argues that if one had to choose between a strategic balance in which a number of countries were allowed to have very large defense budgets, possibly as large as they wished, but with severe limits on the offense, or one in which there were large offense budgets but very severe limits on defense, the first might be preferable for a number of reasons. To recapitulate the most important of these:

(a) It is very cheap to get into the offense business if there is no defense; therefore, with some caveats (which may easily be neglected) any nation can become a nuclear power and may be tempted to do so.

(b)   If deterrence fails and there is war, the amount of damage will be significantly limited.

(c)   It is much more difficult to indulge in nuclear blackmail if one has a small offense and the opponent has a large defense.

(d)   There remains probably more than enough deterrence for normal situations, since nobody is actually going to believe the calculations or, as a practical matter, be willing to risk rocking the boat. On the other hand, if the situation is abnormal— for example, if the other side tries "rationality of irrationality" tactics—resistance to these is likely to be much more credible.[2]

2.   Particularly if the Soviets continue with their ABM program (or can easily go back into it), *it is important for the U.S. to be seriously in the ABM business.* The second most important reason for procuring an ABM system is almost the opposite of the first. The first says we have to start preparing ourselves for a world of arms control and presumably therefore a world of relative peace and cooperation. The second point says that we have to be prepared for a degeneration of international relationships.

It is thus strategically important for the U.S. to be seriously in the ABM business, because even if it is not important to have a large capability in being at this moment, it may be important later. Since we don't want to be in a position from which we have to start from scratch, it is important to go ahead with at least a minimal system. If we go ahead with a thin deployment, an operating military organization would exist, manufacturers would be making equipment, there would be much more serious R&D and planning and consideration of tactics, strategies and policies generally (since engineers, scientists, bureaucrats, analysts and the services would have empirical data and the kind of intuition which only comes with experience, they would not only understand ABM better, they would also have a greater motivation to learn more.) Operators would be trained, reliability problems would be worked out, techniques and standard operating procedures would be devised and tested, the impact of various marginal changes would be noted, and other useful, even vital, data would be collected. In general, our knowledge of many issues would be improved, including estimates of future systems' costs, performance, deployment time, and impact on various situations and contexts. Finally, a base would be created for further improve-

---

[2]There are other reasons the Arms Control Through Defense posture could be a good one, but I cannot go into them here. For some discussion of these see Chapters 3 and 5.

ment, innovation, retrofit, and normal growth, and a capability would exist for rapid expansion and adaptation. All of this would be true even if the system were otherwise useless—and as I argue below, it is likely to be far from useless.

The capacity for "rapid expansion and adaptation" is important. *Deploying a thin cover and "being in the business" should reduce the lead time for the crash deployment of a heavy cover by anywhere from three to five years.* This is a valuable asset. International relations might deteriorate, and the country might want a heavy cover. While I would be against a heavy cover today (mainly on arms race grounds), we may not want to be in a position where it would take five to ten years to acquire a heavy cover if the international situation suddenly required it. With a thin ABM deployment we are, in effect, telling both allies and potential opponents that as long as the detente permits we have no intention of using our superior productive capacity to create a seriously asymmetrical position. But if our opponents choose to cause, or even allow, international relations to deteriorate, we are prepared to move rapidly to a position of asymmetrical strength and will also be in a much better position to alleviate, to some important degree, the consequences of a nuclear war.[3]

3.   While this now seems unlikely, *the system, as deployed, may work unexpectedly well against some potential Soviet attacks.* It is usual, in the United States, when estimating Soviet or other planning, to assume that the other side is intelligent, has good doctrine and understanding of the issues, and suffers from little or no bureaucratic ineptitude or restraint. On the record this has been untrue. One need only examine the postwar record of either the Soviet or American military establishments to note that in many cases they performed much less well than their knowledge, resources, and technological capabilities permitted and the situation required. (As one friend put it, "Our system is incredibly rigid; theirs is transcendentally so!") In other words, while the Soviets doubtless have the ability to design an offensive force that could easily penetrate the proposed light ABM cover, this does not mean that they will in fact rapidly design and de-

---

[3]See Chapter 5 by D.G. Brennan for a discussion of the value of heavier ABM deployments. One important point to note is that, contrary to much current opinion, it seems to take about a dollar of countermeasure to nullify a dollar's worth of defense, and vice versa for heavy defenses.

ploy such a force, or even rapidly modify their existing system. For example, almost every United States defense analyst has believed, roughly since the early 1950's, that day fighters and tube-fired artillery—at least as we and the Soviets have deployed them—are virtually useless to the strategic air defense mission. Yet the Soviets have spent many billions of rubles on these capabilities, at least until very recently.

Even more important than the possibility of demonstrable incompetencies are basic and unavoidable uncertainties, including the possibility of an unpredictable—or perhaps just unpredicted—success of the defense system. Even if both sides believe that the defense system can be penetrated, for a large range of conditions and tactics neither defender nor attacker could be certain. First of all, there are the known or recognized physical, operational and tactical uncertainties of both the offense and defense. Perhaps even more crucial, there is the possibility of unknown, unrecognized, or badly estimated eventualities and effects.

Almost every weapon system the United States has deployed since World War II has had what were at the time unknown defects and/or capabilities which proved of great significance but were only discovered, and corrected or exploited, after deployment. This is likely to be true of future systems as well, particularly with regard to such things as the vulnerability of attacking ballistic missiles to the many effects of defense missile warheads. While both Russians and Americans might be convinced that their own defense system, or their opponent's defense system, did not work, that does not necessarily mean, at least against some important types of attacks, that either or both systems would not in fact work and, of course, vice versa. In the past, every few years has disclosed weapons effects and/or potential failure mechanisms in the attacking missiles which would have made defense systems work better—in at least one case several orders of magnitude better—than planners had estimated (or the system could have been exploited, at least temporarily, to make this happen).

I might also say something about the importance of certain special situations. Probably the most important of these occurs when the ABM is used in circumstances which are technically or militarily advantageous. It should be noted that while such circumstances seem at least as likely to arise as the usual circumstances in which the system is evaluated, they are not normally considered. It is startling that although almost everybody in the

U.S. government is willing, even eager, to hedge if possible against unfavorable circumstances, they are usually not willing to put the same amount of energy or attention into acquiring the ability to exploit favorable circumstances. Such a possibility often is unexpected. (For example, the 10:1 or 16:1 exchange ratio between North Korean and U.S. fighters in 1950-51 was completely unexpected. If anybody had even remotely thought of trying to exploit this possibility in his planning, he would have been laughed out of the building or off the briefing platform.) The difficulty comes less from the basic unpredictability of these possibilities than from the common, almost universal, if unreasonable, unwillingness even to examine them much less to list them as potentially important, if uncertain, benefits. To take one example: recent U.S. doctrine has examined, and even emphasized, the possibility of controlled nuclear wars. One should therefore consider the possibility that such a controlled war might be fought as a "no city war" even to the point where one or both sides' offensive forces have decreased to a very small number of missiles. Under these circumstances even a quite light defense of cities might make a great deal of difference in the bargaining ability and tactics of one or both sides' decision-makers—and in the amount of damage the U.S. or Soviet Union would suffer if there was a final escalation to attacks against cities.

4.   It is important to notice that *even a thin ABM is likely to be able to exploit new discoveries—new weapons effects, new failure mechanisms, new tactics and/or new technology.* That is, even if an ABM system does not work "as is," it may be very simple to make it work if some new element is added, particularly if "work" means in some special situation as described in point 3. If there is no system already deployed which can make use of the new discovery, this could be disadvantageous or, in an asymmetrical situation, even dangerous, e.g. where the Soviets had a deployed system which could apply the new technique. It should be noted that while the Soviets have often been, as suggested earlier, "transcendentally rigid" about the countermeasure business, they have not been anywhere near as rigid about using any new ideas or technologies which they themselves had developed. Even if the Soviets did not discover the new technique, it would be very difficult to persuade our own decision makers that this was so. And, in fact, it could be the height of imprudence for us to assume that the Soviets are less clever than we. Actually, if they have a system in being, they are likely to be more highly moti-

vated than we and to possess better technical conditions for discovering new techniques. It is also possible that the Soviets, being as aware as we are of the basic uncertainties of antiballistic missile systems, may make such claims, either publicly or privately, perhaps correctly, perhaps incorrectly, to have discovered a new technique. They may even, in a crisis, disclose to us the existence of a new technique and their plans to exploit it. In many possible cases it would be difficult for our own people to verify that the new technique worked (or might work). Very likely we would be able to negate this new effect within a year or two and thereby put the strategic balance back to "normal." But in that year or two the Soviets would have a known and very important advantage which could provide a kind of bargaining edge—or if deterrence actually failed, a warfighting advantage— which could be decisive. I am in fact willing to go on record as arguing that there is a high degree of probability, even a near certainty, that such new weapons effects, new failure mechanisms, new tactics, and/or new technologies, will be discovered in the next few years. I am also willing to argue, *but with less confidence,* that these new items may be extremely important to the strategic balance, at least for a short time, that is, until they are negated or otherwise balanced.

The above goes against the fashion current among most defense specialists, who tend to feel any new technology which might be characterized as a "technical breakthrough" is much more likely to hurt than to help active and passive defense measures. Even if one concedes this, it does not follow that there is a zero probability that important technological breakthroughs in defense will occur. Such breakthroughs are much more likely if we have on-going programs in the defense area, and if we have deployed operating systems which increase our "administrative" and "intellectual" capabilities and understanding. Furthermore, we are in a much better position to exploit these breakthroughs rapidly if there is a system in existence. Thus, while we doubtless could continue to work hard to develop and test systems even without doing any procurement or deployment, we will not be in a good position to take advantage of improvements or "breakthroughs" if we have not started all of the necessary associated programs, or if morale and "seriousness" is degraded.

(One of the startling things about the ABM debate today is how many of the civilian "defense intellectuals" who today oppose ABM were willing in the fifties to play an instrumental role in persuading the United States government to spend about five billion dollars a year on air defense. Some of us at the time thought that they were much too enthusiastic about the possibilities of defense then and as a result both oversold their case and ignored or de-emphasized many important issues. This in turn often resulted in unnecessarily inadequate or inefficient programs and in deployments that had many unnecessary weaknesses. Recently it seems to us that many of these same people have overshot the other way and, since they are still as persuasive, it seems likely that their arguments will now result in a failure to deploy things that may work under reasonable circumstances, or otherwise contribute to national security. The fact that excessive enthusiasm for earlier defense systems resulted in excessive frustration, disillusionment, and even an almost emotional allergy to defense should not impress us if this same group now shows an excessive reaction against the "military/industrial establishment" and defense systems in general. This would just seem to indicate that here, as in many human situations, rationality has been replaced by emotion.)

5.   Even if one does not consider seriously the arms control considerations already mentioned, *it seems both imprudent and unreasonable for the U.S. and the Soviet Union to be completely without protection against almost any Nth (nuclear) country, including, of course, China.* While it is conceivable that the United States might be willing to remain so defenseless that any country with ten missiles can destroy its two or three largest cities, it is virtually inconceivable that the Soviet Union would be willing to be so naked. Would they allow a situation to develop in which the Chinese, having procured a dozen missiles or so, would be able to destroy Moscow and Leningrad? There is no hint, no evidence, that the Soviet Union will do so. We have in the past spent something like three or four dollars on offense to every one on defense; the Soviets have probably spent something like three or four to one on defense over offense. On the record, they prefer defense and probably will continue to do so. Except for a few Soviet arms controllers who, having spent time with Americans and Europeans, are heavily influenced by such Western thinking, and who have no serious contact with the Soviet defense effort, no Soviet planner or analyst seems to think of "defense" as aggressive, destabilizing, or arms racing. Almost all seem to think of it as an essential and prudent activity (and their criticism, or more often, lack of criticism, of a U.S. deploy-

ment of ABM almost invariably reflects this attitude).[4] For this reason, unlike the situation in the West, (informal conversations indicate that) many in the Soviet Union would, even today, go along with the current Hudson concept of Arms Control and Defense Emphasis.

It would also seem a major national interest to both the Soviet Union and the United States that there be at most two nuclear "superpowers." But if neither of these nations has even a thin ballistic defense system, any country with a Polaris submarine is a "superpower": it can destroy perhaps ten big cities. (And, as mentioned earlier, a number of methods are becoming available for achieving invulnerability against first-strike or disarming attacks, but while some of them are relatively cheap and simple, they are also, in my judgment, often accident-prone or otherwise undesirable from the arms control point of view and we should not encourage their deployment.) If there is no ABM in the Soviet Union and America the situation may tempt other countries to acquire nuclear missiles. They would then become "superpowers." Not because they would have any kind of a counterforce ability against the Soviet Union or the United States but simply because they could threaten the United States and the Soviet Union with great damage so that deterrence would then become a two-way street between the Nth country and the two superpowers. This of course still leaves open the issue of relative vulnerability and relative damage but both of these may prove to be either unimportant politically or at least not clear cut. At that point, both the Soviets and the United States would probably purchase ABM systems but with real delays and perhaps under destabilizing conditions. On the other hand, it probably would prove fairly easy for the Soviet Union and the United States, if they are in the ABM business, to keep their defenses overwhelmingly ahead of any Chinese offense, and perhaps ahead of the French and the British (or Japanese, or German?) offenses as well, and thus perhaps pre-empt or weaken these nations' desires to acquire or improve nuclear establishments.

I am not suggesting that the desire to be a major or superpower is the only, or even the dominant, incentive for a country to acquire nuclear weapons. It is, however, one which the U.S.

[4]See, for example, the remarks of Premier Kosygin during his news conference in London, February 10, 1967 in *The New York Times,* February 11, 1967.

must take seriously for planning purposes because it is more subject to our control, involving us and our programs more directly than a nuclear weapons program which is generated by local ambitions and conflicts. There may also develop a temptation in some countries to qualify for the "major league" once they are in the nuclear business, even though this did not constitute an important motivation for the initial acquisition of nuclear weapons. It may be important to pre-empt this desire by making it, from the outset, clearly impossible.

6. In a world in which both sides have hundreds, perhaps thousands of alert missiles, ready to be launched on a moment's notice, *one cannot eliminate completely the possibility of an accidental attack.* If such an accident occurred, even a thin ballistic missile defense system is likely to work well, at least against an attack in which there is only one (or a few) offensive missile(s). (However, it is also all too possible that an accident could involve tens of missiles. These too could probably be handled with one hundred per cent effectiveness by the suggested, or a slightly improved, system.) It could repay the entire cost of the missile system several times over if even one of the lesser accidents were prevented from accomplishing its potential destruction or if the effects of one of the larger accidents were diminished by a larger factor. Indeed, this could be considered a simple, but essential and normal peacetime precaution and could, by itself, justify the costs of the system.

I should probably also mention a corollary of this argument, though one which many readers may not be disposed to weigh heavily because they are not likely to take the objective of surviving a nuclear war as an important, or even a low priority, objective. If a war actually occurred there seems fairly good reason to think that neither side might want to hit many, or any, large cities early in the war. (Cities provide the best hostages for bargaining and intrawar deterrence, to keep the other side from attacking or counterattacking against one's own cities.) However, if there are a number of missiles fired at strategic bases it is more than likely that some will go astray; these could easily strike heavily and disastrously in populated areas. Here again a thin ABM cover for our cities could probably prevent or reduce unintended damage, and even much of the unintended but not completely accidental collateral damage that otherwise would occur in the course of attacks on missile sites and other military installations. While this could reduce deterrence against counterforce attacks, it is hard to believe that this reduction in deterrence is significant, and the reduction in destruction could be immense.

7.   Even a thin ABM promotes a *useful "facade" for psychological and political warfare or for defense against such warfare.* Let us assume that one side or the other in a confrontation is naked while the opponent has at least a facade of ballistic missile defense. The side with the facade might then have a number of advantages. First of all, it could claim that it believed that its facade worked. The other side could not be sure that this belief was wrong and might therefore fear to press the first side too hard. Even if the first side were mistaken, and knew it was mistaken, it might still precipitate or prolong some crisis in the belief that this facade of protection gave it an advantage in the bargaining. While this belief might be wrong, a credible argument for asymmetry of resolve, if not of threat, would exist and therefore the first side might easily back down. The effect might be increased further when it comes to outsiders' estimates of the behavior of the two sides. Allies, sympathizers, neutrals or unfriendly powers all might argue that the side with the ballistic missile defense system must believe their defense is of some value, otherwise they would not have spent money on it; consequently they must at least believe they have an edge over their opponent. Since such belief can easily lead to greater resolve, whether or not it is justified, the outsiders are likely to draw some quite unfortunate conclusions. To put it another way, the side with some kind of defense has an excuse for being firm or arguing that it will stand firm. The side without the defense correspondingly has an excuse or a motivation for backing down, or strong incentive for accepting arguments in favor of backing down—or at least allies and neutrals are likely to believe that this is the situation.

It should be noted that this argument still holds, but is substantially weaker, if both sides have ABM. Now the argument must be, my ABM is better than your ABM, or I believe my ABM is better than your ABM. In either case, the asymmetry is nowhere near as stark and the arguments are therefore correspondingly less persuasive, though they may still be persuasive enough to be useful in certain marginal situations. For example, if some of the citizens of a state allied to the U.S. wish to argue that the U.S. would come to their support in an intense crisis, or even wage war to avenge their annihilation, they could point to the existence of the U.S. ABM system as evidence of the credibility of the U.S. commitment. The lack of such a system could make the consequences to the U.S. of intervention so stark that even the most friendly foreign citizen might find it impossible to believe in, or rely on, U.S. protection or retribution—or even pretend, for various political reasons, to defend the concept of U.S. protection or retribution. This is true even if the eventuality of the American commitment being called upon were very remote.

It is important to view this problem of U.S. credibility in an historical perspective, because the situation has really changed dramatically over the last couple of years: as things used to stand, during the fifties and through the mid-sixties, in any serious crisis the Soviets were more likely to back down than the Americans. It is, of course, common to decry both the practicality and value of strategic superiority. Many will argue that since both sides have "overkill" capability, the notion of strategic superiority is meaningless, degenerating to a useless superiority in the number and/or quality of weapons and not bringing in its train any usable capabilities. This view has probably not yet been tested (and could not have been until roughly 1968 or 1969). Up to that point, the United States strategic forces were relatively well protected and, compared to the Soviets, rather numerous and capable. As a result, any U.S. negotiator could explicitly or implicitly say to a Soviet negotiator, "As you know, if this ever came to a serious showdown, you would be unable to launch any serious attack on U.S. strategic forces. You could only attack U.S. cities, which would, of course, be suicidal since it would immediately be followed by a retaliatory city attack of our own. You would, therefore, be deterred from launching such an attack. We, on the other hand, do have a capability to launch a very serious attack on your strategic forces and largely disarm you. Indeed, we can probably do this without killing many Russians. No doubt some of your strategic forces will survive, but they will be relatively limited in effectiveness. While they could do great damage, they could not wipe the United States out. The contrary would not be true of our retaliatory blow if you tried to use your residual strategic forces in this way." While the details were both unknown to most Americans and all-important, it is reasonably clear that both the Americans and the Soviets have had some inkling that something like the above threat was possible. Of course, the U.S. negotiator would have added that all of the above was irrelevant since the two countries were not going to come to that kind of a showdown; nevertheless it was interesting to note that if they ever did, the United States had a rather substantial and important kind of advantage.

The foregoing is intended to emphasize that one new thing about 1969 is that this strategic advantage will either have disappeared or be close to disappearing. For the first time, the Soviets will have a sense of strategic parity with the United States. We know that the last time the Soviets had a sense of impending superiority (during the so-called missile gap period of the late fifties and very early sixties) they tried to convert this into political gains.

It should be noted in this respect that even a pro forma and operationally meaningless superiority may be psychologically very important. The side possessing it is likely to feel entitled to some gains for its extra strength, and in these kinds of negotiations "feeling entitled" is often a very useful card. I will not continue the discussion of the meaning and implications of strategic superiority here but simply note that the seventies will be the first postwar decade in which it seems likely that the Soviets will not feel any such restraints. While few are concerned about this development, any prudent U.S. government must now take some new possibilities into account. Perhaps the least prudent thing it could do would be to allow a stark but seemingly important asymmetry to develop, e.g., the Soviets have ABM and the U.S. does not—or even more important, to leave U.S. land missiles unprotected in the face of the possibility that the Soviets could threaten Minuteman with MIRV's in the 1970's.[5]

8.   Any defense system, including *the proposed thin deployment, is likely to induce significant uncertainties into the opponent's calculations, force him to carry countermeasures in his missiles, and/or make him modify his tactics.* All of the above can result in large extra costs, operational degradations and/or reductions in the yield carried.

Both sides, of course, have to worry about these uncertainties. In the first level of analysis they can play an important role in deterring an attack, since the attacker cannot rely on his plans working and it seems reasonable that, in the nuclear age, an attacker requires a high degree of certainty. If an attack occurs and the attacker does attempt to hedge against these uncertainties, he is likely to have adopted tactics and procured equipment which resulted in significant compromises in performance and was, perhaps, also much more expensive so that less equipment was actually procured.

[5]See Chapter 6 for Albert Wohlstetter's discussion of this issue.

Even the thin ABM system might be reasonably effective in forcing the Soviets to modify their warheads and their tactics (particularly in regard to total megatonnage delivered and the number of groundbursts versus air bursts) in such a way that if deterrence failed and war actually occurred the actual damage to the environment in the U.S. and possibly even to cities and people might be sharply lessened.

It should be noted that the above costs and the reduction in the size of attack will occur even if the ABM system does not work; all that is required is that it seem to the enemy to have a reasonable possibility of working at the time the war actually occurs. In other words, even if the ABM system is totally un-workable at the moment, the enemy still has to be prepared for the possibility that the system will be fixed. The above effects are sometimes called "virtual attrition" because of the character-istic of being independent of the actual attrition that the system can exert.

It should also be noted that while there is some tendency to buy more missiles in order to offset the uncertainties, the more usual and more efficient reaction is likely to be, as described above, simply changing countermeasures and tactics. Therefore while situations exist in which the above effect can result in an increase in the level of arms, most times this increase is either going to be small or in fact does not occur. In fact, the situation is more likely to go the other way.

9.   Even *a thin ABM system could be important to the U.S. ability to protect important assets useful or vital to postwar recuperation.* If instead of asking the question, "Does an ABM system provide one hundred per cent defense?," we ask the ques-tion, "Does it increase the likelihood that in a large war a relative-ly small but extraordinarily useful portion of our assets will survive?," the whole analysis changes.

Such an emphasis on the continuing existence of the nation, on recuperation, could be very important in generating "friendly" criteria for ABM effectiveness calculations and studies. At the minimum, one might wish to utilize the following criteria in evalu-ating ABM: Will it be successful in saving one or two large cities out of a hundred? Will it save the last five of a hundred ports? Will it save the last five of a hundred refineries, the last five of a hundred steel mills, and so on?

Here the fact that the penetration calculation is uncertain now really helps the defender rather than the attacker. It is a relatively trivial problem, compared to normal criteria, to be able to do quite well by these standards.

However, one meets a psychological problem at this point. I used to go around saying that if war occurs it is better to have twenty million dead than sixty million dead, a statement which aroused the utmost hostility (as opposed to the equally descriptive remark that it is worse to have sixty million dead than twenty million dead). The reason for putting the remark in the first manner was to make clear that the survival of the nation is an essential objective. It is practically impossible to get people to devote energy and intensity of effort, to make bureaucratic sacrifices and compromises, if the end result of it all is defined as a total failure. To see this problem clearly, assume that there has been a war and ten, twenty, or thirty million people have been killed, but fifty or one hundred million lives have been saved by active and passive defenses. The defense people will hardly wish to celebrate these results as a success (they will be lynched if they try it), but in some very real sense their efforts, as opposed to those of the deterrent forces, will have been "a success." And it is important to accept this limited definition of "success" as a criteria or objective; otherwise one gets into the same self-defeating situation which air defense experienced in the fifties. Then, in many quarters, only one hundred per cent attrition of the attacking bombers was "respectable," or acceptable as a definition of success.

10. *Having an ABM system might cause a useful change in the threshold against symbolic or exemplary attacks.* One of the fears of the nuclear age, particularly in a balance of terror situation (at least according to many analysts), is that if a nation is naked of defenses there are a great many types of threats which can be made against it by other nuclear powers, particularly very precise and/or explicit blackmail threats, or threats of punitive or exemplary attacks. One can imagine one side or the other is exploding a small nuclear weapon at some point on the other side's territory in order to warn, frighten, or otherwise influence the behavior of its opponent. It seems, on the whole, to be much easier to design such threats (or attacks) to maximize political advantage and to minimize risks (to the attacker) if there is no ABM. In fact, even a primitive, to say nothing of a thin ballistic missile defense system may make such careful design almost impossible.

It is hard to decide how seriously to take these possibilities, but since many serious theorists and imaginative novelists apparently take them seriously, it may be prudent to add some insurance against them. But one must also add that ABM may also create opportunities for new kinds of symbolic or punitive threats and attacks, although on balance it seems to act more against this possibility than for it.

Turn now to a consideration of some cons. Again I take into account only issues which seem to me worth serious concern. And since I am writing what is, fundamentally, a polemical article, I will spend most of my time on answers to these objections.

1. Probably the most frequent and most important argument against ABM is that *even a thin ABM deployment will stimulate an arms race*. I believe that a heavy deployment around cities might well accelerate the arms race. It probably would not do so nearly as much as most people fear, but the matter is serious enough for this to have been one of the main reasons I consistently have advocated only a thin cover. But it is important to realize that the almost fanatic preoccupation which many Americans seem to have with maintaining a fixed number of Russian hostages has not been a reciprocal preoccupation of the Soviets, at least not during the 24 postwar years. And if we deployed a very heavy ballistic missile defense system today, the Russians still would not be as badly off, in respect to the number of hostages held by the respective sides, as they were in the period between 1945 and some two or three years ago. While they have never seemed extremely sensitive to this issue, it would nonetheless be unreasonable not to expect them to react to a heavy American ABM deployment, and such a reaction, with the American counteraction, would accelerate the arms race.

However, the light cover that is being discussed here, whether of the Safeguard or Sentinel sort, is not likely to raise this problem. If the Soviets in fact prove to be deeply concerned about the thin deployment, they could, and probably would, simply modify their offensive missiles to carry countermeasures and perhaps alter their tactics. This should be sufficient to reestablish the level of their threat to the American population. The opponents of the thin ABM system really cannot have it both ways. They point out, presumably correctly, that on paper it is easy to counter and largely nullify the system (subject, of course, to the uncertainties I have already discussed). They then argue that the Soviets will be so concerned (even though no Soviet defense expert or government spokesman has yet expressed such concern, only Americans have) that they will react in a serious and dramatic way, accelerating the arms race.

2. *The deployment of any kind of ABM system marks a new level in the arms race simply because it is qualitatively so different from any system currently deployed.* It is important to realize that simply adding a new kind of equipment does not necessarily represent an escalation in the arms race. Many individuals were very concerned about the substitution of missiles for bombers in the 1950's. This substitution looked like a very serious escalation because it seemed to displace a relatively safe system (it was difficult to keep bombers on alert, and even after they were launched with bombs aboard, five to ten hours had to pass before they dropped their bombs on their target) with very frightening missile systems (frightening because they could be kept on literally fifteen to thirty second alert and because it took only twenty to thirty minutes before they hit their targets). Today almost all analysts are agreed that much of the last decade was—and very likely the next decade will be—significantly safer because of the introduction of missiles. The Polaris submarine system and the hardened, dispersed Minutemen are both superior, from the viewpoint of arms control, to bombers, which were in fact vulnerable, accident-prone and even likely, under some circumstances, to lead to pre-emptive action for purely technical reasons. Arms control experts now concede that the drastic and dramatic change to the current system of hardened, dispersed, and alert missile forces was for their purposes desirable.

Nevertheless, the deepest motivation that many people have for preventing the deployment of a ballistic missile defense is the hope that this will accomplish a slowing of the rapid rate of weapons change. I have indicated elsewhere that, in our day, every five years or so seems to bring a major revolution in the art and technology of central war. As a result, ideas formulated in one period may easily be obsolete and inappropriate, or even dangerous, five years later. This is a most difficult matter to cope with—for example, in trying to negotiate a long-term arms control treaty. People have the very sound instinct that if they could only slow the pace of change, there might be a much greater chance of learning to cope with it.

It is, however, of great importance that if such slowing down be achieved it be done in a way that stabilizes a reasonably viable and desirable situation. This is not an absolute value; I could easily imagine preferring what is basically a poor situation, but one which is somehow understood, to a new situation which might in some objective sense be easier to deal with, but only after some five years of learning and after the situation had changed again. However, I cannot imagine paying a large price for only a slight increase in understanding and only a slight slow-down; particularly not when the scenario actually involves an attempt to stabilize what is inherently unstable. In any case ABM deployment is of lesser importance in this respect than MIRV, new reconnaissance techniques, laser developments, improvements in guidance, etc., all of which are on the way.

I would argue that attempts to stabilize a position of absolute defenselessness are neither feasible nor desirable, and that the specific issue on which so many proponents of arms control have chosen to fight is one of the worst they could have chosen (a reason why I oppose them so strongly on this point, even though I am myself an ardent exponent of many arms control measures). Not only are the general arguments for including defense capability in any stabilized system fairly good, but in particular, in the era of the MIRV and highly accurate guidance systems, it seems most important to be able to defend at least hardened missile sites. (This is, of course, the main objective of the Safeguard program as announced by the President. To that extent Safeguard is probably even less controversial than the Sentinel program, proposed by Mr. McNamara.)

3. *Any system which protects civilians is not directly and simply related to deterrence of direct attack on the United States and is therefore a diversion of effort, perhaps a harmful one.* Thus ABM for civilians is part of what we sometimes call a "war-fighting" system and seems to assume that deterrence may fail. Many people feel that we must put all our bets on deterrence working and make no preparation to alleviate the consequences if deterrence fails. Others feel that anything which decreases the horror and destruction of war makes war significantly more probable. I myself am generally skeptical of both these arguments. While I am sympathetic to those who fear the results of an inordinate preoccupation with being able to survive a war, I still think at least moderate attention should be paid to this issue. Too great a preoccupation with warfighting can obviously stimulate the arms race or even risk-taking conduct. One can easily imagine a very intense crisis in which the existence of a theory of survival—even if only based on uncertainties—might seriously modify behavior towards greater willingness to stand firm, or even towards taking great chances. But surely, reducing the number of probable dead from, say fifty million, to say twenty

million is not going to change many attitudes, particularly given
the uncertainties. In addition, I would also tend to think that one
gets more rational behavior from a government if its policies are
based upon relatively objective capabilities, capabilities which
also hedge against disaster. Simple "resolve"—a simple insistence
on holding firm because one "must" hold firm—can be disastrous
when it is accompanied by a total unwillingness to face the consequences of deterrence failing. In such a case the government
may be forced into illusioned and unthinking rigidity, or even a
reckless optimism, because it cannot afford to make serious
calculations.

I must add that I find it surprising that so many are anxious
to stop ABM and create a situation where if the other side, or
even a crisis situation undesired by both sides, poses credible
threats of nuclear eruption the government cannot possibly delude
itself as to the apocalyptic implications of "standing firm." Almost all of these individuals lived through the Nazi period when
percisely this "war is unthinkable" attitude was exploited by
Hitler. Hitler, of course, said to his opponents, "one of us has to be
reasonable and it won't be me." He proved that deterrence could
be offensive as well as defensive. In an offensive deterrent situation, the irrational or irresponsible have a clear and possibly
overwhelming advantage over the sober, prudential, "reasonable"
people. For this reason alone it is probably wrong to try to make
the balance of terror excessively stark.

4. *The system may cost more than the proposed one or two
billion a year or so.* I have, of course, been in the business of weapons systems studies for almost twenty years and I am familiar with
the likely rise in a system's cost over the original estimates. There
are generally four important reasons for such a rise in cost. These
are inflation, a rise in real costs, an initial mis-estimate of costs involved in the original proposal, and an increase in the scope of the
system beyond that which was originally proposed. I would argue
that the first possibility is irrelevant, the second argues for early
deployment, the third—with the caveats stated below—is relatively unlikely to be large, at least in terms of increases by a factor
of two or so. The Safeguard system includes only well-studied
hardware; it is well past the point of systems definition. We have a
good deal of relevant hard data. It is therefore almost
impossible to believe that this system could not be built fairly close
to the current estimates. (This does not necessarily apply to the
cost of fixing mistakes, insuring reliability, and the cost of the so-

called software such as programming, training, maintenance, etc. These are very uncertain but seem relatively unlikely to exceed estimates by more than one or two billion dollars in the first five-year period.) There obviously are many uncertainties remaining in the proposed missile deployment, but the range of uncertainties does not seem to be as large as was the case in the F-111 project (where we had little idea of what the plane would actually be like or how one would go about designing and building it). On the other hand, it is very possible that the system will change in character. But this is, at least in part, a matter of conscious government decision, and of public and Congressional debate. And while one sympathizes with those who fear allowing the nose of the camel into the tent, I feel, given likely political developments in the future (which is that the American public is likely to be increasingly hostile towards defense projects and expenditures), unless the government can make a good argument for an enlarged or changed system, it seems unlikely that there will be any "quiet" or unnoticed expansion. And I believe that the case for the thin area defense is so good that I would proceed with the deployment even if there was some risk of a later unjustified expansion.

One possible motive for excessive expansion which was very seriously considered and emphasized in the past seemed at the time, and still seems, so remote as to be almost amusing. This is that local communities would demand missile defense because they would fear being left without protection. We know from the experience of the Nike Ajax and Nike Hercules programs that such a demand did not materialize—in the slightest. For a number of technological and political reasons it seems even less likely in the case of the proposed system. In fact, recent public opposition to the location of Sentinel sites in populated areas suggests that political pressures may in fact push in the opposite direction. But this objection is still common. However, I would conclude that it arises more out of hostility towards defense programs in general (or to the "military industrial complex") than out of a rational assessment of the ABM situation.

5. Another common objection to ABM, and one raised recently by a number of knowledgeable scientists, is that *the system is too complex to work*. This is certainly likely to prove true if the system operates on a one-time basis, with no realistic exercises. It is also likely that there may occur very special conditions when it may not work. On the other hand, in this country we have actually been quite good at making complex systems work. We

have not yet lost a man in space. Indeed one reason the U.S. should get into this business is to learn how to make ABM simpler, more dependable and more reliable, and to gain knowledge of how well this can be achieved. This cannot be done without some deployment, nor in a short period of time after such deployment. It takes experience, organization, procedures, manuals, and so on to shake down a system so that relatively realistic exercises and appraisals can be made. All of these are additional reasons why I think the country should go ahead with the deployment of a thin ballistic missile defense. The problem of devising reasonably or adequately realistic exercises is one that the people concerned should be aware of. If they do not neglect the problem (including checking up in a reliable fashion on the likely and natural optimism of the military services) this problem looks solvable, though so long as the system is not used in war there will always be at least a theoretical uncertainty.

It should also be noted that this issue of reliability is in important ways a competitive problem. The other side's offense capability and particularly its penetration tactics are also likely to depend on the efficient operation of many hundreds, perhaps thousands, of relatively complex and largely untried mechanisms. It might therefore happen, in practice, that the defense system will operate an order of magnitude or so better than expected, because of the unreliability of some aspect of the offense. This could happen even if the defense was also degraded because of operational unreliabilities. It is important to notice that the situation is not completely asymmetrical and that to the extent that it is asymmetrical, as long as one does not demand one hundred per cent in the face of a large coordinated attack, the asymmetries probably favor the defense.

A special worry exists among technical people that we will tend to do "defense conservative" calculations in estimating the performance of our defense, and "offense conservative" calculations on offense estimates, and that at the same time the enemy will do likewise. In other words, *we will underestimate our own capabilities and overestimate his and vice versa.* This would certainly cause a spiraling arms race.

While it is true that the United States, in certain specific areas, has underestimated its capabilities and overestimated the opponent's, I would say that the opposite has generally been true in recent history. As far as the Soviets are concerned, I know of no evidence that they have done this kind of thing—rather the opposite. The Soviet military services do not seem to have the "hostile review" by critical civilian authority or analysts which is so typical of our country. (For example, the Hudson Institute has virtually a vested interest in finding things wrong with the government systems and policies which we study, but little or no vested interest or advantage in arguing that they are right). Even if we make the overestimation/underestimation error, there seems to be little or no tendency for the Soviets to do so as well—and we are not likely to make this mistake just because of the deployment of the ABM system.

6. One can also argue that *any ABM system is inherently untestable.* This is likely to be at least equally true of the offense system of the opponent. I have argued that exactly this kind of uncertainty may be desirable.

7. It would be much *better to apply this five or ten billion dollars to be spent over the next five years to various domestic problems that urgently need funds.* Indeed our domestic programs are crying out for much larger sums, and this is of course an important aspect of the issue: one or two billion dollars may not be enough to make a real difference. But this issue should be debated in more general terms. Do we wish to have an eighty billion dollar or so defense budget, and, if we wish to cut it, do we wish to return these funds to the taxpayer or to reallocate them to various other federal, state or local functions? I would not care to try to settle this general issue; I am prepared to argue that if a cut of one or two billion dollars per year is made in the defense budget it is much better to take the cut out of some of our less useful Vietnamese operations or from other U.S. military expenditures than from ABM. To cut the ABM system because of pressures on the military budget is very much like cutting the lean and leaving the fat. I believe this is so unless you are prepared to argue that, for some specific political or bureaucratic reason, we must choose between ABM and, say, specific and urgent improvements in our educational system. If such specific trades must be made I can easily imagine being against ABM; but there seems to me no reason why the problem should be formulated in this way.

To say this should not be taken as being for or against an over-all cut in the current military budget. I would have to do a much more serious study than I have done to comment very usefully on this issue, but I do note that there are a number of places where there seems to be either "fat" or relatively low priority items in the military budget, while in other areas the costs are going up.

Clearly some programs are going to have to be squeezed, even some worthwhile programs, in order to allow for increased costs. ABM strikes me as one of the more important programs and therefore one of the last that should be squeezed.

8. *The defender must try to outguess the opponent's tactics.* For many purposes the opponent must also try to outguess the defender's tactics. From the technical point of view, unlike almost any other imaginable system, it is relatively easy for the ABM system to revise tactics at the last minute, indeed the last second, to its operative best estimate of the requirements of the situation. Last minute data can be evaluated and tactics more easily changed in the middle of the battle by the proposed ABM than by any offense system I know of. The question of asymmetry is important here. For example, it often is said that one cannot have one hundred per cent defense and therefore we cannot rely on defense. This is correct. But we cannot have one hundred per cent confidence in deterrence, one hundred per cent confidence in arms control, or one hundred per cent confidence in any thing else. We live in an uncertain world and many of the general remarks that are made against ABM are perfectly appliable to every other aspect of modern military planning, and, in fact, to most of modern life.

9. *The proposed ABM is not the best technological alternative, particularly so far as protecting strategic forces is concerned.* This may or may not be correct. It is practically impossible in these studies ever to make a serious argument that a certain proposal is "best." Serious people in this field tend to use the term "preferred" by which they mean that there seem to be many arguments in favor of the recommended system and no particularly overwhelming reason for choosing any other. From the viewpoint of arms control, which I believe to be the most serious consideration here, some of the alternatives that have been suggested are extremely undesirable. The worst (and it is typical of how extreme some people have gone in their opposition to this system) is that we fire our Minuteman missiles on fifteen minutes warning of an attack rather than follow the current procedure which is to have a capability for such firing but basically to expect to ride out any attack on our strategic forces before making any decision to fire. It is still worthwhile to have the capability to fire in a minute or so for a number of reasons. For one thing, it makes the opponent cautious. He can't be sure that you won't fire. For another, you may, in various circumstances, have to change doctrine at the

last moment. But almost all who have looked at this problem agree that once we make it an accepted or standard procedure to fire ICBM's on warning, it begins to get very easy to write scenarios for accidental war. Indeed, one of the main reasons the current system can be considered relatively stable and in any way "acceptable," is that we assume the doctrine of both sides is not to fire on warning.

In fact, one of the reasons we fear Nth nuclear countries is that small countries may find it possible to achieve relative invulnerability for their forces only by a doctrine of firing on warning or by hiding missiles in such a way (e.g., under the sea or in a lake in unmanned sites) that a degree of control and monitoring is lost.

Another technological alternative which might work is simply to multiply the number of Minutemen. But even if this saves money it would seem to be undesirable for other obvious reasons. Another possibility would be to phase out Minuteman and shift our dependence completely to the Polaris submarine. This also seems a mistake, partly because there are conceivable certain vulnerabilities that the Polaris submarine may have, particularly in the future; partly because the Polaris submarine is ordinarily deployed outside the continental waters of the United States, which can raise certain kinds of jurisdictional difficulties; and, in part, because we may wish for a number of reasons to have diverse methods of retaliation.

10. *The proposed system will be obsolete in five or ten years.* This certainly will be true if no changes are made in the system. Much more likely is that we will be able to retrofit and upgrade the system in ways that hold back obsolescence for at least another five or ten years. And then of course we will probably have either to have a major retrofit or a replacement system. This of course is true of every weapon system that the United States has deployed since World War II. One reason for having an ABM system is so we can learn how to retrofit and improve it, learning what its capabilities are and are not, and how to replace it with even better systems. As far as the U.S. government is concerned, it tends to estimate what it calls "five-year operating costs" with the specific assumption that at the end of the five years the system is obsolete and must have justified the total capital invested and the five years of operating costs. Unless a proposed system can meet this standard it generally is not procured. We thus should not be surprised that at the end of five years retrofit or change is necessary. Retrofit, typically, is relatively inexpensive, but eventually

there comes a time when retrofit is insufficient and replacement must occur. This will undoubtedly occur within ten to twenty years of the deployment of the system.

I have somewhat arbitrarily discussed only ten pros and ten cons. On the pro side of the house I have had to rely on my own intuition as to which arguments are the most important. I believe the reader can therefore take that discussion somewhat more seriously than the con side. For the latter, I may have ignored arguments which will seem to many to be of extreme importance. I do not, in any case, claim there are no good arguments against the deployment of a thin ABM system of either the Sentinel or Safeguard type. What I do claim is that the arguments in favor of such deployment are weighty—weighty enough so that even if one comes to a decision against this deployment, one should at least feel some doubt: one may well be wrong. The thing which has disturbed me most about the current debate is the extreme dogmatism found on both sides, but more common among opponents than among the advocates. Those who favor ABM actually seem on the defensive. One result of this is that they often have shifted their ground, which can arouse skepticism. Some of those who favor a thin deployment also do so because they originally wanted a heavy deployment. The accusation that they think of this as a "toe in the water" or as a "camel's nose in the tent" is not completely wrong. But let me re-emphasize my belief that the compromise on the thin deployment was not fortuitous or accidental. As often happens in a democratic give and take, the program which comes out is much better than the one which went in. The thin system is, in my judgment, from the points of view of technology, strategy, arms control, and international politics, perhaps the best compromise that could have been achieved, and almost certainly is the "preferred choice" of those which have any chance of adoption.

Chapter 5

THE CASE FOR POPULATION DEFENSE

by Donald G. Brennan

INTRODUCTION

The subject of defense against ballistic missiles occupies, in terms of the debate about it, a unique position among strategic issues of the nuclear era. Missile defenses have been more intensely debated in the U.S. than any other weapon system selected for deployment, such as the air defense system or the Polaris and Minuteman offensive missile systems, or any arms-control measure adopted to date, including the ban on nuclear tests. In fact, the decision to deploy defenses may well be more important than any other single decision made to date concerning our strategic nuclear forces.

But the published literature of this debate has been one-sided. With few exceptions, and those few mainly confined to journals not noted for their opposition to any weapon system whatever, most of the articles and editorials relating to ballistic missile defense (BMD for short—sometimes, but not here, denoted ABM) published before the spring of 1969 have opposed U.S. deployment of missile defense. For example, there have been three articles in *Foreign Affairs* prior to the April 1969 issue concerned in whole or part with BMD, and all three opposed U.S. deployment.[1] In view of the facts that the U.S. Administration clearly supports American deployment of BMD, and that most of the senior American academic strategists and many prominent students or advo-

[1] J.I. Coffey, The Anti-Ballistic Missile Debate, April 1967; Robert L. Rothstein, The ABM, Proliferation and International Stability, April 1968; and Carl Kaysen, Keeping the Strategic Balance, July 1968.

91

cates of arms control favor deployment at least under some conditions, it is odd that so much of the early published material was single-mindedly in opposition to BMD.[2] The present article is an attempt to clarify for a larger audience some of the reasons why many analysts think it entirely reasonable to favor American deployment.

Missile defenses can have either or both of two major applications: for the protection of people and resources, and for the protection of strategic offensive forces. The Safeguard program announced by President Nixon on March 14, 1969 has important elements of both kinds. The defense of strategic forces has been discussed elsewhere[3], and I shall concentrate mainly on the protection of people and resources.

I shall discuss several considerations relating to a U.S. BMD system intended to have substantial effectiveness against major Soviet attacks, rather than discuss only a so-called "light" or "thin" system intended to be effective only against Chinese or other marginal attacks. Much of the support (both inside and outside the Government) for the original deployment decision for the former Sentinel system came from quarters that believed the system would eventually have significant capability against large Soviet attacks. It seems both possible and desirable that whatever system finally emerges will eventually have such a capability, and therefore it seems appropriate to provide some discussion here of the policy issues this prospect presents. However, I shall also mention a number of points that relate equally to a "light" defense of cities.

In the next section I shall take up the technical-effectiveness issues and state several positive reasons favoring BMD deployment. The section following provides an examination of certain fundamental problems of deterrence and attempts to show that some of the arguments about deterrence made by some critics of BMD are unsound. Arms-control issues are then taken up and it is argued that BMD deployment can contribute positively to

[2]An important exception is in Charles M. Herzfeld, Ballistic Missile Defense and National Security, *Annals of the N.Y. Academy of Sciences,* vol. 134, pp. 119-25, November 22, 1965. Beginning in the spring of 1969, a substantial amount of material favorable to deployment began appearing in various sources.

[3]See especially Albert Wohlstetter, Statement before the Senate Armed Services Committee, April 23, 1969, and supplementary statements submitted by Wohlstetter for the record of those hearings, included as Chapter 6 of this book.

traditional objectives of arms control and, in particular, need not lead to a new arms race.

SOME TECHNICAL ESTIMATES

In an important sense, the key issues in the debate about BMD are not technical. The sense is as follows. There are certain estimates generally believed within the community of people who have carried out the U.S. BMD development to characterize the plausible range of technical and economic effectiveness of systems achievable in the near future. These estimates are subject to some controversy. The sense involved is that even if the uncertainty and controversy concerning the prevailing estimates were wholly removed, most of the articulate critics of BMD deployment would remain critical: their objections are rooted in other concerns, which I shall discuss below.

On the other hand, there is an important sense in which technical issues are vital to the debate, namely that most of the support for BMD deployment, at least within those quarters in which such opinion is subject to change, depends on the fact that the prevailing estimates indicate that a defense of substantial effectiveness is feasible. Indeed, I myself was shifted from being a mild opponent to something of a proponent of deployment in part by a substantial shift in the estimates of effectiveness prevailing in the 1963-65 era. (The other major reason for my own shift stemmed from an improved understanding of Soviet perceptions of these matters, which will be taken up below.)

With this perspective on their role in the debate, let us consider briefly some of the prevailing technical estimates. The main published sources of such information are the unclassified "posture statements" issued annually in recent years by the Secretary of Defense, especially those issued by McNamara in 1967 and 1968, although some supplementary information has been contained in Government hearings and speeches.

A useful way of characterizing the effect of a substantial BMD system is to estimate the number of lives it might save in various specified circumstances. In a table of such estimates given in McNamara's 1968 posture statement, it was indicated that there could be one hundred twenty million American fatalities in certain possible wars of the mid-1970's if no significant BMD were deployed in the U.S. Against the same Soviet forces and attacks, it was indicated that BMD systems costing from ten to twenty billion dollars could reduce expectable fatalities to between ten and forty million Americans, depending on the level of the defense and the details of the war. Damage to production and transportation resources would, of course, be similarly reduced, a result not achievable with economically feasible civil-defense shelter programs. Thus, such a defense might change the postwar U.S. situation from one in which over half the population was gone and recovery in any time period would be problematical to one in which perhaps ninety per cent survived and economic recovery might be complete within five to ten years. This difference would be enormous.

It is this possible difference that constitutes the major motivation for deploying heavy defenses, at least in the minds of many analysts, myself included. In effect, procuring such defenses is like buying "insurance" that would limit the consequences of a war; the outcome would still be a disaster, but probably one of a very different order than the result of having the same offensive forces expended in a war with no defenses. The immediate survivors of the war would certainly notice this difference—indeed, it would probably make all the difference in their own long-term prospects for survival and economic recovery.

It is possible that a BMD system might perform in an actual war much less well than expected, because of some unforeseen technical failure; it is, however, about equally likely that the opposing offensive forces will perform against the defenses much less well than expected, which is to say that the defenses may perform much better than expected. (Critics of BMD are prone to emphasize the first of these points much more than the second.) And, as I shall indicate below, the deployment of defenses may result in saving many millions of lives in a war even if they fail altogether in the war itself.

Of course, the U.S. defense might have to face a Soviet offensive force larger than the one that would have existed if the U.S. defense did not exist. In other words, the Soviets could increase their offensive force so as to nullify, partly or wholly, the U.S. defense. I shall later discuss whether it seems likely that the Soviets would do this; let us here consider how difficult it would be for them to do it. This is one of the important technical characteristics of offense-defense interactions.

A useful way of characterizing the degree of difficulty is with a parameter called the "cost exchange ratio," defined as follows.

The U.S. might deploy a particular defense system at a particular cost. It would generally be feasible for the Soviets to add an increment to their strategic offensive forces that would offset or nullify the opposing defense, and this increment of offense would also have a particular cost. The ratio (cost of the offsetting increment of offense) / (cost of the defense) is called the "cost exchange ratio." Thus, relatively ineffective defenses would have a relatively low cost exchange ratio, while a defense system that would be relatively difficult to penetrate would have a relatively high ratio.

Several years ago, it was widely believed that missile defenses were easy to penetrate, so easy that offensive increments costing only one or a few per cent of the opposing defense would serve to nullify it. In recent years, however, it has become apparent that cheap forms of decoys and other penetration aids cannot be relied upon to nullify modern defense techniques. A good defense can be overcome, but it is difficult. This is reflected in the fact that cost exchange ratios for a good defense are in the region of 1:1, i.e., unity. Thus, *it is about as expensive to nullify a good defense as to build it.*

Some specific examples were provided in the 1967 posture statement. Two postulated defense systems were considered, one costing ten billion dollars and the other twenty billion dollars. Under the conditions of a hypothetical war in which the U.S. fatalities were estimated to be one hundred million without any missile defenses, these BMD systems reduced the fatalities to thirty million and twenty million, respectively, if the Soviets did not change their offensive forces in reaction to the defenses. If the Soviets added an increment to their offensive forces costing one-quarter as much as the BMD, they could raise American fatalities to forty million; if they spent one-half the cost of the defenses, they could raise the level to sixty million; and if they spent as much as the full cost of the defense, the fatalities would rise to ninety million. To raise the level of fatalities back up to the undefended level (one hundred million)—the usual criterion of offsetting a defense—would require an incremental Soviet expenditure on their offensive forces that would exceed the cost of the defense. These calculations assumed that the Soviets had advanced technology for their offensive forces and made effective use of it.

It is worth pointing out that these estimates were published by McNamara, who was an intense critic of missile defenses. It is therefore in no way to be expected that these estimates are biased in favor of missile defenses.

Although McNamara published information showing that exchange ratios were about unity as far back as January 1967, and although information to this effect was known in the Government for perhaps two or three years before that, many critics of missile defenses continue to assert that it is cheaper to offset defenses than to build them. For example, Kaysen, in his July 1968 article in *Foreign Affairs,* said: "Were we to deploy much stronger and more costly defenses [than the initial Sentinel program] it would remain within the Soviet capability to counter them by corresponding increases in the size of their offensive deployments —*which could probably be made at significantly less cost than that of our increased defenses.*" (Emphasis added.) If "counter" means "wholly or largely offset," as is usual and as Kaysen's context suggests, there is no objective basis for the italicized statement, and there has not been for some few years. As additional examples of peculiar reporting of this matter, an unambiguous misstatement of fact concerning exchange ratios was contained in a much-cited article by Garwin and Bethe,[4] and a very misleading statement was made by Wiesner.[5]

Some remarks on these estimates of effectiveness and cost are in order. To begin with the matter of cost, the two deployments considered above were estimated to cost ten and twenty billion dollars. McNamara, in speaking about the latter program, several times referred to the fact that many weapon systems proved to cost twice as much as originally estimated, as indeed they have, and suggested that this program would more likely cost forty billion

---

[4]"[McNamara] finds invariably (in the 1968 Posture Statement) that the offense, by spending considerably less money than the defense, can restore casualties and destruction to the original level before defenses were installed," Richard L. Garwin and Hans A. Bethe, Anti-Ballistic Missile Systems, *Scientific American,* March 1968, pp. 21-31. (Quotation at p. 31.)

[5]"Secretary McNamara . . . concede[s] that an anti-Soviet ABM defense would not be worth the huge expense, because the Russians could nullify its effectiveness at considerably lower cost to themselves." Jerome B. Wiesner, The Case Against an Antiballistic Missile System, *Look* Magazine, November 28, 1967, pp. 25-7. (Quotation at p. 26). The Secretary had perhaps quoted such estimates in earlier years, but ten months preceding Wiesner's article he had published a posture statement including unity cost exchange ratios.

dollars when completed.[6] Some journalists and others have in turn doubled McNamara's estimate once again, and one can find articles and newspaper editorials referring to BMD systems alleged to cost eighty to one hundred billion dollars. It is difficult to escape the feeling that these latter estimates are made purely for their political effect, and have no significant basis in reality. Missile defense systems had been much more extensively studied at the time these estimates were worked out than was true of many of the weapon systems whose early cost estimates proved much too low. Moreover, it is possible for the Secretary of Defense to decide to spend no more than a certain sum, say fifteen billion dollars, on investment cost in missile defense, and to instruct the services to produce the best possible defense within that budget, rather than to commit himself to a deployment specified in quantities and characteristics of equipment of possibly uncertain cost.

Obviously the relationship between cost and performance of a system as large and complex as those considered here cannot be specified in advance with anything like precision. This should not obscure the fact that the range receiving major consideration or advocacy is, say, eight to twenty billion dollars.

For some perspective on this range of costs, it is instructive to consider that the U.S. has spent perhaps fifty billion dollars on air defense since World War II.[7] We are currently still spending almost two billion dollars per year on air defense. And, while estimates of the impact of the air defense system on U.S. casualties from Soviet bomber attacks are not available, it is a good bet that the current air defense system is and has been less important as insurance for the country than the major proposed BMD systems would be.

It would be fair to ask how stable these estimates of effectiveness are likely to prove in the future. That is, while it now appears that a U.S. BMD system costing between ten and twenty billion dollars could reduce American fatalities from one hundred or

[6]The Polaris program, with a total hardware cost of about fourteen billion dollars through Fiscal Year 1969, is an example of a major program in which the actual costs were very close to the estimated costs.

[7]Herbert Roback, Staff Administrator of the Military Operations Subcommittee, U.S. House of Representatives, in E.P. Wigner, (ed.), *Who Speaks for Civil Defense?* Scribner's, New York, 1968, p. 95.

one hundred twenty million to perhaps ten to forty million in possible wars of the mid-1970's if the Soviets do not substantially increase their offensive forces in reaction, and that the cost to the Soviets to substantially nullify the defense would be at least comparable to the cost of the defense, is it likely that these estimates will still seem reasonable when we get to the mid-1970's?

A question of this form does not admit an unequivocal answer; one cannot say with confidence whether inventions not yet made or developments not yet realized will more favor offense or defense, although there are some reasons for thinking the trend will continue to favor the defense. But a parallel may be useful. In the U.S., we have had fairly high confidence for over a decade that the Polaris submarine force is a reasonably secure component of our strategic offensive forces. The main reason for this confidence resides in the fact that we have conducted a major research and development program—on the order of one-half billion dollars per year— in anti-submarine warfare for many years, and no cheap and reliable way of attacking such submarines has been found. A similar statement is beginning to be true in relation to BMD: we have conducted a major research and development program—on the order of one-third billion dollars per year— in means of penetrating missile defenses for several years, and no cheap and reliable way of penetrating a good defense has been found. This does not guarantee that one cannot be found, and it does not say that expensive ways of penetrating are not known— as are expensive ways of attacking Polaris submarines. But it does suggest that the technical prospects for missile offense-defense interactions, while not yet as stable as the submarine-antisubmarine situation, are likely to prove acceptably stable, and in particular should be a great deal better than the early estimates of air defense proved.

It is worth noting that a BMD system may possibly have important effects even if it later failed to perform as expected in a war. If the Soviets were to react to a U.S. defense by retrofitting their existing missile force with decoys and other penetration aids, without a major increase in the number of rockets, they would reduce the total payload available for warheads, and thereby reduce the potential damage the U.S. might incur in a war even if the defense failed utterly. This effect, which is known in the trade as "virtual attrition" and is often encountered in defensive systems of other kinds, is likely to be quite modest. A more important possibility could arise through re-targeting of the Soviet offensive force because of a U.S. defense; the Soviets might concentrate most or all of their offensive missiles (apart from those used for missile bases or other military targets) on the largest cities to be sure of destroying them, and leave unattacked many medium and small cities. Or they might attack only undefended areas, and leave aside most or all the largest (defended) cities. In either case, the mere presence of the defense could result in saving many millions of lives no matter whether it "worked" or not. Freeman Dyson has summarized this possibility with the amusing observation that BMD is very good at protecting cities that are not attacked; the real point, of course, is that it may sharply reduce the number of significant cities that are attacked.

Let us mention briefly here three other positive reasons favoring U.S. BMD deployment. First, the time may soon arrive, if it is not already here, when there will be some possibility of attacks of anonymous or disguised origin. Since these would not be subject to standard threats of deterrence, active defenses may be the primary protection against such attacks. Second, the possibility of a purely accidental launch of some part of the Soviet force is probably very remote, but the possibility of an unauthorized launch, especially during an intense crisis, may not be so remote and should be protected against. Even a modest defense might be very effective against such an attack; this has been one of the arguments used—rightly, I believe—in support of the current Safeguard program. Third, missile defenses (even light defenses) considerably complicate the planning of an attacker who would penetrate them; this phenomenon seems likely to serve as an additional "firebreak" to the initiation of a strategic nuclear war.

It may be useful to expand briefly upon one of these points, viz., the possibility of a disguised attack, or what is sometimes called a "catalytic" attack—an attempt by some third country to trigger a war between two countries by attacking one in such a way that it will be thought to have been done by the other. Some strategists have been skeptical of the possibility that such an attack could or would be carried out. While it does seem unlikely that disguised attacks would be a serious threat in periods of low international tension, the possibility could be very real—and correspondingly dangerous, in a period of acute crisis.

Consider, for example, the Cuban missile crisis. At the onset of that crisis, President Kennedy said: "It shall be the policy of this nation to regard any nuclear missile launched from Cuba against any nation in the Western hemisphere as an attack by the Soviet

Union on the United States requiring a full retaliatory response upon the Soviet Union." If the Chinese had had a missile-launching submarine near Cuba at that time, they might well have been tempted by what would have appeared, as a consequence of that statement, to be a possibility of eliminating both of their major opponents with one stroke. And if they *had* been tempted, the strategem might, as a consequence of the intense tension within the U.S. government at that time, possibly have worked.

It is not possible to protect against threats of this kind by ordinary deterrence; indeed, the major hazard of a catalytic attack arises out of, and is motivated and made possible by, an existing posture of deterrence. The potential role of active defense against such attacks is twofold. First, since such an attack would be relatively "small' (perhaps a few tens of missiles might be plausible in some circumstances), there is a good chance that even a light defense would completely or almost completely eliminate the damage the attack would have produced in the absence of any defense. Second, eliminating or greatly reducing the possible damage the attack might cause would greatly reduce the likelihood that the attack would trigger a near-reflex catastrophic, and catastrophically mistaken, response.

It should be noted that there are still other possibilities of undeterrable attacks, apart from the disguised variety, but construction of the relevant scenarios would take us too far from the main path.

PROBLEMS OF DETERRENCE

One of the main areas of concern to critics of missile defense has to do with the impact of missile defense on fundamentals of deterrence. While it is certainly natural that this concern should arise, I believe that any specific justification for the concern largely evaporates on examination. Let us consider this area.

The problem has often been related to what McNamara termed the "Assured Destruction" mission of the U.S. strategic forces, identified by him in his 1968 posture statement to mean "an ability to inflict at all times and under all foreseeable conditions an unacceptable degree of damage upon any single aggressor, or combination of aggressors—even after absorbing a surprise attack." (p. 47.) McNamara recognized that what constituted "an unacceptable degree of damage" was not subject to precise specification, and in spelling out this requirement, he said (*ibid.,* p. 50): "In the case of the Soviet Union, I would judge that a capability on our part to destroy, say, one-fifth to one-fourth of her population [i.e., about fifty million Russians] and one-half of her industrial capacity would serve as an effective deterrent."[8]

Let us note here that in this and in every other context in which McNamara discussed this issue, he defined the "Assured Destruction" requirement *without any reference to the nature or scale of the Soviet threat.* I shall come back to this fact.[9]

Because McNamara came to regard the ability to destroy fifty million Russians as the keystone of Western security, he viewed Soviet deployment of BMD as a potential threat to that security, and intended to nullify any Soviet defenses with added U.S. offensive forces. He also appeared to believe, and frequently asserted, that the Soviets had a similar requirement for an "Assured Destruction" capacity, and that any U.S. interference with this requirement would in all likelihood only cause the Soviets to increase their offensive forces. It appears that this perception was at the core of McNamara's opposition to BMD deployment, as it was for many other opponents of missile defenses. The U.S. strategic posture that has evolved from this perception in recent years has been aptly dubbed a posture of "Assured Vulnerability" by Steuart Pittman.[10] I shall later discuss the evidence concerning Soviet views on this matter; let us first review the origin and nature of the alleged American requirement for a fixed large number of Russian hostages.

The U.S. first became involved in the business of strategic nuclear deterrence in the very late 1940's and the early 1950's, say up through 1953. The Soviets had no major ability to attack the U.S. directly in this period and the primary perceived requirement of the American stategic forces was to deter a Soviet assault

[8]However, in his table on p. 57 of Soviet population and industry destroyed at various levels of attack, McNamara underlined the entries for 74 million fatalities and 76 per cent industrial capacity destroyed.

[9]It will appear throughout that I am highly critical of McNamara's handling of BMD—as, indeed, I am. I should like to add that, in spite of this fact, I still believe he was the greatest Secretary of Defense the U.S. has had, at least until 1964 or 1965.

[10]Government and Civil Defense, Steuart Pittman, former Assistant Secretary of Defense for Civil Defense, in Wigner, *op. cit.*

on Western Europe. This requirement (among others) was articulated by John Foster Dulles in his famous "massive retaliation" policy early in 1954. The U.S. offensive forces that were intended to provide the deterring threat were changing in this period, but the U.S. threat may be roughly summarized as a few hundred bombers armed with pure fission (not thermonuclear) bombs with a yield of a few tens of kilotons, for a total deliverable threat of a few tens of megatons. It is doubtful if the Soviet fatalities that this force would have produced were accurately estimated in that period, and they certainly were not publicized, but it is most unlikely that they would have exceeded a few million, at least until quite late in the period.

Now, there were many criticisms made of the "massive retaliation" policy when it was first publicized, but there were few if any criticisms to the effect that the U.S. threat was inadequately deterring. It is therefore instructive to recall the perceived Soviet threat of that period: It was the Soviet Union of Stalin, believed to have a six-million-man army, a Soviet Union which had only recently subjugated Eastern Europe, and which was believed to have instigated or at least approved the Korean war. Not even the recent Czech invasion makes the Soviet Union of today seem nearly as threatening. And this was the threat that was widely judged to be adequately deterred by a few tens of megatons.[11]

Beginning in about 1954, two important changes occurred. The first of these was what can fairly be called a technological accident, namely, it was found that thermonuclear bombs could be made to work. This made it possible to increase the explosive yield achievable in a given weight of bomb by factors such as twenty or fifty or one hundred. The other (and more important) change was that the advent of a Soviet long-range bomber force armed with substantial numbers of nuclear weapons presented the threat of a direct attack on the U.S.

In the period when the Soviets could not mount a major attack on the U.S., an implicit part of the U.S. threat to protect Europe was the fact that, even if the Soviets overran Europe at a time when U.S. strategic forces could not have put an immediate

---

[11]As McNamara and others have rightly pointed out, the total yield in megatons does not adequately reflect the total effect of a force. We have, however, no better measure readily available with which to make these comparisons, and the comparisons in these terms will at least not be grossly misleading.

full stop to the Soviet production and military establishments, the Soviets would have been unable to prevent the continuation of the U.S. as a fighting society and the continuation of U.S. attacks against Soviet facilities and forces. The Soviets could scarcely have counted on any net gain from an attack on Europe in this situation and could not have eliminated their principal opponent.

When major direct Soviet attacks on the U.S. became possible, the structure of the situation changed considerably. It might then have become possible for the Soviets to have eliminated the U.S. as a fighting society, and thereby to secure Europe and eliminate their principal opponent at one blow. Thus, many strategists judged that there were two reinforcing reasons why it was appropriate to react to this possibility with a large strategic threat to deter it: On the one hand, this possibility might in some crisis have loomed as extremely valuable to the Soviets, a possibility for which they might have been prepared to pay large costs, such as a few million fatalities; on the other hand, if such a possibility came to pass, it would have been essentially and promptly lethal for the whole of the West—in a political sense, in a literal physical sense for many millions, and in an economic sense for the survivors.

The Soviets might in some circumstance have badly wanted to do it, and we certainly wanted badly that they should not do it. Moreover, there appeared to be no technical defense in sight that would have substantially reduced the possible Soviet motivation to do it, or our motivation to deter it. This was the fundamental driving force behind the evolution in the late 1950's and early 1960's of a U.S. strategic threat measured in thousands of megatons—a deterrent threat for which "Assured Destruction" was indeed the correct phrase. It was the result of designing a force that would assure the Soviets that they could not mount a lethal attack against the West without encountering lethal retaliation.

It is clear from the origin of this perfectly reasonable logic that, to the extent the maximum possible Soviet motivation for such an attack might have been reduced, or to the extent the U.S. motivation to deter it might have been reduced, the scale of the retaliatory threat might have been reduced in some corresponding degree. It is this linkage that appears to have been wholly absent from McNamara's thinking about strategic forces in recent years. So far as can be seen from the record, at least when missile defense was under consideration, McNamara was determined to be able to kill fifty million Russians *no matter what* the maximum Soviet threat.

If a maximal Soviet strategic attack were capable of destroying, say, ten million Americans and fifteen per cent of our industry, they would no doubt be more deterred by the threat of losing fifty million Russians and fifty per cent of their industry than if our retaliatory threat were "only" fifteen million Russians and twenty per cent of their industry, other things being equal. There is therefore a certain attractiveness in trying to forget about any linkage between threat and retaliation, and fixing once and for all some intended level of "Assured Destruction" which is believed capable of deterring the Soviets from any actions whatever that might bring this force into play. Among other things, this would spare the necessity of thinking through some difficult issues (though it brings in some new ones of its own, notably the question of how much "Assured Destruction" is "enough"). But there are a number of problems resulting from such a posture, of which the most immediate for our purposes is that it tends to make it difficult for us to limit damage to *ourselves*—i.e., it tends to force *us* into a posture of "Assured Vulnerability."

In particular, a determination to maintain a large fixed level of "Assured Destruction" capability against the Soviets led McNamara to respond to incipient Soviet missile defenses by increasing U.S. offensive-force capabilities, and the theory that the Soviets would do likewise led McNamara to oppose the deployment by the U.S. of an anti-Soviet BMD system. In view of the effectiveness of modern defense, we might better have used the U.S. resources committed to increasing our offensive forces to increase our defenses instead. By thus reducing the Soviet threat, rather than increasing our own, we should have reduced both the extent to which the Soviets might gain by attacking us, and the extent to which we are intensely motivated to deter the attack.

It is easy to understand the effects involved here in a simplified case. Consider a situation in which Soviet and American offensive forces are fixed at similar unchanging levels on each side, and in which both the U.S. and the Soviet Union are building comparable levels of defenses. If the American and Soviet defenses are both "light," then our BMD would not much diminish Soviet ability to destroy us, but the Soviet BMD would not much reduce the effectiveness of our assured-destruction forces either; if both American and Soviet defenses are "heavy," then our assured-destruction forces would be significantly degraded, but so too would the capability of the Soviets to eliminate the U.S. as a fighting society.

This points to the following formulation of a reasonable requirement for a conservative American strategic posture:

> Following any plausibly feasible strategic attack by the Soviet Union, the U.S. should have the capacity to inflict as much or more total damage (of similar kind) on the Soviet Union as the Soviets had inflicted and could still inflict on the U.S.[12]

In short, we should have a reliable capability to do at least as badly unto the Soviets as they had done or could do unto us. This would imply that, if the Soviets started a strategic war with us, they would be guaranteed to come out worse, a powerful deterrent to starting such a war. The Soviets could not achieve a significant military advantage by a strategic attack, and an irrational, coercive, or punitive attack—whether large or small—would risk bringing as much or more destruction on the Soviets as they could or did bring on us. This would make the initiation of nuclear blackmail unattractive to any reasonable decision-maker at any effective level of strategic forces.

Let us note explicitly that this posture does not imply that a U.S. capability to destroy fifty or seventy-four or one hundred million Russians is a fundamental requirement of nature, without regard to the circumstances. It indicates that both the U.S. and the Soviet Union might reasonably engage in some measures to limit the possible damage of a war without necessarily impairing U.S. security in the process. Such measures might include, for instance, direct reduction of strategic offensive forces by agreement, or deployment of defenses with or without explicit agreement.

It is interesting that the U.S. has, in fact, proposed direct reductions in strategic offensive forces. For several years, we have had a proposal before the Geneva disarmament negotiations to reduce such forces by cutting a substantial percentage from each side in each of two stages.[13] It is obvious that this proposal must have been evaluated with regard to some criterion for a strategic posture similar to the one discussed just above; one cannot carry out unlimited reductions in offensive forces and still be able to

[12]This principle implies that the strategic offensive forces must be quite well protected, which appears to be feasible.

[13]U.S. Draft Treaty of April 29, 1965.

guarantee the capability to kill seventy-four million Russians, or whatever such number is selected. Now, if certain necessary requirements are met, as they can be, a symmetric increase in active defenses deployed by each of the superpowers would have approximately the same kind of potential impact on possible war outcomes that percentage cuts in offensive forces would have. It seems odd that McNamara (among others) never appeared willing even to consider possibilities of missile defense in the light of the strategic criteria he applied to percentage cuts in offensive forces.

One may ask: If BMD deployed in both superpowers would have roughly the same effect on possible war outcomes as direct reductions on both sides in offensive forces, why not simply reduce the latter, and save the money and trouble of the BMD? The answer is that in some circumstances one might, but the circumstances are not those now prevailing. To reduce U.S. and Soviet offensive forces to a level where the possible casualties on each side (without defenses) did not exceed, say, twenty million would likely be acceptable to the U.S. only with a degree of inspection that is most unlikely to be acceptable to the Soviets. In other words, there appears to be no current political feasibility of offensive-force cuts on such a scale, while there seems to be ample feasibility of suitable BMD deployment—which, rather than increasing U.S. needs for inspection of Soviet offensive forces, might actually *reduce* our sensitivity to such information. This effect, indeed, would facilitate later direct reductions in offensive forces. (There are other motives for BMD, such as protection against Chinese or anonymous attacks, that would not be affected by Soviet-American reductions. These motives, however, might be satisfied by a light defense.)

From the mid-1950's to the mid-1960's, the strategic postures of the superpowers were dominated by the logic that, since we could not defend, we had to deter. This position, for which there was originally ample justification, now seems to be interpreted in some minds, chiefly certain American ones, to mean that, since we must deter, we cannot defend. This should count as the *non sequitur* of the decade.

ARMS RACES AND ARMS CONTROLS

The final major area of concern to critics of missile defenses is that of arms races, and correlated arms-control problems. The kind of arms race involved here is what is called an offense-defense race. The usual image of this is that if, say, the U.S. procures some missile defenses, the Soviet Union will feel obliged to respond by increasing its offensive forces sufficiently to nullify the defense. This increase in Soviet offense capability might in turn motivate the U.S. to increase its defense capability still further, and so on. For example, McNamara said (in his 1967 posture statement, p. 53): "It is the virtual certainty that the Soviets will act to maintain their deterrent which casts such grave doubts on the advisability of our deploying the Nike X system for the protection of our cities against the kind of heavy, sophisticated missile attack they could launch in the 1970s. In all probability, all we would accomplish would be to increase greatly both their defense expenditures and ours without any gain in real security to either side." (The whole of this passage is underscored in the original.)

If arms-race responses of this kind occur, they will not be because of some fundamental law of nature, but will result from interactions of achievable technology with prevailing attitudes and budgets. Each of these factors is of importance.

It is useful to discuss this problem in terms of the concept of cost exchange ratios. If cost exchange ratios were as low as .01, or one per cent, there would be little doubt that, within the present political environment, a defense system deployed by one superpower would be nullified by the other. For example, if the Soviets built, say, a twenty billion dollar system, and if it would cost the U.S. only two hundred million dollars to neutralize it, there would scarcely be any debate about the matter within the U.S. bureaucracy, the Congress, or the public: the Defense Department would simply go ahead and neutralize the Soviet defense. In this world, the technology (as linked to budgets) would surely dominate the attitudes, and deterrence would reign supreme; defense could have at most a marginal role, at least as between the superpowers. There would be very slight motivation in either country to build defenses against the other, and most likely they would not be built.

On the other hand, if cost exchange ratios were in the neighborhood of one hundred or more, there would again be little debate, but in this world, defense would reign supreme, and deterrence would rest on very different threats and counter-threats than those that loom as dominant today. In this case, to nullify a twenty billion dollar Soviet defense would cost the U.S. $2,000 billion. The expenditure of such a sum within foreseeable budgets is not, of course, a realistic possibility, and the U.S. would instead be building its own defense—about which there would be little controversy, and which the Soviets could not offset either. Again, the technology would dominate prevailing attitudes.[14]

In the actual world that is upon us of cost exchange ratios near unity, perhaps one-half or three but not one-tenth or ten, the attitudes prevailing are not driven by the technology toward either deterrence or defense, but may (and do) go in either direction. It is much more a matter of preference and conscious decision whether we and the Soviets wish to spend our strategic-force budgets chiefly to increase the level of "hostages" on the other side, or to decrease our own. Thus, whether we are to have an offense-defense arms race or not depends in the first instance on whether Soviet and American attitudes are lined up the same way or not. If both governments are willing to accept a high level of hostages on each side, with modest or no defenses, there will be no great pressures for an offense-defense race; similarly if both are willing to live with substantial defenses and relatively low levels of hostages, with modest or no attempts on either side to offset the defense of the other. But if one side attempts to reduce its own hostages below the level demanded by the other, or attempts to increase the hostages of the other above a level the other considers acceptable in the circumstances, and especially if both happen together in any combination, the resulting pressures for an arms race might well be limited mainly by budgetary forces.

The fact that these issues are importantly influenced by attitudes is not always clearly recognized. There is, however, something of a "fashion" in some circles against interfering with the so-called requirements for "Assured Destruction" capabilities on either side, especially when (almost only when) the interference comes from missile defense. But, as I have argued earlier, maintaining very high levels of possible Soviet damage does not seem to be a requirement of U.S. security in circumstances where we

---

[14]Experts may recognize that this discussion is simplified. The principle illustrated, however, remains valid when the complications are taken into account.

can correspondingly limit damage to ourselves, and indeed it is in some degree antithetical to the objective of limiting our own possible damage. Still less, of course, is it a requirement of U.S. security to maintain high levels of U.S. hostages on behalf of the Soviets. Outside of the group who have been actively opposing defenses, I believe that these facts are generally recognized among people concerned with national defense. "Assured Vulnerability" has characterized the trend of our strategic posture in recent years because of the views of McNamara and a few others, not because of the defense community as a whole, most of which has opposed the trend. Therefore, while the kind of fashion mentioned above has and has had important adherents, it seems unlikely to prove dominant in the U.S. policy process in the future. American attitudes in this regard are mixed, but there is at least a fair chance that views favoring more emphasis on defense, views which are in fact rather widely held, will prove important in the evolution of the U.S. strategic posture.

Soviet attitudes concerning hostage levels seem much less mixed, so far as can be seen; they are much more friendly to the deployment of defenses. In particular, contrary to many statements made by American critics of U.S. BMD, it appears that the Soviets are not substantially antagonized by the prospect of U.S. BMD. I shall mention some of the evidence for this.

Let us begin with the passage of McNamara's quoted above, in which he implied that it was a "virtual certainty" that the Soviets "will act to maintain their deterrent," i.e., will act to nullify any U.S. defense by increasing their offense. Now, if the Soviets were in fact committed to a response of the sort McNamara said they were, which would at least cost them substantial money, the first ones we should expect to hear making such statements would be, not McNamara, but the Soviets themselves. So far as can be seen, the Soviets have never been bashful about making political and diplomatic statements designed to deter publicly known U.S. programs they did not like, or to embarrass the U.S. over programs that at least were not advantageous to them. For example, they have repeatedly made public statements opposing the operation of U.S. Polaris submarines in the Mediterranean, and the operation of nuclear-armed air-alert bomber forces.

In the light of past Soviet political offensives against unwanted U.S. programs, it would be remarkable in the extreme if the Soviets had the attitudes attributed to them by McNamara and yet did absolutely nothing to discourage U.S. defenses. The fact is, however, that there seems to be no reliable report of any Soviet attempts to deter our BMD by such statements, either public or private, official or unofficial.

There is a great deal of additional evidence, beyond this negative but persuasive fact, indicating that Soviet attitudes have not been at all in McNamara's direction. There have, for instance, been many statements by individual Russians at both official and unofficial levels, both impromptu and carefully considered. In a press conference in London on 9 February 1967, Premier Kosygin was asked: "Do you believe it is possible to agree on the moratorium on the [deployment] of an anti-missile defense system [a then-current American proposal] and if possible on what conditions?" He replied in part: "I believe that defensive systems, which prevent attack, are not the cause of the arms race, but constitute a factor preventing the death of people. Some argue like this: What is cheaper, to have offensive weapons which can destroy towns and whole states or to have defensive weapons which can prevent this destruction? At present the theory is current somewhere that the system which is cheaper should be developed. Such so-called theoreticians argue as to the cost of killing a man—$500,000 or $100,000. Maybe an anti-missile system is more expensive than an offensive system, but it is designed not to kill people but to preserve human lives. I understand that I do not reply to the question I was asked, but you can draw yourselves the appropriate conclusions." Indeed, one can.

A detailed rebuttal to the standard arguments against BMD was given by the late Soviet military publicist Major General N. I. Talensky in the quasi-official Soviet journal *International Affairs* in October 1964. It may be interesting to note that the Talensky article, though not so identified, was at least partly a response to a paper presented to Talensky and other Russians earlier in 1964 by a group of Americans that included the present writer, a paper opposing defenses written by Jeremy Stone but which I had a good deal to do with. I have, of course, since changed my views, although Stone has not.[15] Many other contacts with Russians at official and unofficial levels, including several meetings I personally have had the chance to observe, illustrate that the attitude exemplified by the Kosygin quotation above is very

[15]Stone's paper was later published, with modifications, in his book. See J.J. Stone, *Containing the Arms Race,* The M.I.T. Press, Cambridge, Mass., 1966, especially Chapter One, Antiballistic Missiles and Arms Control.

widely held in the Soviet Union, while the attitude held by American critics of BMD, such as McNamara or Kaysen, toward the alleged importance of matintaining high hostage levels seems not to be held at all. Soviet strategic literature also does not reflect a McNamara-like view. So far as can be seen, the Soviets simply do not adhere to such a model of deterrence.

The main criticisms of BMD that have been expressed by any Russians, so far as I am aware, have come from a few scientists who have been skeptical of the effectiveness of defenses and therefore regarded them as wasteful of resources. It is probably significant that these scientists seem not closely associated with current Soviet weapon programs; I believe it likely that they are following the lead of some of their Western friends and counterparts, except that even these Russian critics seem not to share in the theoretical opposition to BMD. One major Russian scientist who *is* closely associated with the Soviet missile program has said (to Americans) that effective missile defense is on the whole probably realizable. Other Soviet criticisms, arising out of the March 1969 "Safeguard" decision, have been political (rather than strategic) in character.[16]

One additional bit of evidence is worth mentioning. After McNamara announced the decision to deploy the Sentinel BMD system in September 1967, the U.S. came under attack from several of our allies and neutral friends, especially from several countries participating in the Eighteen-Nation Disarmament Committee then meeting in Geneva, who complained that the American deployment decision would be bad for the incipient non-proliferation treaty and would only heighten the arms race. There was one country that came to our assistance in that context, holding that the decision would not harm the prospects for the non-proliferation treaty: that country was the Soviet Union.[17] So far as I am aware, this is the only case on record in which the Soviet Union has defended us diplomatically against our friends and allies. This is all the more remarkable in view of the fact that the Soviets did not, then or since, believe that the Sentinel system was intended only for Chinese attacks. (In some sense, as will be evident from this article, their skepticism was well placed.)

[16]See Johan J. Holst, Missile Defense, the Soviet Union, and the Arms Race, Chapter 7.

[17]See Thomas J. Hamilton, U.S. Says Nike Net Will Spur Atom Pact, *The New York Times,* September 20, 1967.

The fact that the Soviets apparently do not share the view of McNamara and some of his associates toward deterrence and "Assured Destruction" requirements does not, of course, mean that they are disinterested in military matters. It appears that Soviet strategists generally emphasize the importance of maintaining a good position in relation to the U.S., but seem not to understand this to mean that they must maintain some large fixed number of American hostages without regard to the circumstances. The sharp increase in Soviet offensive forces that has taken place in the recent past is evidence that they did not wish to remain in a position inferior to the U.S. in such forces; it provides no evidence whatever that they have come to hold the "Assured Destruction" dogma that has held sway here.

Some American critics of BMD have described these Soviet attitudes as "unsophisticated," and argued that the Soviets will "get over it," and come to respond to an American defense as McNamara predicted even if they are not yet committed to it. It is true that strenuous efforts to "educate" the Soviets have been made by McNamara and others, and one cannot say with certainty that these efforts will fail; it would not be the first time that the Soviets lost their senses over some issue just as we were coming to ours. But their views in the past should not be denigrated; it seems to me, and to many other Western strategists, that the defense-oriented philosophy exhibited by the Soviets makes good sense. As to matters of fundamental approach to deterrence and defense, I should say that we in the U.S. might better acquire some "education" from the Soviets.

In view of the fact that Soviet attitudes already seem to favor defenses, and that American attitudes, while currently mixed, *ought* to favor defenses, the obvious way of trying to improve prevailing strategic postures through arms control arrangements is to limit offensive forces primarily, and to limit defenses only secondarily, if at all. This is exactly the reverse of the order of priorities frequently suggested in the U.S. in the past few years. It is, however, more in keeping with the traditional aims of arms control. The primary objectives of arms control have often been stated to be reducing the likelihood of war or mitigating its consequences if it occurs.[18] In view of the arguments of the preceding

[18]See my introductory chapter, Setting and Goals of Arms Control, in D.G. Brennan, Ed., *Arms Control, Disarmament, and National Security,* Braziller, N.Y., 1961. The definitions given there have been widely used.

sections, it seems to me highly probable that deployment of missile defenses will contribute to both of these objectives, while abstaining from defenses will likely contribute to neither. If the deployments are managed with at least modest intelligence in both the U.S. and the Soviet Union, there need not even be arms-race responses that would further add to prevailing arms expenditures.

This is not the place for detailed examination of technical issues, but I should remark that a suitable way of limiting offensive forces in such a context might well be to have an understanding between the U.S. and the Soviet Union, preferably an informal and flexible one, that the total weight of all offensive forces on each side, missiles, planes, and tankers, should be held within some ceiling. This ceiling should be the same for each side and set high enough, at least initially, to include forces on hand or already in procurement. In that case, it would impose no new inspection requirements, i.e., beyond those we already try to satisfy in the present world. My personal inclination would be to exempt defensive forces from controls altogether, except perhaps for interceptor missiles that were large enough to serve as offensive missiles, but if there were a suitable consensus that some mild limitation was desirable, such as limiting the rate of deployment to (say) one thousand interceptors per year, I should not oppose it.

Many opponents of BMD have agreed that an arms-control program of this form seemed fundamentally preferable to a posture of abstaining from defenses and leaving the offensive forces unconstrained; they argue that a program of the type suggested here will not prove feasible, because it will not prove acceptable to the U.S. military "establishment."[19] This assertion is subject to investigation, and considerable investigation suggests it is incorrect. Many senior military officers, in the U.S. Air Force as well as in other services, are favorably disposed to a suitable ceiling on offensive forces (at prevailing levels) providing it is possible to deploy defenses.

A more important objection to postures with a heavy component of defense that is sometimes encountered is the following. The Soviets might, it is argued, find some way of attacking our offensive forces with sufficient effectiveness so that their defenses could intercept most or all of our remaining offensive forces. By thus initiating the first strike, they might escape relatively unscathed—which, if true, could motivate the initiation of the strike

[19]For instance, this seems to be the main point of difference between J.B. Wiesner and myself.

in an intense crisis. It should be noted that the major studies of BMD performance do not show a dramatic dependence on who attacks first, so this concern has no current substantial basis; it is rather an apprehension about some future possible vulnerability that might occur.

Obviously, no one could give an absolute guarantee that such a weakness could not occur. It requires, however, a vulnerability in our offensive forces of the kind that people have been trying to prevent for years; only the degree of vulnerability that would be significant would be changed by a heavy Soviet defense. If the U.S. were to provide added protection of its offensive forces by BMD, there would seem to be no reason whatever for believing that postures with heavy defense in both the U.S. and the Soviet Union would leave us more vulnerable to this type of problem than we are at present.

In fact, such vulnerabilities might be reduced. It is important in considering problems of this type to evaluate the risks of proposed postures in comparison to realistic alternatives, which are not without some risks themselves. In particular, our offensive forces of the present and recent past may well have had important vulnerabilities, including the possibility of undetected ones. For example, Senator Henry Jackson, in a Senate speech of September 25, 1968, discussed electromagnetic-pulse phenomena from nuclear bursts in terms that suggest these phenomena are a continuing source of concern for the security of our offensive forces. A potential vulnerability of a different type might have threatened the fixed component of our offensive forces if the Soviets had developed multiple, independently guided reentry vehicles (MIRV) before we had understood the concept ourselves. There is nothing in the public record that suggests that these have been the only vulnerabilities of major or potentially major concern in our strategic postures of the past. In view of this, it is not at all obvious, to say the least, that a posture of pure deterrence, based wholly on offensive forces, would be more secure against unpleasant surprises (such as a suddenly-discovered extreme vulnerability to a first-strike) than postures with heavy emphasis on defense. Even if there were some added risk associated with the defensive posture, this would have to be weighed against the possibility that the defense might save fifty or eighty million Americans in the event of a major war, and make possible much more rapid economic recovery.

It will be clear that I believe an arms-control program giving first priority to constraints on offensive forces, and second priority to limitations on defensive forces, is in the national interest of the U.S.; in particular, it would sharply reduce any remaining pressures for an offense-defense arms race. It is no contradiction that I believe such a program would also be in the interest of the Soviet Union, and therefore in our common interest. Moreover, as recently as September 1968, I have heard senior Russians suggesting unofficially exactly this order of priorities. There is thus some reason to believe that U.S.-Soviet discussions about stabilizing strategic forces may prove fruitful.

This discussion has mainly concerned near-term limitations on strategic forces. In the longer term, it may prove possible to bring about major disarmament of the offensive forces. I mentioned before that suitable BMD deployment, by reducing our sensitivity to inspection information, would facilitate direct reductions in offensive forces. Indeed, I believe the only possible routes to major reductions in offensive forces—i.e., to a degree that would make a large difference in the scale of possible damage—that could prove feasible in the next decade or so all involve substantial defenses.

It may be useful to illustrate the effect involved with numerical examples. At 1969 levels of offensive forces, an uncertainty of, say, one hundred missiles in the number of Soviet missiles deployed would be of relatively little consequence for the United States. However, if it were decided to reduce offensive forces by agreement to a level that could not cause more than, say, twenty million fatalities, then the allowed forces themselves would have to be limited to something like one hundred missiles on each side, if there were no defenses. At *this* level of offensive forces, a clandestine stock of one hundred missiles could be of great—indeed, literally overwhelming—significance, again if there were no defenses.

Now, an inspection system that would reliably detect as few as one hundred clandestine missiles does not seem likely to be politically feasible within the next decade or more. On the other hand, a BMD system that would reliably intercept all or almost all of one hundred or two hundred missiles is highly feasible, and, if deployed, would substantially reduce or wholly eliminate the threat a modest clandestine force could constitute. (A large clandestine force probably could be detected by inspection.) Thus, defenses would make possible major disarmament of the offensive forces, as well as reducing the possible impact of forces in being when the defenses were deployed.

In contrast, I do not believe that any of the critics of BMD have even the beginnings of a plausible program for achieving major disarmament of the offensive forces by, say, 1980. Many of them seem committed to support forever a strategic posture that appears to favor dead Russians over live Americans. I believe that this choice is just as bizarre as it appears; we should rather prefer live Americans to dead Russians, and we should not choose deliberately to live forever under a nuclear sword of Damocles.

Quite apart from offense-defense races, a different mechanism that might lead to an arms race—perhaps a defense-defense race, or simply a one-sided race of escalating requirements—is sometimes said to reside in the possibility of generalized public pressures for "more." This line of argument is sometimes summarized by saying that, in matters of defense, one cannot be "a little bit pregnant." Our experience in both air defense and civil defense is so much against this idea that it should be dismissed without further discussion. Similarly, it is sometimes said that the American public would not tolerate any inequalities in local defense effectiveness.[20] We have had a major air defense system with substantial inequalities in local defense effectiveness for perhaps fifteen years, and scarcely anyone other than experts associated with the system is even sure of whether his own home city even *has* a local defense, much less how it compares to other cities. The degree of awareness of these matters that has prevailed in the past in the general public is reflected in a public-opinion poll conducted in 1964, which found that two-thirds of the U.S. public believed we had a BMD system all deployed and ready for action!

[20]A good design objective for a BMD planner is to make all targets equally unattractive for the opposing offense. This requires that large cities be more heavily defended than smaller ones, but has the effect of protecting everyone equally in a suitable sense. Actual BMD deployments can approximate this objective, so the alleged problem is of limited relevance even in its own terms.

THE CASE FOR POPULATION DEFENSE   117

CONCLUSION

Space has not permitted here a discussion of several other problem areas sometimes associated with missile defense, such as the implications of U.S. BMD for the Western Alliance, or the frequently-repeated assertion (which I believe is false) that BMD would require as a prerequisite a major expansion of civil-defense programs. Several scholars have, however, studied these problems, and I believe it is fair to say that, on examination, they seem even less likely to prove troublesome than the problems already considered.

It seems to me there is little doubt about which way the policy process in the U.S. ought to evolve in relation to BMD. The American body politic is unlikely to judge that pursuit of "Assured Vulnerability" is a proper objective of the Department of Defense.

Chapter 6

THE CASE FOR
STRATEGIC FORCE DEFENSE[1]

by Albert Wohlstetter

THE ROLE OF ABM IN THE 1970'S

Since I believe the Safeguard program warrants the sums involved, and I support it, perhaps I should begin by saying that I am entirely sympathetic to a rigorous review of the Defense Budget. I favor getting our safety as cheaply as we can. Moreover, I believe the Defense Budget has a good deal of fat that can be cut without substantial harm. I would recommend, for example, a careful look at the equipment and support costs of our ground forces, and at our tactical air forces, both land and sea-based. Some of these seem ineffective, or levelled at threats that are poorly defined or not grave enough to be worth the cost.

Sensible efforts to reduce the Defense Budget, however, would not center on the strategic offense and defense force. There are, of course, arguable choices about strategic offense and defense. But the eight billion dollar plus strategic budget makes up a small part of the total Defense Budget. It has a paramount importance for the safety of the country, and, indeed, of international society. Deterring nuclear coercion and nuclear attack on ourselves and our allies, reducing the damage done in case deterrence fails are complex and uncertain functions; but because they are crucial, the part of the Defense Budget devoted to them has been the most studied and is better understood than any of the rest.

Nonetheless, sizable uncertainties are intrinsic. They affect the predictions of scientists as well as the military and limit the

[1]This chapter constitutes a slightly edited version of my Statement to the Senate Armed Services Committee, April 23, 1969 and a supplement submitted May 23rd, 1969.

reductions we can make without excessive risk. The strategic forces will need continuing adjustment to predicted and to some unanticipated changes in the state of the art. But such adjustments need not entail drastic changes up or down in long term levels of spending.

A start in deploying ABM, I believe, is a prudent response to changes in the state of the art available to ourselves and to our adversaries. As strategic systems go, it is a modest program. It is subject to review and can be halted or stretched out. The average annual cost of the completed program on a five year basis is less than one-fifth of what we were spending for active defense against manned bombers at the end of the 1950's. Nor is it at all likely to start a quantitative arms spiral. Indeed, despite the stereotype, there has been no quantitative arms race in the strategic offense and defense budget, no "ever-accelerating increase," nor, in fact, any long term increase at all. The budget for strategic offense and defense forces in fiscal 1962 was 11.3 billion dollars.[2] The proposed fiscal 1970 budget, as of June, comes to about 8 billion dollars. Adjusted for price changes, the 1962 figure was well over fifty per cent higher than that for 1970, perhaps even as much as two-thirds higher.

There is an important difference between making qualitative adjustments to technical change and expanding the number of vehicles or megatons or dollars spent. The difference has been ignored in a debate on ABM that seems at the same time impassioned and very abstract, quite removed from the concrete political, economic, and military realities of nuclear offense and defense and their actual history. For example, one alternative to protecting Minuteman is to buy more Minutemen without protection. But adding new vehicles is costly and more destabilizing than an active defense of these hard points, since it increases the capacity to strike first. A one-sided self-denial of new technology can lead simply to multiplying our missiles and budgets, or to a decrease in safety, or to both.

Active defense against ballistic missiles in the 1970's will have an important role to play in maintaining a protected and responsible second-strike capacity. The projected Safeguard defense of the national command authority and of the bomber and

[2]*DoD Appropriations for 1969,* Hearings, Part I, Financial Summary. Expenditures in the 1950's were not then broken down by mission but strategic budgets were even higher in the late 1950's than in 1962. In constant prices, for example, 1959 was more than double 1970.

Minuteman bases are directed to this end. And it has a useful function in providing an area defense against attacks involving modest numbers of apparent incoming missiles.

There have been so many charges that the Safeguard program was invented in bad faith in March of this year as a gimmick to answer critics of the Sentinel city defense that I would stress that in 1967, long before the present Administration quite independently decided on Safeguard, the evidence of advancing technology convinced me that ABM in the 1970's would have essentially the uses the Administration suggests for Safeguard, and in the same order: to defend the offense and, given this, at a small extra cost to provide a light area defense of population.[3] In fact, there is a substantial continuity between the ABM decisions of the present and past Administrations. The last Administration called for an ABM area defense but said it would furnish an economic basis for defending Minuteman if the threat grew. It had been weighing and it continued to weigh this decision for some time—indeed itself requested some funds for hardpoint defense in its own version of the 1970 fiscal budget.

Like the Republicans now, the Democrats in 1967 were charged with directing their ABM decision against the opposing party. I would recommend to opponents of ABM that they contemplate the possibility that the decisions were made in good faith in both cases, and that we turn to the substance of the issues.

There are other political and military functions of an ABM system than protecting the offense and offering an area defense of civilians against light attack. I would like to say something about each of these two latter roles and also something about the

---

[3] . . . "*First*, an offense force with such increased accuracies and reliabilities and with an extensive use of MIRV's is very much more efficient in attacking the fixed offense force or the important fixed elements of the mobile force of an adversary . . . *Second*, one result of this sort of change in Russian offense forces is to make improved anti-ballistic missiles (rather than simply more hardening or more missiles) an economic way for the United States to protect the hard fixed elements of a strategic force . . . *Third*, at a minor increment in the modest cost of a hard-point ABM defense, it is possible to make available a light ABM for defense of civil societies against a small submarine or land-based missile force or part of a large one launched by mistake or without authorization . . ." Address to the September 1967 Institute of Strategic Studies Conference on the Implications of Military Technology in the 1970's at Elsinore, Denmark. Strength, Interest and New Technologies, in *Adelphi Papers*, No. 46, p. 4.

doctrine of Minimum Deterrence on which much opposition to the ABM is based, but time permits comment mostly on the protected offense function.

ABM as a Part of a Second-Strike Force in the 1970's

For one superpower as against another, getting and keeping a responsible second strike force is feasible but hard. It requires thought, effort, and continuing realistic adjustments to technological change. Minimum Deterrence theorists, who call for no defense of our civilians and nearly total reliance on a threat to bombard enemy civilians, have always claimed that the attacker inevitably must expend many strategic vehicles to destroy only one of the vehicles attacked. No such generalization holds. It has depended and always must depend on the changing capabilities of the offense and on the kind and degree of protection of the force attacked. At one time, for example, both we and the Russians had very many unprotected aircraft concentrated on a base within the lethal radius of a single bomb. On a two-wing base, for example, we had as many as one hundred thirty aircraft; on a one-wing base sixty-five medium bombers and tankers. And the planned response time was too slow for the reliable warning likely to be available. Small numbers of vehicles could have destroyed much larger numbers of the vehicles they attacked. Under some realistically determined conditions, the ratio would have favored the attacker by one to eight or more. These vulnerabilities had nothing to do with the supposed missile gap. In fact they preceded such predictions.

There is always a temptation in such circumstances to resort to responses that are automatic or that bypass national command. Advocates of sole reliance on city bombardment forces have from the time this doctrine first gained currency been tempted to prove that response was certain by making it automatic, by shortcutting responsible political decision.[4] But the decision to launch ICBM's against Russian cities would be perhaps the most momentous choice ever made in all of history. It would be the decision for World War III. If this awful decision is ever made it should be based on as much information as we can get and it should be made

---

[4]See, for example, one of the first classic sources of Minimum Deterrence Doctrine, National Planning Association, *1970 Without Arms Control.* Special Committee Report, Planning Pamphlet No. 104, Washington, D.C., 1958, pp. 32-3, 44.

by as high a political authority as possible. It is the last decision we should contemplate delegating to a computer.

The revival today, by several distinguished senators and some able physicists opposing ABM, of the suggestion that, rather than defend ICBM's, we should launch them at Russian cities simply on the basis of radar represents a long step backward. If we were willing to do this, we would dispense with silos or Poseidon submarines or any other mode of protecting our missiles. And we would increase the nightmare possibility of nuclear war by mistake.

Understanding of the complex problems of designing a protected and responsible nuclear strategic force has grown slowly among scientists as well as laymen, civilians as well as soldiers, Democrats as well as Republicans. But it has grown, and decisively. The United States has designed and deployed a second-strike force capable of riding out an attack, and there have been large improvements in protecting responsible command. This was accomplished not by merely expanding nuclear bombardment forces, but in essence by shifting to forces with protection against the changing threat. The stereotype repeated throughout the 1960's that our security has declined while our strategic force grew at an accelerating rate is grossly wrong on both counts. In the past some key programs increased the protected second-strike capacity of the force, while cutting at the same time billions of dollars from the spending projected.

In the 1970's unless we continue to make appropriate decisions to meet technological change, once again the viability of a large part of our second-strike force will be put in question. Several related innovations, but in particular the development of a rocket booster carrying many reentry vehicles each aimed precisely at a different target, raises once again the possibility of attack ratios favoring the attacker. One reentry vehicle may kill a booster carrying several. One booster can carry the means of destroying many boosters.

Raising a question about the future second-strike capacity of any part of our strategic force implies nothing about the present intentions of an adversary to strike first or even to be able in the future effectively to strike first. The recent debate on whether the Soviet missile, SS-9, is a "first-strike weapon" or whether the Russians intend it to be seems beside the point. If by maintaining our second-strike capability we can make the risks of striking very great, this can affect an adversary's intentions favorably to ourselves. It can deter him even in a crisis, like the one over missiles in Cuba, when the alternative to striking may look bad, but not, if we are careful, as bad as striking. Moreover, we ought not to talk of "first-strike weapons" and "second-strike weapons" as if this could be settled simply by looking at the weapons on one side. Whether or not a weapons system can preclude substantial retaliation will depend on many uncertain future performance characteristics of the forces on *both* sides. The test of whether one has a responsible second-strike capacity is whether one can, under nuclear attack, preserve vehicles, decision centers and the flow of communications among them, whether one can transmit the order to retaliate and penetrate adversary defenses to reach targets. If we were unwilling even to entertain the hypothesis of a first-strike, we would do nothing to protect any part of our strategic forces or its control centers by making them mobile or hard or by ABM. Some leading scientists who oppose currently deploying ABM say they will favor it for the defense of Minuteman when precise MIRV's and the related offense technologies are likely to be available to the Russians. That calendar date, and not present Soviet intent, is then a major substantive issue for these opponents. And their position recognizes that we want to maintain the second-strike capacity—not of just one, but of all major vehicle types in our strategic force: Minuteman, bombers, and Poseidon.

In designing a second-strike force, there are excellent reasons for making it a substantial mixture of vehicles of several quite different types: land as well as sea-based, manned as well as unmanned, each with its own mode of protection. Such systems have differing limitations, are subject to varied and independent uncertainties, require distinct modes of attack and, if each type is protected, greatly complicate the attack. It is a serious matter, then, if a large part of this mixture is badly affected by changing adversary forces and technologies. The forces deployed and the state of the art available to the Russians will influence other parts of our strategic force than Minuteman silos. And ABM has a role to play, for example, in protecting the important fixed elements of a mobile force, including the politically responsible command centers. Preserving command, control and communications is always hard, and particularly so for mobile sea-based systems.

My remarks, however, center, so far as the second-strike function of ABM is concerned, on the problem of protecting Minuteman. We have good cause to preserve the second-strike capability of so large a proportion of our strategic force. Even if it were true that the United States needed only a few strategic vehicles surviving, buying and paying for the operation of a great many that had become vulnerable to attack would be a very poor way to obtain those few surviving. There are safer and cheaper ways of getting a force of a given size than to buy a much larger one, most of which is susceptable to annihilation.

How does the planned timing of our ABM deployment compare to the date when it is reasonably likely that Russian offense technology could badly worsen the effectiveness of our projected Minuteman III? The first point to note is that the proposed Safeguard deployment has extended lead times. It can stretch out further if continuing review of intelligence suggests it should, but the shortest schedule calls for completing this program early in 1976. If, as ABM opponents stress in other connections, there is likely to be a substantial shakedown period, we are talking of 1977 or later. If, as has been suggested, we delay decision for another year or more and then proceed to design and develop an entirely new ABM we are talking of the 1980's.

Second, predicting exact calendar dates at which technologies will be available to adversaries and what their strategic significance will be is very hard, and we are not very good at it. Moreover, we have erred not only on the side of overestimating Russian capabilities, but often by underestimating them. At earlier dates we were surprised by the rapid Soviet achievement of the A-bomb, the H-bomb, advanced jet engines, long-range turbo-prop bombers, airborne intercept radars, and large-scale fissile-material production. And scientists have been surprised; not only military men.[5]

[5]We have not been very good at predicting our own or our adversary's technologies. These matters are intrinsically uncertain. Eminent scientists at the end of the 1940's predicted that fusion weapons would be infeasible, and, if feasible, undeliverable, and, if delivered, of no strategic significance, since it was thought (erroneously) they could be used only against cities. Some of those who then thought the threat of fusion bombs against cities neither moral nor important strategically now take it to be both. Compare, for example, Hans Bethe's present views with those in The Hydrogen Bomb, *Scientific American,* 182(4) April 1950, pp. 18-23. In February 1953 an important scientific study group expected the Soviets would have no ICBM's before the late 1960's—a prediction plainly in error by the end of the year. See the final report of the Lincoln Summer Study, among whose prominent members were James Killian, Jerome B. Wiesner and Carl Kaysen. Writing in October 1964, Jerome B.

Third, the public discussion has not stressed how sensitively the accuracy of attack affects the viability of the hardened force attacked. Accuracy affects the number of weapons required to destroy a hard target very much more than the bomb yield or the overpressure resistance of the target. Roughly speaking, for such targets, improving accuracy by a factor of slightly more than two is the same as increasing bomb yield tenfold and serves essentially to offset a tenfold increase in overpressure resistance.

I have tried to reconstruct various numerical proofs recently presented or distributed to the Congress that purport to show that Minuteman will be quite safe without any extra protection; these proofs depend heavily on optimistic estimates of limitations in Russian delivery accuracies, reliabilities, and associated offense capabilities and sometimes on very poor offense tactics.[6] Suppose, however, that by 1976 when Safeguard is deployed, or by 1977 when it may be shaken down, the Russians have:

1. accuracies like those of the systems we are deploying now[7]
2. over-all reliabilities currently attributable to them
3. methods familiar to us for using extensive and timely information as to which missiles have failed so that others can replace them
4. continued production of SS-9 boosters at past rates
5. modest numbers of MIRV's per booster (e.g., the three five-megaton reentry vehicles stated by Secretary Laird for the SS-9)

then the percentage of the Minuteman force that would be destroyed, if undefended, comes to about ninety-five per cent.

These results are based on quite moderate assumptions about Russian capabilities. Better accuracies, for example, may be expected in the late 1970's, and higher degrees of MIRVing. Reliabilities of any given offense missile system improve with use. Do those who favor a hardpoint defense but would postpone a

---

Wiesner and Herbert York, National Security and the Nuclear Test Ban, *Scientific American,* 211 (4) Oct. 1964, pp. 18, 27-35, were quite sure that no technological surprises could substantially change the operational effectiveness of intercontinental delivery systems, and thus entirely missed the major strategic potential of precisely aimed MIRV's, a concept that had already emerged in the classified literature. These were able and informed men. But exact prediction on these matters defies confident assertion.

[6]See next section for elaboration.

[7]Poseidon and Minuteman III have been test flown and are in the process of deployment (the first of these should be operational in about a year and a half).

start really consider these Russian capabilities I have outlined "extremely implausible"? Or at *all* implausible?

There is a striking inconsistency in the way ABM opponents treat the Chinese and the Russians. In contemplating the possibility of a Russian offense against our Minuteman, they assume Russians who cannot by 1976 or 1977—twenty years after Sputnik—do what we know how to do now. When considering the ability of the Chinese to penetrate an ABM defense, they attribute to them penetration systems that cost us many billions of dollars, a dozen years of trials and many failures to develop, and they assume this for the first generation Chinese missiles. These are rather backward Russians and very advanced Chinese. Moreover since in the Russian case we are considering a potential threat to our second-strike capability and we want this to be highly reliable, we want particularly to avoid underestimating the threat. But we should undertake a modest defense of population if it works in the expected case, even if on extremely pessimistic assumptions it might not. Here again it seems to me the ABM critics get things exactly backwards.

Finally, the fact that such impending developments in Russian offense may make it necessary to do something more to protect the fixed elements of our force should come as no surprise. It was the sensitive effects of missile inaccuracy that in the early 1950's suggested to the original proponents of programs for hardening strategic vehicles against ICBM attack

    a.   that hardening would be an important and effective method of protection against ICBM attack in the 1960's

    b.   that by itself hardening would not be adequate for much past the 1960's.

The ICBM's then expected in the 1960's were, of course, enormously faster than manned bombers, and therefore would outmode some programs that served very well in the 1950's; but the early ICBM's were likely to be much less accurate than the manned bombers. They were expected to have inaccuracies measured in miles, perhaps, it seemed then, as large as five miles, compared to the quarter of a nautical mile or fifteen hundred feet median miss distance associated with manned bombers. Since just doubling inaccuracy could affect weapons requirements by a factor of four, hardening clearly seemed a good idea. The paper proposing hardening for the 1960's was entitled "Defending a Strategic Force after 1960" and was put out on February 1, 1954. That paper included a very short section called "After After 1960" that is quite relevant for understanding why we should expect that we will have to adapt the current Minuteman to impending changes in opposing offense technology. The section read in full:

> The foregoing also suggests that even against the ballistic missile this defense would have a finite life. The missile might improve drastically in accuracy and payload. However, the date at which the Russians will have a missile capable of carrying a 25 MT bomb with a 1500 ft CEP appears sufficiently far removed to make the defense good, let's say, until the end of the Sixties. (p. 91)

That the numbers cited in this paper of February 1954 so closely match some of those being talked of for the SS-9 is, of course, purely a coincidence. They were performance characteristics of bombers then current. However, the quotation illustrates that, from the outset, it was to be expected that sooner or later and probably in the 1970's, hardening would not be enough by itself. The discussion also suggests that to depend merely on further hardening would make the system vulnerable to further improvements in accuracy.

Hardening can be outpaced by further development in precision. This does not mean that for some possible threats a combination of ABM and extreme hardening might not be useful. It might. But as a complete substitute for ABM extreme hardening has drawbacks. It is subject, in my opinion, to much larger uncertainties as to both performance and costs than the ABM.

The major components of the Safeguard system have received elaborate study and testing. Ideas for brand new ABM systems to defend hard points that I am familiar with are not serious competitors in this time period. We should start deploying the system now on the schedule suggested and we should expect, as in the case of every other offense and defense system, that we shall learn a great deal from operational experience, make some changes and retrofits. This seems to me a sound way to supplement the protection of the Minuteman in a period when we can expect it to be endangered.

ON THE COUNTERFORCE CALCULATIONS OF
SOME PROMINENT ABM OPPONENTS[8]

In preparing the preceding portion of this chapter on the role of ABM in the 1970's, I undertook to review and test my past views on the subject and once again to form my own independent judgment. I, therefore, did not rely on calculations of either the government or its critics. I took the relevant classified and public data and performed my own analysis.

The kind of analysis involved in obtaining a protected and responsible strategic force has been my principal concern for eighteen years starting with the study that gave rise to the first-strike/second-strike distinction and to a good many other concepts and modes of protecting and controlling strategic forces cited by both sides in the present debate. The ABM has other functions that I support, but my chapter in the space available focused on its role in defending Minuteman. As I stressed there, these are complex and intrinsically uncertain matters. Where scientists differ on them, laymen may be tempted simply to throw up their hands and choose to rely on the authority of those scientists they favor. I feel, however, that the substantive differences among the scientists, if carefully explained, are quite accessible to the interested reader and that such careful explanation can help them form their own judgment as to which conclusions are sound.

On the Safety of Minuteman

In my statement to the Senate Armed Services Committee on April 23, I said, "I have tried to reconstruct various numerical proofs recently presented or distributed to the Congress that purport to show our Minuteman will be safe without any extra protection; these proofs depend heavily on optimistic estimates of limitations in Russian delivery accuracies, reliabilities, associated offense capabilities, and sometimes on poor offense tactics." In response to questions from members of the Committee, I illustrated several troubles with these attempted proofs of the safety of Minuteman, but there was no time to explain their defects adequately. I would like to try to do that now, and to comment specifically on the calculations of Dr. Rathjens, Dr. Lapp,

[8]This section is a slightly edited version of a May 23 supplement to my April 23 Statement to the Senate Armed Services Committee.

and of the Federation of American Scientists. Some of the comments, particularly those of Dr. Lapp, bear also on some unevidenced statements on this subject by Prof. Chayes and Dr. Panofsky and, more recently, by Dr. Wiesner.

Though my own calculations were based on classified as well as public data, my summary of results, like that of Dr. Rathjens, was unclassified and so are the comments I am about to make. This will prevent explicit specification of some of the numbers assumed by Dr. Rathjens and by myself and inevitably it forces some roundaboutness of expression. I am able to state, for example, that Dr. Rathjens and I assume the same accuracy for the Russian SS-9 in the mid- and late 1970's. I can say that the SS-9 is now expected (and, before the Nixon Administration, was expected) to achieve that accuracy years in advance of this late time period. And I can say, as Dr. Rathjens did, that the accuracy we have assumed for the Russians, in this late time period, is essentially the same as that estimated for our own MIRV carrying missiles, namely Poseidon and Minuteman III.[9] But I cannot say what that accuracy is.

I, therefore, submitted a classified statement in which the essential numerical assumptions are explicit and related to intelligence estimates. However, even without the classified statements, some essential defects of the calculations of Dr. Rathjens, Dr. Lapp, and the Federation of American Scientists can be made clear.

Dr. Rathjens' Calculations

Dr. Rathjens has stated "Even if the Soviet SS-9 missile force were to grow as rapidly as the Defense Department's most worrisome projections, even if the Soviet Union were to develop and employ MIRV's with those missiles and even if they achieved accuracies as good as we apparently expect with our MIRV forces (according to figures released in late 1967 by former Deputy Secretary of Defense Nitze), a quarter of our Minuteman force could be expected to survive a Soviet preemptive SS-9 attack. That quarter alone would be more than enough to inflict unacceptable damage on the U.S.S.R.[10]

[9]See footnote 7 above.

[10]Testimony of April 23, before the Senate Armed Services Committee. See also his testimony of March 28, Part I, p. 359 of *Strategic and Foreign Policy Implications of ABM Systems,* Hearings before a subcommittee of the Senate Committee on Foreign Relations.

My own parallel calculations for the mid- and late 1970's, using what I described as moderate assumptions, show about five per cent surviving. What explains the difference? Since Dr. Rathjens and I compared notes on April 22, I am able to fix quite precisely where we agreed and where we differed.

Our assumptions agreed in the accuracy assumed for the SS-9, in the over-all reliability rate, in the numbers of SS-9 boosters (500) and in the use of several independently aimed reentry vehicles in each booster. Our assumptions differed on three key points: in the degree of blast resistance assumed for our Minuteman silos, in the yield of the Russian reentry vehicles, and in the use or non-use by the Russians of substantial information about what missiles are unready at launch or fail in early stages.

On the first point, I have explained that Dr. Rathjens assumed that Minuteman silos were two-thirds more blast resistant than I did, and two-thirds more blast resistant than they are officially estimated to be. He derived his assumption by reading several points off an unclassified chart showing the probability of a Minuteman silo being destroyed as a function of accuracy for various bomb yields. Then by using standard rules for weapons effects he inferred the overpressure resistance of Minuteman silos. However, the curves on the unclassified chart cannot be correctly read to imply the overpressure resistance Dr. Rathjens infers. His reading of the curves was in error.

Second, I assumed three 5-megaton reentry vehicles for each SS-9, as in Secretary Laird's public statements. Dr. Rathjens assumed four 1-megaton reentry vehicles. More than four reentry vehicles can be fitted on the SS-9, if the payload is only one megaton. However, the three 5-megaton reentry vehicles, given the accuracy we both assume, and given the actual blast resistance of the Minuteman, do enough for the attacker. Using his lower Russian bomb yield and his overestimated Minuteman blast resistance, Dr. Rathjens derived a probability of about sixty per cent that one arriving Russian reentry vehicle would destroy one Minuteman silo. If he had used the officially estimated 5-megaton reentry vehicle and the actual blast resistance of the Minuteman silo, the probability would have been nearly ninety-nine per cent. If he had used three 5-megaton reentry vehicles per booster for the SS-9 and the correct estimate for blast resistance, he would have found only sixteen per cent, instead of twenty-five per cent of the Minuteman force surviving. Alternatively, if he had used the classified estimates of the number of 1-megaton reentry vehicles that can be fitted on an SS-9 booster, his calculations would have shown about 7.3 per cent surviving. The combined significance of these first two points of difference between Dr. Rathjens and myself is then considerable.

The third point of difference between our calculations is that Dr. Rathjens assumes that the Russians would have to salvo all of their missiles with no information as to which had been un-ready or failed in time to be discovered, or at any rate with no use of such information. However, it is familiar that better methods are available and are of considerable utility for an offense that wants to assure a very high percentage of destruction of the force attacked. Most missiles that are counted as "unreliable" (excluded from the figure of over-all reliability) are either not ready for launch or fail at launch, and this information can be made available immediately. A substantial additional fraction that fail do so at burnout, and information as to whether burnout velocity is within expected tolerances can also be made quickly available. For radio-guided missiles this is almost automatic, but inertial systems can also radio this information back, as the telemetering in a missile flight test program shows. Later flight information is also feasible. While some fraction of the failures will remain unknown, a large proportion can be known. There-fore, instead of salvoing all extra missiles blindly, to make up for all unreadiness and all failures without knowing where they occur, one can reprogram some extra missiles to replace the large pro-portion of known failures. Using a current planning factor for the proportion of the unreliable missiles that cannot be replaced on the basis of timely information, the calculations using three 5-megaton reentry vehicles show considerably greater destruction. Instead of sixteen per cent surviving, the approximate five per cent survival that I mentioned previously results. It should be ob-served that this ability of the 5MT force to destroy five per cent of the Minuteman force presumes that only about one-half the failures after launching are replaced—a figure well within the state of the art. Moreover, even limiting the use of information to mis-sile malfunctions before or during launch, the 5MT MIRV force would leave only eight or nine per cent surviving.

Finally, such techniques of using substantial timely informa-tion as to which missiles cannot be relied on are less important for cases where smaller yields and larger numbers of reentry vehicles per booster are used. For the 1-megaton multiple reentry vehicle case I have referred to, the expected number of Minutemen surviv-ing reduces from approximately 7.3 per cent without using such

TABLE I

CALCULATIONS ON THE VULNERABILITY OF THE
MINUTEMAN FORCE IN THE LATE 1970's
IF NO EXTRA PROTECTION

*Difference Between Assumptions Used by
Dr. Rathjens and Myself*

Number of SS-9's	: Same (500)	
Over-all reliability	: Same	
Accuracy	: Same	
Minuteman Blast Resistance	Dr. Rathjens'	: 2/3 higher than official estimate
	Mine	: Official estimate
SS-9 payload	Dr. Rathjens'	: 4 reentry vehicles at 1 MT (less than SS-9 capability)
	Mine	: 3 at 5 MT (SS-9 capability)
Use of partial information on missile malfunctions	Dr. Rathjens'	: Not used
	Mine	: Used

*Effect of Assumptions on
Minuteman Survivability*

	Minuteman Surviving
Dr. Rathjens' result	25%
Adjust for correct Minuteman blast resistance and three 5 MT MIRV per SS-9	16%
Alternatively adjust for correct Minuteman blast resistance and number of 1 MT MIRV warheads the SS-9 is capable of carrying	7.3%
Using correct Minuteman blast resistance, three 5 MT MIRV per SS-9, and information as to missile malfunctions before or during launch only	8.7%
Using correct Minuteman blast resistance, the correct number of 1 MT warheads per SS-9, and information as to missile malfunctions before and during launch only	6%
Using correct Minuteman blast resistance and *either* the 5 MT MIRV or the 1 MT MIRV option, and information as to missile malfunctions including one-half those that fail after launch	5%

techniques, to five per cent using them. The errors in Dr. Rathjens' calculations are not amended simply by taking into account the possibility of reprogramming.

The table above summarizes the differences between Dr. Rathjens' and my calculations.

Dr. Lapp's Calculations

Dr. Ralph Lapp's calculations were not presented at a Senate Hearing. However, one set of his calculations was presented as a two page appendix to his statement called "The Case Against Missile Defense," and they were featured in front page stories early in April in leading newspapers, describing Dr. Lapp as science advisor to the Senate opposition. These calculations attacking the credibility of a threat to Minuteman themselves apparently achieved widespread credence. They contain several grave errors, some of which have been pointed out independently by myself on April 23rd before the Senate Armed Services Committee, by Dr. Lawrence O'Neill before the House Armed Services Committee, and by Professor Eugene Wigner before the American Physical Society on April 29th. Yet these statements pointing out Dr. Lapp's errors have received little or no newspaper notice. It is therefore worth reviewing Dr. Lapp's calculations, particularly so since one of his most blatant errors appears to have been adopted uncritically by some of the other witnesses before the Committee, specifically Professor Chayes and Dr. Panofsky.[11]

Dr. Lapp states that his calculations are based on "maximum values" for Soviet capabilities. He shows seventy-six per cent of the Minuteman surviving, compared to Dr. Rathjens' twenty-five and my five per cent. Moreover, he has several assumptions that agree with my own:

1. Three 5-megaton reentry vehicles per SS-9, and
2. An accuracy estimate derived, like Dr. Rathjens', from public indications of the great precision of our Poseidon or Minuteman MIRV's.

His combined assumptions about the yield and accuracy of an SS-9 reentry vehicle and the blast resistance of the Minuteman result in very high probabilities that a single arriving reentry vehicle will destroy a Minuteman silo.

---

[11]It is an error that is repeated also in Abram Chayes & Jerome B. Wiesner (eds.), *ABM—An Evaluation of the Decision to Deploy an Anti-ballistic Missile System,* Harper & Row, New York, 1969.

He suggests that two and one-half warheads of 5-megaton power with a half nautical mile inaccuracy or CEP[12] are needed to destroy a 200 psi target with a ninety-five per cent probability, and 1.1 warheads would have that probability if the CEP were a quarter of a nautical mile. In fact, using standard methods of calculation, at a half-mile inaccuracy, two warheads would yield a ninety-six per cent destruction probability and at a quarter of a mile inaccuracy one warhead would have a more than ninety-nine per cent probability of destroying a 200 psi target. Either Dr. Lapp's calculations are based on some rather exotic and unspecified method, or they are in error. But in any case it is apparent that, even using his methods, he derives a very high single shot kill probability, roughly comparable to my own.

How then does Dr. Lapp's Minuteman force, faced by supposedly "maximum" Russian capabilities, come out so much better than even Dr. Rathjens' Minuteman force? First, Dr. Lapp assumes a much smaller number of SS-9's than Dr. Rathjens and I. He assumes three hundred thirty-three SS-9's. This is hardly a maximum force. It is less than the number that would be produced at past rates by continuing production into the relevant 1976-77 time period. At three reentry vehicles per booster, Dr. Lapp's assumption would give the Russians about one thousand reentry vehicles.

Second, he assumes that the Russians would use only three-fourths of their SS-9 force, that is, about two hundred fifty SS-9's (or 750 reentry vehicles). This extraordinary failure to use a fourth of the force most adapted to the purpose of destroying Minuteman is attributed to a supposed universal rule that military strategists always keep forces in reserve. This may or may not be true for tank battles or aircraft attacks in a conventional war. (The June 1967 war in the Middle East suggests it is not a sound generalization even about attacks with aircraft at the start of a non-nuclear war.) But as a universal rule for a nuclear first-strike? Dr. Lapp does not say for what these SS-9's would be reserved.

[12]CEP is the acronym for "Circular Error, Probable," a commonly used measure of the inaccuracy of weapon systems. In repeated firings, 50% of the weapons would miss their targets by less than the CEP (or median miss distance) and 50% would miss by more than the CEP. A frequent misinterpretation assumes that all weapons miss their targets by a distance equal to the CEP—which is like assuming that all students score at the 50th percentile on an exam.
A nautical mile is 6080'. It, rather than a statute mile, is a standard dimension for measuring CEP or median miss distance.

Most important, Dr. Lapp forgets that the Soviet Union has a great many intercontinental missiles besides the SS-9 and exceeding the SS-9 in numbers by a large amount. These missiles would seem to furnish a reserve that might satisfy a military strategist.

Third, he assumes over-all reliabilities that are quite a bit lower than the reliabilities that Dr. Rathjens and I assumed, also lower than those attributed to the SS-9. As a result of the three assumptions, Dr. Lapp's Russians would have substantially less than half as many reliable arriving reentry vehicles as our thousand Minuteman silos. More than half the Minuteman force would then be untouched by SS-9 reentry vehicles.

Finally, Dr. Lapp makes an assumption that is plainly absurd. He supposes that even though each warhead has a very high probability of destroying a single silo, "any military realist" would fire two of his outnumbered attacking reentry vehicles at each silo that is attacked. This would leave three-fourths of the silos untouched. But if each warhead has a ninety-nine per cent probability of destroying a single silo, firing two at one silo would merely increase the probability of destroying that specific silo to 99.99% but would make it quite certain that a silo that could have been destroyed will go unscathed. If a more sensible tactic were followed, namely to fire each of the two missiles at a different silo, there would be a probability of ninety-eight per cent of destroying both silos and a probability of 99.99% that at least one of the two would be destroyed. (This latter is the same probability that Dr. Lapp would have achieved against the specific one that he was aiming at.) In short, Dr. Lapp's tactic would greatly reduce the expected level of destruction achieved by the attack, and it would not increase the probability of achieving some minimum level of destruction. I know of no military realist who would regard Dr. Lapp's tactic as a sensible one for the attacker. I must agree with Dr. Wigner that Dr. Lapp has presumed that his adversary would be unbelievably stupid.

It should be observed that the absurdity of the tactic is not dependent on the roughly ninety-nine per cent single shot kill probability implicit in Dr. Lapp's accuracy, yield and resistance assumptions. If one were to use a ninety-five per cent shot destruction probability, the point is equally obvious. In this latter case, an adversary who assigned one missile to each of two targets would have a better than ninety per cent chance of getting them both and a probability of 99¾% of getting at least one; and he could get no better than a 99¾% probability of getting one silo if he sent both missiles against one silo. In the latter case, however, he could destroy at *most* one silo.

Professor Chayes and Dr. Panofsky have made statements suggesting they also accept the principle of sending at least two missiles to each silo.

Professor Chayes said in his statement to the Senate Armed Services Committee on April 23:

> . . . it is agreed that the attacker would need at the very minimum 2,000 accurate warheads—two for every one of our silos—before being able to think about a first strike.

Professor Panofsky in his statement to the Senate Armed Services Committee on April 22 stated:

> Moreover, an attacker would have to compensate for the limited reliability of his force by targeting at least two and possibly more warheads against each of the 1,000 Minuteman silos.

The reason behind these two statements is less explicit than Dr. Lapp's. Dr. Panofsky is talking about compensating for unreliability rather than inaccuracy, but it seems plain that no such universal rule makes sense.

Dr. Lapp has a second set of calculations published on May 4, 1969 in *The New York Times Magazine*.[13] There he assumes the Russians may have five hundred rather than three hundred thirty-three SS-9's. Since he again assumes three reentry vehicles per booster, this makes a total of 1,500 reentry vehicles per booster. He apparently avoids the obviously bad strategies of reserving a quarter of the force, and then using the remainder to attack only half the targets they are capable of destroying with high probability. Nonetheless, once again his calculations show very high survival rates: "500 to 750 operable Minuteman." With these changed assumptions, how does the outcome continue to remain so favorable to Minuteman's survival?

Dr. Lapp has made some other changes. He has reduced the yield of the SS-9 reentry vehicles by twenty per cent, increased his estimate of the hardness of the Minuteman by fifty per cent, and

[13]Ralph E. Lapp, From Nike to Safeguard: A Biography of the ABM, *The New York Times Magazine,* May 4, 1969.

most important, he now uses very large inaccuracies for the SS-9, 3,600 feet in one case and 5,500 feet in the other. The latter great inaccuracy assures him his seven hundred fifty operable Minuteman surviving. But there is no justification for assuming such great inaccuracies in the mid- and late 1970's. One of the few constants in Dr. Lapp's various calculations appears to be his conclusion.

Calculations of Dr. Steven Weinberg and Dr. Jerome Wiesner in ABM: An Evaluation of the Decision to Employ an Anti-Ballistic Missile System edited by Abram Chayes and Jerome Wiesner, New York, 1969

Dr. Weinberg and Dr. Wiesner present variants of the same calculation to show the safety of the Minuteman force. Dr. Weinberg supposes that at least 2,100 reliable arriving reentry vehicles "with megaton yield and high accuracy" would be needed to destroy all but 42 of our 1,050 ICBM silos. He appears to assume an eighty per cent single shot kill probability. Dr. Weinberg doesn't indicate the exact blast resistance, yield, and inaccuracy assumptions that go into his eighty per cent hypothetical kill probability and the testimony of Deputy Secretary Packard that he cites in that connection offers no basis for such a determination.[14] Mr. Packard there shows for three different bomb yields a spectrum of probabilities varying from less than ten per cent to one hundred per cent as accuracy varies from a mile or so down below one-tenth of a mile. Mr. Packard does not say what the accuracy of any SS-9 reentry vehicle is expected to be so that no specific single shot kill probability can be inferred from his testimony.

Dr. Wiesner assumes five hundred reliable SS-9's, each carrying three MIRV's; or more exactly fifteen hundred reliable MIRV's. And he also assumes an eighty per cent kill probability for each arriving reentry vehicle. He justifies this with the statement that a 5-megaton reentry vehicle would have to be used and that "at best the MIRV guidance system will be accurate enough

[14]Chayes & Wiesner (eds.), *op. cit.,* pp. 86-93.

to give only a 0.8 kill probability for the unit."[15] One can read directly from Deputy Secretary Packard's chart that Dr. Wiesner is thus implying that accuracies less than about 2,400 feet are not possible in the time period in question. Dr. Wiesner has given no technical argument to support this assertion; it is at variance with expected accuracies for our own MIRV systems, and it is at variance with the accuracy that the intelligence community has *for some time* expected the SS-9 to achieve years before the late 1970's time period, and with the accuracy assumed by Dr. Rathjens. At the 5-megaton yield and with the expected SS-9 accuracy the single shot kill probability for each reliable arriving reentry vehicle would be very much higher than eighty per cent as I have already pointed out elsewhere.

If Dr. Wiesner had used three 5-megaton reentry vehicles, the expected accuracy of the SS-9's and, furthermore, had incorporated expected reliabilities his calculations would have shown only sixty-three out of 1100 hard targets surviving, that is 5.7%. Or if he had used the expected accuracy and reliabilities and the number of 1 megaton vehicles deliverable by the SS-9, he would have arrived at substantially the same result: sixty eight out of 1100 surviving.

There are a number of less critical flaws in Dr. Weinberg's and Dr. Wiesner's calculations. The essential, however, is that they both assume combinations of accuracy, yield and number of reentry vehicles per booster that are less effective than intelligence expects (and for some time has expected) of the SS-9.

The Calculations of the Federation of American Scientists, March 8, 1969

These calculations of the FAS were published nearly a week before the President's decision on the Safeguard System was announced. The FAS statement was intended to refute in advance the need for extra protection of the Minuteman force. However,

[15]Professor Wohlstetter's critique is based upon the manuscript version of the book which was distributed prior to its publication. In book form, Dr. Wiesner replaced the explicit .8 kill probability with a vague reference to an "accuracy estimated by Secretary Laird." In the manuscript, he incorrectly calculated (on the basis of a .8 kill probability) that 270 missiles would survive (the correct number is less than 150). The book version retains the "conclusion" of 270 survivors but does not make any explicit probability assumption— and thus implicitly now assumes a kill probability of about .65. Chayes and Wiesner (eds.) *op. cit.,* p. 73. *Editors.*

the calculations it presents are basically irrelevant since they use only the Russian force "at the present time," and they assume larger inaccuracies than intelligence attributes to the Russians' SS-9's for the later time period. They do not use MIRV's and in fact, according to their author, they do not use the SS-9 at all.

In the first section of this chapter,[16] I said that the many confident assertions current that Minuteman will be safe without extra protection in the late 1970's are unjustified. These supplementary comments have illustrated and analyzed some essential flaws in these assertions: they depend on erroneous estimates about the blast resistance of our own forces or wishful estimates about Russian lacks either in accuracy or in other capabilities or in competent tactics in that time period; they do not, as they claim, use "the most worrisome projections" and the "maximum capabilities" for Russian forces. In fact even my own calculations showing that the Minuteman will be vulnerable if extra protection is not provided do not use "maximum" Russian capabilities. Greater accuracies, for example, are quite feasible in the late 1970's for the Russians. I have used the CEP attributed to the SS-9 in the early 1970's. If the SS-9's CEP should be two hundred fifty feet smaller than that estimate, then only four hundred SS-9's using megaton range reentry vehicles would destroy about ninety five per cent of the Minuteman force. Or with the larger force even greater percentages of the Minuteman force could be destroyed if we do nothing to supplement its protection. As I emphasized in my statement on April 23rd, the expected vulnerability of a hardened force is extremely sensitive to the accuracy of the force attacking. The accuracy assumed by Dr. Rathjens and myself is not only attributed to the SS-9 in the early 1970's, it is also the accuracy we estimate for our own MIRV's. Programs for achieving still greater accuracies for some of our MIRV's have been drawn up though not funded.

I have focused on the problem of protecting Minuteman, because, as I have stressed, we need a mixed force and have good reason to preserve the second-strike capability of so large a proportion of our strategic force. Even if it were true that the United States needed only a few strategic vehicles surviving, buying and paying for the operation of a great many that had become vulnerable to attack would be a very poor way to obtain those few surviving. There are safer and cheaper ways of getting a force

[16]i.e., my testimony on April 23, 1969.

of a given size than to buy a much larger one, most of which is susceptible to annihilation. To maintain a force, most of which could then be used only in a first-strike hardly contributes to stability.

It is sometimes said that such analyses of the potential vulnerability of Minuteman are like the talk of the bomber gap in the early 1950's and the missile gap at the end of the 1950's. Nothing could be further from the truth. Most of those who talked of bomber gaps and missile gaps raised these possibilities to argue for expanding the number of our own bombers or missiles to close the gap. They thought of the problem as one of matching first-strike forces. But how to maintain a second-strike force cannot be adequately understood in these terms. Whether or not we have it depends, as I have said, not simply on the relative size of two opposing forces, but on a great many characteristics of the attacking force and of the force attacked and its protection. It is the opponents of the ABM today who, rather than defend the offense, would simply expand it. Moreover, many of these same opponents of the ABM were among the chief propounders of the missile and bomber gaps in the past; some scientists are now willing to state that they helped "create the myth of the missile gap." My own record on this matter is quite clear. Throughout the 1950's I pointed out the essential irrelevance of matching first-strike forces and of all the gap theories that flowed from such matching. For example, in 1956 I wrote:

> Exaggerated estimates of Russian force size, for example, might be used directly to suggest emulation. But we have already made clear that determining who has the best or second best Air Force in being in advance of attack by simply matching numbers or quality is not to the point. Those who assert that we may have fewer and perhaps inferior planes than the enemy and still have a deterrent force must also recognize that we may have more and even better vehicles and yet have inadequate deterrence.[17]

The propensity simply to list Russian and American pre-attack forces measured in various arbitrary ways continues to be exhibited on both sides of the present debate. On one side, first-strike capabilities are sometimes matched against adversary cities in the discussions of "overkill." On the other side, first-strike

[17]Albert J. Wohlstetter and F.S. Hoffman, *Protecting U.S. Power to Strike Back in the 1950's and 1960's,* R-290, The RAND Corporation, Santa Monica, Cal., September 1, 1956.

forces of Russia and the United States are sometimes matched against each other to show "superiority" or "inferiority" or "parity" or the like. My point is quite different. Foreseeable technical change in the 1970's compels sober thought about improving the protection of crucial elements in our strategic force. Such change can affect our second-strike capability. In that connection, I have centered my discussion on the protection of the Minuteman, but the problem of protecting our bombers is also important and even more we must improve our protection of the national political command vital to the control of sea as well as land-based strategic forces.

Part III

INTERACTIONS WITH OTHER POLICY AREAS

Chapter 7

MISSILE DEFENSE, THE SOVIET UNION, AND THE ARMS RACE

by Johan J. Holst

THE DEFENSIVE TRADITION

There is very little evidence that ballistic missile defense has been the subject of any major policy debate in the Soviet Union. Whatever bargaining has taken place over the allocation of limited funds, has focused on the relative priority to be accorded the various components of the Soviet military posture at a particular point in time. It is likely that some time in the early or mid-sixties, a basic decision was made to expand the offensive missile forces in a major effort to catch up with the U.S. and that this decision had the effect of slowing down the Soviet BMD effort. There is, however, no evidence that there exists within the relevant decision-making strata any ideological or doctrinal hostility to ballistic missile defense. In fact, the available evidence suggests that the very opposite attitudes prevail.

The Air Defense Legacy

Many observers have noted a strong emphasis on defensive weapon systems and deployments in the evolution of the Russian military posture since the Second World War. The tradition could be extended much further back in history and explained in part with reference to Russian national experiences, particularly the long history of painful foreign incursions into Russia. We shall, however, limit our perspective to the cold-war period.

Stalin had reportedly been impressed by the damage effected by the Allied strategic bombing against population targets in World War II. This impression, coupled with the fact that the United States possessed both a long-range bomber force and the atomic bomb, probably accounts for the top priority which was accorded the task of establishing a modern air-defense system in the immediate postwar years, with heavy investments in early warning radars and jet fighter interceptors. The first jet fighter which entered service in quantity was the MiG-15 "Fagot," and it is estimated that as many as fifteen thousand of this aircraft was produced.[1] By 1955, the Soviet air defense forces comprised some four thousand jet interceptors and a reasonably comprehensive early warning radar system providing warning in depth through a three-tier line of stations ranging from the Arctic coast to central Russia and other lines covering the southern, western, and eastern approaches.

It remains a curious characteristic of the considerable Soviet investments in aircraft interceptors that the capabilities procured were substantially limited to clear-weather day interception; at least until the late fifties. (MiG-17 "Fresco," which entered service in 1952, was a subsonic day-fighter. MiG-19 "Farmer," the first Soviet supersonic interceptor, which entered service in 1955, was also designed as a day-fighter and later versions had only limited all-weather capability. This was also true of the MiG-21 "Fishbed," which entered service in 1959. The first all-weather fighter was the *sub*sonic YAK-25 "Flashlight," entering service in 1955. A supersonic improvement, YAK-28 "Firebar," is believed to have entered service in 1962-63. Another supersonic all-weather fighter, SU-9 "Fishpot," entered service late in 1959.[2]) One possible, but conjectural, interpretation of the Soviet failure to procure all-weather, day-night fighters could be that it was based on the assumption that Moscow would be able to choose the time of war by striking first during a time of the year when the light in the Arctic would enable Soviet interceptors to operate against U.S. bombers on retaliatory strike missions. A "bureaucratic," and more likely explanation is that the procurements reflected in large measure the vested interests and weight of the tactical air force for whose purposes day fighters were valuable.

[1]Róbert A. Kilmarx, *A History of Soviet Air Power,* Frederick A. Praeger, New York, 1962, p. 230.

[2]Recent additions to the operational inventory of all-weather interceptors include MiG-23 "Foxbat" and TU-28 "Fiddler." The Russians have shown several experimental VTOL (vertical take-off and landing), STOL (short take-off and landing) and variable geometry fighters at the Tushino (1961) and Domodedovo (1967) airshows.

Another *apparent* "anomaly" in the Soviet air defense posture was the heavy investments in tube-fired anti-aircraft artillery. Most Western analysts believed such equipment to be largely ineffective against modern strategic bombers. (The Russians may now be phasing out guns over 57 mm in favor of surface-to-air-missiles.) Again the explanation may lie in the realm of bureaucratic inertia rather than in that of measures-countermeasures analysis. The Soviet air-defense forces, PVO (Protivovozdushnaya Oborona), grew out of the artillery forces. In 1948, the PVO was officially raised to the level of a main branch of the armed forces equal to the ground forces, the air force and the navy. The reorganization which took place after the death of Stalin resulted in a centralization of the PVO organization and the appointment of its first main commander in 1954 (Marshal of the Artillery Govorov).[3] Our comments on the apparent anomalies—and many more could be found—suggest, with reference to the current BMD debate, that there is nothing automatic or predictable about Soviet reactions to developments in the U.S. military posture. There may be a lot of traditional, bureaucratic and doctrinal obstacles to optimized off-set response measures.

The strong artillery tradition in the Soviet air-defense effort may account to some extent for the early emphasis on surface-to-air (SAM) missiles. According to a recent authoritative Soviet source, SAM technology became available to the PVO in 1952.[4] The deployment of the first-generation SA-1 "Guild" around Moscow became visible by 1956. It is interesting to note, in connection with the current speculation about Soviet intentions in the BMD field and how the latter may be extrapolated from the current Soviet deployment, that the SA-1 deployment was limited to the area around Moscow. However, by 1958 deployment of the second-generation SA-2 "Guideline" was started. This missile, which has undergone substantial improvements, has been widely deployed in the Soviet Union. A third SAM, SA-3 "Goa" was first shown in public in 1964. It is believed to be a Soviet counterpart to the American Hawk missile, designed for short-range defense against low-altitude attacks. It is deployed in fixed sites

[3]The postwar history of the PVO is authoritatively covered in P.F. Batitsky (ed.), *Voyska Protivovozdushnoy Oborony Strany,* Voenizdat, Moscow, 1968, Part Three, pp. 337-409.

[4]General of the Army P. Batitsky. Voyska Protivovozdushnoy Oborony Strany, *Voenno-Istoricheskii Zhurnal* (8) 1967, pp. 26-7.

around cities and exists also in a mobile version mounted on a truck chassis. There are also two other mobile SAM systems, SA-4 "Ganef" and SA-6 "Gainful," which are launched from tracked vehicles. The current construction of the SA-5 "Griffon"/ Tallinn-Line in northwestern Russia—now generally believed to be an advanced anti-aircraft missile network—testifies to the continued Soviet concern about active air defense. The total Soviet SAM force probably numbers in the region of one thousand sites.[5] (The United States Continental Air Defense maintains some sixteen battalions of Nike Hercules surface-to-air missiles and two Hawk battalions. There are also one hundred eighty-eight long-range/Bomarc missiles.) The total personnel of the PVO numbers about 500,000 (compared to 90,000 in the U.S. Air Defense Command), of which the ground elements account for some 250,000. The PVO fighter interceptors number about 3,700 (there are 1,250 interceptors under NORAD (North American Air Defense Command).[6]

The Soviet Union has since World War II, spent two and a half times what the United States has spent on anti-aircraft defense,[7] which means they have spent on the order of 125 billion dollars.[8] According to recent estimates, the Russians are spending from three and one-half to four dollars to each one dollar that the United States spends on defensive strategic weapon systems.[9] The current U.S. expenditures on strategic defense systems amount to about two billion dollars per annum, so that the Soviet Union is spending the equivalent of seven to eight billion dollars per year in this sector.

[5]Malcolm Mackintosh, *Juggernaut: The Russian Forces, 1918-66,* Macmillan, New York, 1967, p. 309.

[6]Figures from *The Military Balance 1968-1969,* published by the Institute for Strategic Studies, London, 1968.

[7]According to former Secretary of Defense Robert S. McNamara, *Military Procurement Authorizations for Fiscal Year 1968,* Hearings before the Committee on Armed Services and Subcommittee on Department of Defense of the Committee on Appropriations, U.S. Senate, 90th Cong. 1st Sess., 1967, p. 303.

[8]Herbert Roback, Civil Defense and National Defense, in Eugene P. Wigner, *Who Speaks for Civil Defense?,* Scribner's, New York, 1968, p. 95 gives the U.S. figure as $50 billion.

[9]Press Conference, February 18, 1969. Secretary of Defense Melvin R. Laird.

The Soviet BMD Effort

There is not a great deal of solid information available about the Russian BMD program. There is, as indicated above, a rather strong tradition of substantial expenditures on active strategic defense systems. This tradition has created a strong active defense lobby within the Soviet decision-making structure. The active defense tradition is probably reinforced also by a basic doctrinal antagonism to dependence of the kind which is implicit in the concept of mutual deterrence. Communist doctrine has consistently warned against the dangers of hostile manipulation, and mutual deterrence could, of course, harbor all kinds of potentials for manipulative strategies. The following statement by the late Russian strategist, General Nikolaj Talenskij, is revealing in this context: "The creation of an effective anti-missile system enables the state to make its defenses dependent chiefly on its own possibilities, and not on mutual deterrence, that is on the goodwill of the other side."[10]

It is certainly consistent with a dialectical view of technological developments within the historical process for the Russians to commit substantial resources to the development of the counter-weapon to the long-range ballistic missile. The development and procurement of such a weapon system is also consistent with the Soviet view of the requirements to a winning strategy in a wartime environment. Finally, the Kremlin is likely to view the acquisition of a BMD system as consistent with the psychological projection of Soviet strategic prowess.

Russian behavior in the past seems to indicate some preference for early deployment as part of the research-and-development phase in order to gain operational experience for subsequent large-scale deployments of improved systems. Such a mode may also reflect the natural biases of a defense establishment where the military control such "technical" policy decisions (the Soviet Ministry of Defense is run by military officers). This pattern was, as we noted in the previous section, observable in the Russian anti-aircraft missile deployments and it may very well be repeated in the Russian BMD program. One indication of the strong Soviet interest in ballistic missile defense is the considerable number of

---

[10]Nikolaj Talenskij, Anti-Missile Systems and Disarmament, *International Affairs,* Moscow, (10), 1964, p. 18.

monographs which have been published on that subject in the Soviet Union over the last two years.[11]

Officially expressed Soviet interest in BMD systems dates back at least to the mid-fifties, when Marshal Malinovskij replaced Marshal Zhukov as Minister of Defense. He stressed the need to devote greater attention "to the problems of air defense and anti-missile defense."[12] The technical feasibility was not, however, considered particularly promising in the short-term perspective, although optimism was expressed that the problem was soluble in principle.

In 1961, Khrushchev remarked in an interview with a correspondent of *The New York Times* that he was "very satisfied with the work of those who are producing the means of combatting such (ICBM) rockets."[13] The first claim of success was made, however, by Marshal Malinovskij at the 22nd Party Congress in October 1961, when he claimed that "the problem of destroying missiles in flight . . . has been successfully solved."[14] In July 1962, Khrushchev made his famous remark that the Soviet Union had a missile which could "hit a fly in outer space."[15] Subsequently, several Soviet military leaders made assertions about alleged Soviet BMD capabilities.

The first public display of a weapon which was claimed to have a BMD role was in the November Day parade in 1963. The missile, which was subsequently given the Western designation "Griffon," is a two-stage missile capable of reaching an altitude of twenty-five to thirty miles, a slant range of about one hundred miles and an estimated speed of Mach 3-5. It could be fitted with a

[11]M.N. Nikolayev, *Snaryad Protiv Snaryada,* Voenizdat, Moscow, 1960; M.N. Goncharov, *Rakety i Problema Antiraket.* Izd DOSAAF, Moscow, 1960, 258 p. (30,000 copies); M.N. Nikolayev, *Raketa Protiv Rakety,* Voenizdat, Moscow, 1963; N.F. Shibayev, *Bor'ba s Rake-tami,* Voenizdat, Moscow, 1964; E.K. Bragin and A.G. Kubarev, *Protivoraketnaya Oborona,* Voenizdat, Moscow, 1966, 95p. (17,-000 copies); P.V. Morozov, *Bor'ba s Vozdushno-Kosmicheskimi Tselyami,* Voenizdat, Moscow, 1967, 142p. (10,000 copies). These are all technical monographs based largely on materials obtained from Western sources.

[12]*Krasnaya Zvezda,* November 27, 1957.

[13]Interview with C.L. Sulzberger, *Izvestia,* September 9, 1961.

[14]*Pravda,* October 5, 1961.

[15]*The New York Times,* July 17, 1962.

conventional or a nuclear warhead.[16] There remains considerable doubt as to the anti-missile capability of this missile and its estimated performance does not compare at all to the American high-acceleration Sprint missile. Western newspapers reported in 1963 that the "Griffon" was being deployed around Leningrad.[17] Subsequent evidence suggests that the deployment was ultimately halted, persumably because of unsatisfactory technical performance.[18] It may, however, have constituted an initial (research and development) deployment of the SA-5, "Tallinn system."

In November 1964, the Russians paraded another large missile for which the commentators claimed a long-range ballistic missile defense capability. This missile, "Galosh," has been shown also in subsequent parades, but always in a protective cannister. It was claimed capable of intercepting ballistic missiles at long distances from the defended targets and it has been suggested that it has exo-atmospheric range similar to the Spartan,[19] although the missile is otherwise comparable to the U.S. first-generation Zeus missile. The missile container measures some sixty feet and the missile is believed capable of carrying a large thermonuclear warhead.

It is likely that no definite deployment decision was made in regard to BMD under Khrushchev, although a substantial effort had been undertaken in order to provide the option of deployment. It is possible that the promotion of Marshal Biriuzov to Chief of the General Staff in 1963 indicated a commitment to the build-up of Soviet missile strength, including BMD. Biriuzov had been head of the air defense forces for many years and it was under him (1955-62) that the large-scale deployment of surface-to-air missiles was undertaken. Marshal Biriuzov had for a short period (1962-63) also commanded the strategic missile forces. The initial deployment decision may have been made sometime in 1963-64.

It is interesting to note that the second (1964) and third (1968) editions of Marshal Sokolovskij's *Military Strategy* dropped a formulation from the first edition according to which ballistic missiles "are still practically invulnerable to existing means of air

[16]*Aerospace Technology,* 21(3), July 31, 1967, p. 99.

[17]*The New York Times,* November 11, 1963.

[18]*The New York Times,* January 29, 1967.

[19]*The New York Times,* February 13, 1969.

defense."[20] The first edition contained the statement that "in principle, a technical solution to this (i.e., antimissile defense) has now been found. In the future this form of defense must be perfected."[21] In the second and third editions the last sentence was deleted.

During 1965, films of alleged missile interceptions were shown on Soviet television and, in July of that year, Brezhnev declared that the Soviet Union had achieved significant results in the procurement of anti-missile systems and that it would shortly be possible to make important progress which would significantly improve their performance.[22] At the 23rd Party Congress in April 1966, Marshal Malinovskij asserted that Soviet air defense forces guarantee a certain destruction of all aircraft and many of the enemy's missiles.[23]

The Soviet leadership evidently has made the decision to assign first priority to the build-up of the Soviet long-range missile forces. The corollary of this position may have been a decision to keep the BMD deployment initially limited to a ring around Moscow. There is little evidence of substantial conflict over this decision which constitutes a decision allowing further research-and-development efforts and postponing the question of large-scale deployment. It is, however, possible that Air Marshal Sudets' (Commander-in-Chief of PVO) failure to be re-elected to the Central Committee in April 1966 and his subsequent retirement in July, when he was succeeded by Army General (since promoted to Marshal) Batitsky, is connected with a decision to go slow on the BMD deployment. Marshal Sudets had been an ardent advocate of BMD. A go-slow decision is, however, probably not the result of any doctrinal dispute about the value of active defenses but rather an interim compromise in the internal bargaining over the allocation of limited funds. [Marshal Zakharov (born 1898) became Chief of the General Staff once more after the death of Marshal Biriuzov in an air accident in October 1964, and he is

[20]V.D. Sokolovskij, *et al., Soviet Military Strategy,* RAND Edition, Prentice Hall, Englewood Cliffs, N.J., 1963, p. 298. *Voennaya Strategiia* (2nd ed.), Voenizdat, Moscow, 1964, p. 241.

[21]*Ibid.,* p. 345.

[22]*Pravda,* July 4, 1965.

[23]*Krasnaya Zvezda,* April 2, 1966.

likely to have given strong support to the traditionalist opposition to cuts in the ground forces.]

A major work on Soviet strategy, published in 1967, contained a formulation which suggested that there was still room for improvements in the Soviet BMD technology. "Simultaneous with the improvement in missiles, the problem of anti-missile defense, the chief means of which is the anti-missile, is being solved."[24] An authoritative history of the Soviet military establishment, for which Marshal Zakharov headed the editorial committee, makes the following observation and proud claim: "The arrival of ballistic missiles and space vehicles required a nuclear air defense system to respond not only against the aircraft threat, but first of all to provide anti-missile and anti-space defense. Technically this problem was solved very quickly in our country."[25] Soviet statements about the efficacy of missile defense have stabilized over the last years around the relatively sober assertion that "the air defense forces are capable of destroying *any* aircraft and *many* missiles of the enemy at both long and short ranges from the defended targets."[26] There was some evidence of divergent estimates regarding the expected effectiveness of BMD among top Soviet military leaders in the spring of 1967. The differences in formulation may be related to a debate associated with the U.S. proposal for strategic arms talks, but it is rather characteristic that the positions taken by the military spokesmen reflected, or could be interpreted as reflecting, particular service biases and interests. Thus the Commander-in-Chief of the PVO, Marshal Batitsky, asserted that BMD could reliably protect the country while the Commander of the Strategic Missile Forces, Marshal Krylov, and the head of the Soviet Civil Defense Program, Marshal Chuikov, asserted that some missiles would always get through and that Soviet missiles employed *en masse* were practically invulnerable. The Minister of Defense, Marshal Grechko, formulated his position in similar terms and Marshal Zakharov has recently reiterated the assertion that Soviet missiles are capable of penetrating U.S. missile defenses (a

[24]N. Ya. Sushko and T.R. Kondratkov, *Metodologicheskie Problemy Voennoy Teorrii i Praktiki,* Voenizdat, Moscow, 1967, p. 68.

[25]*50 Let Vooruzhennykh Sil S.S.S.R.,* Voenizdat, Moscow, 1968, p. 510.

[26]Marshal N. Krylov, in *Selskaya Zhizn,* February 23, 1968 (emphasis added).

position which is not denied by U.S. officials).[27] It should be emphasized, however, that although Soviet military spokesmen may differ in their current estimates of BMD capabilities, none has questioned, at least publicly, the desirability of building and perfecting such defenses.

There have been very few references to BMD in Soviet statements or professional literature over the last two years. This silence certainly reflects the difference in style between the flamboyant Khrushchev and the rather cautious and terse posture of the Brezhnev-Kosygin regime, but it may also indicate a postponement of the crucial decisions, as well as possible shifts in perspectives and leverage within the decision-making structure generated by the transformations in the Soviet strategic posture, wherein offensive missile forces are assuming a more dominating role. We should also expect that the issue is deliberately being handled with some circumspection because of clear signals from Washington that in American eyes the BMD question is a key issue in the future course of Soviet-American strategic relations. It is likely that the rather persistent efforts of the Johnson Administration to "educate the Russians" about BMD did, at least, have the effect of causing the Soviet BMD decisions to be made at a high political level rather than in the Ministry of Defense. Hence, the Soviet decisions in this field will now have to be made with reference to the expected impact on U.S. perceptions and reactions in regard to the weapons competition, as well as the general contours of the political relationship between the two superpowers.

Mr. McNamara announced in November 1966,[28] that the Soviet Union had initiated the deployment of a BMD system around Moscow based on the "Galosh" missile.

There has been some basic disagreement in Washington about the real nature of another system which is being deployed extensively in the northwestern parts of the U.S.S.R. and some other places. This so-called Tallinn system is presumably based in part on the SA-5 "Griffon." It is now generally believed that it is designed and its radars deployed to counter high-flying aerodynamic threats rather than ballistic missile threats to the Soviet Union. It is, however, somewhat curious that the Russians should decide to invest substantially in a system against high-flying air-

[27]*The New York Times,* February 21 and 23, 1967; *Pravda,* February 17, 1968; *The New York Times,* May 1, 1969.

[28]Transcript in *The New York Times,* November 11, 1966.

craft at a time when the U.S. bomber force is declining, the B-70 is dead, the B-52's are obtaining low-flying capabilities, and the actual and potential follow-ons (FB-111 and AMSA) would also be designed to carry out low-flying attacks. Hence, it seems reasonable to hedge judgments about the real and prospective nature of the system, taking into account possible retrofit and upgrading of the system to provide it with substantial BMD capabilities. The residual uncertainties about the system are evidenced by the following formulation in a recent Department of Defense "fact sheet" on ballistic missile defense: "A majority of the intelligence community believes that it is designed against high-performance airplanes rather than ballistic missiles, *although the latter is a possibility*"[29] (emphasis is added).

The Russians have never officially released information about their BMD deployment efforts, but allegedly improved versions of the "Galosh" missiles have been shown in recent May Day and November Day parades in Red Square (the 1969 May Day parade did not include a military display). The present "Galosh" deployment has apparently been slowed down and presently consists of sixty-seven anti-missile launchers around Moscow. The total system will presumably include some one hundred launchers. Given the estimated range of the "Galosh" missile, such a deployment would provide a thin area defense for substantial portions of western Russia. In its original configuration the radars were deployed against U.S. strategic attacks only,[30] but recently the radars have been directed also toward Communist China.[31] The Russians apparently stopped building new ABM sites some time in 1968 and then proceeded with changing the configuration of the radars and with testing an improved interceptor missile.[32] This long range interceptor reportedly has a "loiter" capability, which means that it is able to coast for a short while after it has been fired until it has selected a target, at which

[29] *DoD Fact Sheet on ABM,* April 1969.

[30] Mr. McNamara in *Military Procurement Authorization for Fiscal Year 1968, op. cit.,* p. 303.

[31] President Nixon at his press conference, March 14, 1969. Transcript in *The New York Times,* March 15, 1969.

[32] *Safeguard Antiballistic Missile System,* Hearings before the Subcommittee of the Committee on Appropriations, House of Representatives, 91st Cong. 1st Sess., 1969, pp. 55,61.

point it will be restarted and maneuvered to the target.[33] Thus the issue of Soviet intentions in the BMD area is still ambiguous, perhaps even to Soviet decision-makers. The current preoccupation with China seems likely, however, to provide strong incentives to obtain at least a thin area defense system. Historical tradition and outlooks are likely also to structure strong biases in favor of a more substantial effort.

RUSSIAN REACTIONS TO THE AMERICAN BMD DECISIONS

It has been rather curious, and perhaps telling, that the Soviet Union refrained for so long from commenting on the sharp debate which has developed in the United States over the ballistic missile defense issue during the last year or so. Thus the Soviet press remained silent until the eve of President Nixon's announcement about the revised deployment schedule and configuration, which subsequently obtained the designation "Safeguard."

The prolonged silence may reflect a basic equivocation in the Soviet assessment of (1) what U.S. decision would be preferable from a Soviet interest perspective; (2) the expected impact of Moscow's taking a stand on the outcome of the U.S. debate; (3) what posture would be most consistent with the objective of reopening the dialogue with Washington and, in particular, with the objective of having bilateral strategic arms talks. The equivocation on these issues remains.

The Soviet approach to arms control has always reflected a basic preoccupation with the manipulation of politics, particularly the domestic politics of the adversary. It is presumably no accident that, for example, most Russian books and pamphlets on the subject of arms control and disarmament contain the word "struggle" (bor'ba) in the title, suggesting the need to mobilize political pressures so as to force otherwise hostile or reluctant decision-makers to consent to arms control agreements.

This perspective does, of course, reflect some basic ideological presuppositions about the distribution of roles, interests and power in the non-communist world. We are not suggesting that Soviet arms control policy is based entirely or even predominantly on ideological suppositions, but we do need to recognize that

[33]*Ibid.,* pp. 10-11.

for any decision-maker certain basic assumptions about the roles, interests and power in the world are necessary as a kind of explanatory or organizational framework facilitating the interpretation of experiences, observations and goals. Thus ideology constitutes *inter alia* an image of the world which defines the major actors and their preestablished roles.

In view of Soviet ideological predilections, it was rather surprising that Soviet commentators would remain silent so long in regard to the Sentinel controversy, particularly as it became increasingly clear that the controversy was to some important extent becoming divorced from the concrete BMD issues and converted into a confrontation between the "Liberal Establishment" and "the military industrial complex." Such a political texture would seem to fit Communist expectations and interpretational categories rather well. In addition, it was clear that the widespread mistrust of the military and the civilian defense management was related to public opposition to the war in Vietnam and to the perceived incompetence with which the U.S. was conducting this war. The increasing evidence of multifold alienation in American society and the unpredictable elements they introduce into Soviet calculations seem to have frightened Soviet observers who have, for instance, criticized the radical student activists in the U.S. There is a sense in which it is extremely uncomfortable to confront what might be construed as confirmatory evidence of apocalyptical predictions when the troubled party is a major nuclear power!

It is, on the whole, not unreasonable to assume that the Soviet failure to exploit the American controversy propagandistically may reflect a general assessment that the Sentinel deployment (or a variation thereof) would not necessarily be an unwelcome move. In any event, the Soviet Union was not exactly the most innocent censurer of ballistic missile defense deployments.

The prolonged silence was broken on March 13, 1969 with the publication of a lengthy article in *Izvestia*[34] by the paper's prominent political commentator Vikenty Matveyev. The same day *Pravda*[35] published a shorter article by one of its New York correspondents. The publication date suggests that the articles

---

[34]V. Matveyev, Vooruzheniya i Razoruzhenie (Armaments and Disarmament), *Izvestia,* March 13, 1969.

[35]B. Orekhov, Sentinel: Parol' voennogo Buma (Sentinel-Password for Military Boom), *Pravda,* March 13, 1969.

were probably not meant to have any serious influence on
Mr. Nixon's decisions.

The Matveyev article is critical of the Sentinel program, but
it is important to notice which criticisms are made and the arguments which are not employed. Essentially, Mr. Matveyev presents the pro-Sentinel lobby as being the spokesmen for the
"military industrial complex" which remains intrinsically hostile
to any slowdown of the arms race and arms control arrangements
with the Soviet Union. His article is not an attack on BMD as
such. It does not argue, for example, that the American BMD
effort constitutes an arms race generating system in terms of its
interactions with the Soviet strategic posture. The arms race
argument is focused rather on the alleged interests and inimical
objectives of the so-called "military industrial complex."[36]

It is worth noting that the nature and tenor of the Matveyev
article may have been chosen also for purposes of rationalizing
Soviet decision making *vis-a-vis* whatever internal opposition may
exist in the decision-making system in Moscow. Hence the article
appears to justify the Soviet willingness to enter into strategic arms
talks by emphasizing (1) the "progressive" forces in the U.S. which
will force the government in Washington to make a deal, (2) the
economic incentives for making a deal which are present in the
West and hence not confined to the Soviet Union, and (3) recent
advances in Soviet missile capabilities: "the balance of forces
which has been reached now offers a possibility to conclude agreements on the freeze and reduction of nuclear armaments." There
is also the added consideration of polemizing against the Chinese
position.

It is interesting that the Tass report of President Nixon's
BMD decision, which was carried by *Pravda* and *Izvestia*,[37] did
not contain any criticism of the decision, and it quoted the President approvingly to the effect that the U.S. remained willing to
enter into strategic arms talks. We should note also that no official

[36]A brief Tass report in *Pravda,* March 19, 1969, quoted Drew
Pearson and *The Chicago Tribune* in support of this perspective.
It was also formulated in similar terms by Yury Zhukov in *Pravda,*
March 25, 1969.

[37]*Pravda,* March 15, 1969; *Izvestia,* March 16, 1969. It was note-
worthy that a major article on the resumption of the ENDC talks,
which devoted considerable space to the urgency of strategic arms
limitation, did not even mention the decision. Article by R. Mikhailov
in *Pravda,* March 17, 1969.

Soviet spokesman has commented publicly on the American decision. It may be an overstatement to write as did James Reston of *The New York Times* that the Russians "even reacted to President Nixon's latest decision to build an anti-missile system as if we were doing them a favor."[38] But the Russians have adhered rather strenuously to the proposition that active defenses are, in fact, a peace-promoting value. It was only four days after the U.S. Senate voted favorably on construction funds for Sentinel in June 1968 that the Soviet Union officially agreed to hold strategic arms talks with the U.S.

The Soviet reaction to Mr. McNamara's Sentinel deployment speech at San Francisco, September 18, 1967, and his subsequent elucidation of his policy rationales in an interview with *Life* Magazine,[39] was even more sparse than the reaction to Mr. Nixon's Safeguard decision. The few commentaries depicted the decision as a concession to pressures from the arms industry and expressed concern lest the domestic pressures for growth would prove irresistible.[40] Again the arguments were taken from the domestic debate in the U.S. It is interesting to note, however, that the Soviet commentators did not even mention the China rationale for Sentinel. The commentator in *Pravda* quoted profusely from *The New York Times* editorial opposing Sentinel (September 20, 1967) but neatly omitted the *Times'* arguments about Soviet-American strategic force interactions and arms races.

A second article by Matveyev on March 27 reiterated several of the perspectives which he had elaborated in his first commentary. There is again no assertion that BMD as such will generate an arms race by inducing off-set augmentations in the offensive force arsenals. The arms race concerns are focused rather on the escalation of expenditures (strange argument to be coming from Moscow these days) and the alleged concessions to the arms industry.[41] The Congressional hearings on BMD and the expansion of the public debate in the U.S. have caused Soviet commen-

---

[38] *The New York Times,* March 19, 1969.

[39] *Life,* September 29, 1967, pp. 28, a, b, c.

[40] *Pravda,* September 24, 1967. *Izvestia,* October 4, 1967.

[41] V. Matveyev, Put' Vpered (The Road Ahead), *Izvestia,* March 27, 1969.

tators to revert to the BMD issue in increasingly critical terms. It seems rather clear that the contextual framework of the American Administration's posture on the BMD issue as elaborated by Messrs. Laird and Packard contributed rather significantly to the crystallization of the critical attitudes of the Soviet commentators. Instead of arguing for the limited deployment in terms of prudential objectives such as the need to protect the second-strike option, the value of simply being in the business, the value of damage-limiting capabilities if deterrence should fail, the need to establish some flexibility for purposes of improving the chances of arms control, the importance of providing dissuasion and protection vis-a-vis new nuclear powers (without any specific or exclusive reference to China), etc., Secretary Laird chose to invoke the imminent threat posed by alleged Soviet first-strike intentions. Public extrapolation of intentions from potential capabilities (and we are not suggesting that they may not be serious) is bound to obscure many complexities and likely to be diplomatically unwise. By invoking Soviet first-strike intentions a framework of stark conflict was established as the underlying rationale for the decision to go ahead with BMD. It is also not so long ago that Mr. McNamara and most of the important experts in strategic analysis went to some lengths to explain and elaborate the difference between counter-force capabilities and first-strike intentions in respect of the American posture and proceeded to present a rather persuasive case for a counterforce strategy being consistent with an arms control emphasis in the event that deterrence should fail. We should note also that Soviet discussion of targeting has tended to emphasize counterforce and economic countervalue perspectives and never reflected the deliberate annihilation of population targets as a primary objective of Soviet strategic planning.

Hence, the way the American Administration chose to argue its case for BMD tended to produce Soviet concerns lest the BMD decision be used as a vehicle for expanding the strategic arms competition. This perspective tended to be reinforced, of course, by the observation that much of the political support for ballistic missile defense in the U.S. emanates from quarters which are not known to be particularly friendly to arms control. There are exceptions, of course, but analysts, like the present author, who tend to favor some BMD on arms control grounds have good reasons to feel uncomfortable about their "allies" on the subject (and their friends in the opposite camp) and we should not be surprised that the Russians are similarly concerned (and in addition motivated to some degree to manipulate the "contradictions"). Thus *Pravda's* commentator, Georgij Ratiani, wrote that "one gets the impression that in the interests of the arms industry there is a desire to deliberately mislead American society, to once more fan up an arms race psychosis," and he observed that the speeches of the Secretary of Defense "include deliberately pointed phrases about some kind of mythical 'Soviet challenge'. "[42] And a commentator in *Red Star,* Colonel A. Leontyev, concluded that "we admit (understand) that Americans may have differing views as to whether they need anti-missiles or not. But they hardly need the fantasies which aim at slandering the Soviet Union."[43]

SOVIET-AMERICAN INTERACTIONS:
ARMS RACE ISSUES

One of the major issues in the current controversy over ballistic missile defense is the implications for the further velocity and direction of the strategic arms race. We should note right away that the degree and nature of the interactions between Russian and American strategic force postures is one of the most poorly understood and under-researched processes of international politics. Even the most cursory investigation of the historical development of the basic contour of the Russian and American strategic force postures should suggest, however, that there has been much less reactivity involved than is most often assumed.

Alternative Hypotheses and Some Evidence

It seems useful for heuristic purposes to distinguish among several alternative hypotheses about the nature of Soviet budget decisions in regard to the composition and size of the strategic forces: (1) The reactive hypothesis, (2) the institutional hypothesis, (3) the adaptive hypothesis and (4) the blueprint hypothesis.

For purposes of analysis we may distinguish between *imitative* reactions and *off-set* reactions. An *off-set* reaction

[42]*Pravda,* March 27, 1969. *Pravda* carried one of its most extensive articles on the Safeguard controversy, March 31, 1969. The article, entitled "Dangerous Safeguard" by B. Strel'nikov is a rather factual, albeit partisan, description of the U.S. debate but it does not include any specific Soviet evaluation of the issues. This is also true of a subsequent article by the same author in *Pravda,* June 10, 1969.

[43]*Krasnaya Zvezda,* April 2, 1969.

could imply that Soviet planners would react to American defenses by augmenting Soviet offensive forces so as to reestablish
status quo ante in terms of their ability to inflict damage upon the
United States. Such a pattern of interaction might be generated
by a theory which associates deterrence with fixed levels of
assured destruction capacities. Another kind of off-set reaction
would be the deployment of hard-point BMD to counter improvements in the accuracy of offensive missiles. In terms of timing,
the reaction to the actions and plans of the adversary may be either
sequential (i.e. follow such actions and plans) or *anticipatory* (i.e.
precede or coincide with such actions and plans).

The institutional hypothesis focuses on the Soviet strategic
posture as an outcome of the particular traditions, outlooks, concerns, and distribution of bargaining power which prevail in the
Soviet decision-making system. The adaptive hypothesis views
Soviet decision-making in terms of a pragmatic adaptation to and
exploitation of the perceived constraints and opportunities at any
particular time. The constraints and opportunities may inhere
in economic conditions, political developments in the external
arena, technological developments, prevailing fashions, etc.
Finally, the blueprint hypothesis assumes that Soviet decision-
making may be understood in terms of a long-range plan for world
domination and strategic superiority.

Before we examine the various hypotheses we should note a
couple of characteristics of the Soviet decision-making system
which seem relevant to an evaluation of the BMD issues: Soviet
hardware decisions appear to be more difficult to unmake than
are similar decisions in the United States. Furthermore, the Russians appear to have a distinct tradition of having military doctrine
follow hardware procurements. Finally, the Russians have the
great advantage of generally knowing when the decisions are
made in Washington while the Americans most of the time are
confronted with circumstantial evidence of Soviet decisions made
some time ago.

We can at this point offer only some general observations in
regard to how the evolution of the Soviet strategic posture con-
firms or rejects the various hypotheses which could be made.

There does not seem to be any evidence of a defense-offense
interactive pattern with the Russians responding to American
strategic defenses by augmenting their offensive forces. Thus the
construction of the U.S. continental air-defense in the mid-fifties
and its subsequent improvement with the introduction of the

SAGE (semi-automatic ground environment) system did not cause Moscow to expand its long-range bomber force. Certain adjustments in armaments—such as the introduction of air-to-surface missiles—were eventually made, but it is far from clear that this constituted an *off-set* rather than an *imitative* reaction, nor is it clear that the absence of U.S. strategic defenses would have prevented the introduction of such capabilities.

Somewhat more of a case can be made for the hypothesis that the heavy Soviet investments in air-defense constituted a reaction to the U.S. expenditures on strategic bomber forces. However, it is hard to demonstrate consistent correlations over time and, as we have noted, the Russians have not always acted in an optimal way in their efforts to counter U.S. offensive capabilities.

The particular configuration of the Soviet offensive forces seems to reflect certain traditional Soviet outlooks. We have already referred to the heavy emphasis on active defense. Another characteristic—at least until the mid-sixties—was what we could call a proximity emphasis. Thus the Soviet Union never acquired a large long-range bomber force, but allocated substantial resources into the build-up and maintenance of medium-range bombers. Such a scale of priorities is likely to reflect in part the perspective of a regional power whose historical memories were focused on the threat from contiguous power centers—particularly in Europe.

The strategic Air Force in the Soviet Union, D.A. (Dal'naya Aviatsia), was created in 1946 and by 1947 the Russians had already managed to produce their own copy of the American B-29, TU-4 "Bull." This medium-range bomber was eventually produced in large numbers generating an operational force of some one thousand aircraft by 1953.[44] The TU-4's were potentially able to strike U.S. targets on one-way missions but the available evidence cannot indicate whether such a strategy was part of the Soviet war plan. The TU-16 "Badger"—a twin-jet medium-range bomber—was first shown in 1954. It eventually replaced the TU-4 and the operational inventory included some one thousand of this aircraft by 1959. The third generation medium bomber, the supersonic TU-22 "Blinder," was first shown in 1961 and is currently replacing the TU-16 at the rate of one "Blinder" for every three "Badgers." The present medium bomber force comprises

[44]Robert A. Kilmarx, *A History of Soviet Air Power,* Frederick A. Praeger, New York, 1962, p. 230.

some seven hundred fifty aircraft with the TU-22 constituting somewhat less than a quarter of the force.[45]

Until the introduction of the B-52 in 1955 the American strategic bomber force was dependent on bases within the range of Soviet medium bombers. However, the Soviet Union did not choose to imitate the U.S. procurement of a large bomber force or to off-set it by procurement of a substantial counterforce capability (they may, however, have been closer to the latter than they realized). The four-jet long-range bomber, M-4 "Bison," which was first shown in 1954, and the four-turboprop heavy bomber, TU-20 "Bear," which was shown in 1955, were not procured in large numbers. The demonstration of Soviet capabilities and Soviet assertions about alterations in the relation of forces, did, however, nurture U.S. fears of an impending "bomber gap." In 1956 it was estimated e.g. that the Russians could have some six hundred to seven hundred "Bisons" in operational units by 1959[46] but as it turned out they only built a fraction of that number. The present D.A. force consists of some one hundred ten M-4 "Bisons" and ninety TU-20 "Bear." Some fifty of the total are used in the tanker role.[47]

During the 1950's a large number of forward bases were constructed in the Soviet arctic for the long-range air force, and during 1956-57 the Russians revealed an aerial refuelling capability. However, it is again one of the apparent anomalies in the development of the Soviet force posture that they took a very long time to introduce a serious operational capability.

A similar pattern to that which characterized the Soviet strategic bomber force was to shape the Soviet missile posture until the mid-sixties. The decision to move into the missile age is likely to constitute an adaptation to the opportunities of available or near-available technology. The decisions may also have been focused by the tradition of emphasizing artillery and fire power. Artillery officers dominated in the Soviet missile program which produced the first improvements of the German V-2, SS-1 "Scunner" (1947) and SS-2 "Sibling" (1951). It is likely that the first generation medium-range ballistic missile was in small-scale

[45] *The Military Balance, op. cit.,* p. 8.

[46] Kilmarx, *op. cit.,* p. 325, note 27.

[47] *The Military Balance, op. cit.,* p. 8.

production by 1955-56.[48] The first MRBM SS-3 "Shyster" (600 mi. range) was shown in the November Day Parade of 1957. By 1958 they had begun deployment of the IRBM SS-4 "Sandal" (1,100 mi. range). The missiles were deployed in fixed sites above ground. The 2,000 mile range SS-5 "Skean" was first shown in 1964. The number of MRBM/IRBM's grew from two hundred to seven hundred in 1962 and stabilized around seven hundred fifty in 1963.[49] In 1965, the Russians for the first time showed mobile IRBM's SS-XZ "Scrooge" (3,500 mi.) and in 1967 the SS-14 "Scamp" system with the "Scapegoat" (2,500 mi.) missile. The Soviet MRBM/IRBM program does not have any U.S. counterpart. (45 Jupiter missiles were deployed in Italy (30) and Turkey (15) by 1961 but they were withdrawn in 1963 due to their vulnerability. This was also true of the sixty Thor missiles deployed in the United Kingdom.) Again we may be confronted with an expression of the proximity preoccupation of Soviet decision-makers.

The Russians fired their first ICBM SS-6 "Sapwood" in August 1957 but this missile was, as it turned out, mounted quickly only in very small numbers. In fact the Soviet Union only had a handful by 1961 (the U.S. had twenty-eight).[50] In the meantime they were working on improved ICBM's and the SS-7 "Saddler" designed to use storable liquid fuel, was first displayed publicly in the November Day Parade in 1964. Another second-generation ICBM, the SS-8 "Sasin" was also deployed in the early sixties. It is estimated that some two hundred SS-7 and SS-8 missiles were deployed by the mid-sixties. In the May Day Parade 1965 the Russians showed a smaller ICBM, the SS-11, "Savage" which was reminiscent of the American Minuteman except that it was based on storable liquid instead of solid fuel. It carried a warhead with an estimated yield of 1 MT (megaton) compared to 5-10 MT estimated for the SS-7 and SS-8. In the same parade was shown the large "Scrag" missile which was claimed to be a global missile. In the 1967 November Day Parade the Russians displayed for the first

[48]Asher Lee, *The Soviet Air Force,* John Day, New York, 1962, p. 235. Marshal Krylov has claimed that the Soviet Union had operational MRBM's as early as 1955: Marshal N. Krylov, Raketnye Voiska Strategischeskogo Naznacheniya, *Voenno-Istoricheskii Zhurnal* (7), 1967, p. 21.

[49]See successive editions of *The Military Balance.*

[50]*The New York Times,* April 15, 1964.

time the large SS-9 "Scarp" missile which it was estimated could carry a warhead of some 25 MT.[51] The present buildup of the Soviet ICBM force started some time in 1965 and may reflect a series of decisions made after the Cuban missile crisis and the subsequent ouster of Khrushchev. The buildup consisted of the SS-9 and the SS-11 which were deployed at an approximate rate of two hundred fifty a year, about two hundred SS-11's for each forty to fifty SS-9's.[52] Thus the Soviet ICBM force numbered 340 in October 1966,[53] 720 in October 1967[54] and 900 in October 1968.[55] Some time early in 1968 the Russians evidently slowed down the pace of the SS-11 deployment and stopped the deployment of the SS-9. At the same time they started putting in about twenty-five of the new solid-fuel SS-13($<$1 MT. warhead). It looked like they were about to level off at about numerical parity with the U.S. However, in December 1968 they resumed the construction of SS-9 sites and the current ICBM force is estimated to comprise some 1,200 missiles in being or in the process of being put in silos.[56] Thus for the first time the Soviet Union has chosen to allocate her defense budget to procure and maintain a large intercontinental strike force.

In November 1967, Secretary of Defense McNamara announced that the Russians had been testing a so-called FOBS

---

[51]The information on the Soviet missile forces has been obtained by piecing together information from such sources as *Jane's All The World's Aircraft, Aviation Week and Space Technology* and *Missiles and Rockets (Technology Week).*

[52]William Beecher, Soviet Missile Deployment Puzzles Top U.S. Analysts, *The New York Times,* April 14, 1969.

[53]*1967 Posture Statement* (FY 1968-72 Defense Program and 1968 Defense Budget), Secretary of Defense Robert S. McNamara, p. 41.

[54]*1968 Posture Statement* (FY 1969-73 Defense Program and 1969 Defense Budget), Secretary of Defense Robert S. McNamara, p. 54.

[55]*1969 Posture Statement* (FY 1970-74 Defense Program and 1970 Defense Budget), Secretary of Defense Clark M. Clifford, p. 42.

[56]William Beecher, *op. cit.* Mr. Beecher's story, which appears to be "inspired," is consistent with public statements by Mr. Laird and Mr. Packard.

(fractional orbital bombardment system).[57] A missile which is fired in the FOBS mode (SS-9 "Scarp" is believed to be the booster) is fired in a low orbit about one hundred miles above the earth (the apogee of a normal ICBM trajectory is about eight hundred miles). At a given point a rocket engine is fired to deorbit the reentry vehicle and set it on its course towards its target. By coming in so low it would avoid detection by the BMEWS (Ballistic Missile Early Warning System). There are some severe penalties associated with this mode of attack in terms of reduced accuracy and payload. It might, however, be a fairly good first-strike system against airfields and command centers.

The Soviet Union has maintained a very large ocean-going submarine fleet during the post-war years. This posture is in many ways natural for a heartland power confronting an island power with allies on the rimland (to use Mackinder's terminology). The retention of the large fleet beyond the mid-fifties could, however, look anomalous to an outside observer who did not share the professed Soviet expectation that a future war would be a prolonged war of attrition.

Until very recently the Russians did not have any program to match the U.S. Polaris missile program. A 700-mile missile "Sark" was first shown in 1962 and the 1,000-mile "Serb," allegedly capable of underwater launch, in 1964. They were emplaced in diesel-powered submarines. Twenty-five "G"-class submarines with three missiles each and ten "Z"-class submarines each carrying two missiles were eventually constructed for this purpose. In the mid-sixties the force was augmented by ten "H"-class nuclear-powered submarines, each equipped with three missile firing tubes. Thus by October 1966 the SLBM force numbered one hundred thirty missiles.[58] A third generation SLBM, "Sawfly," was first shown in the November Day Parade in 1967. This missile is currently being emplaced in the new "Y"-class nuclear-powered submarine which went into production in 1968. Like the U.S. missile-carrying submarines, the "Y"-class vessels carry sixteen under-water launched missiles. Eight or nine of these vessels have been launched and the current production program is presumably geared towards turning out seven new "Y"-class submarines per

[57] *The New York Times,* November 4, 1967.

[58] *1967 Posture Statement, op. cit.*

year.[59] Beginning in 1967, Secretary McNamara did only count the Soviet SLBM's which were deployed in nuclear-powered submarines in his comparison of U.S. and Soviet strategic power, on the philosophy that the other missiles were primarily targeted against strategic European land targets and against shipping. Thus the Soviet Union was credited with only forty-five SLBM's in October 1968. If we add the missiles in conventional submarines the number would be one hundred forty. In addition twenty-five of the "E-1" and "E-2"-class nuclear powered submarines are equipped with cruise missiles (six and eight each respectively) as are twenty of the conventional "J" and "W"-class (four and one to three respectively) so that the total force of submarine based cruise missiles amount to approximately two hundred twenty.[60]

The Russians have now clearly assimilated the importance of protecting their missiles and they are putting them in hardened silos as well as employing certain concealment techniques such as constructing mock villages and planting grass and bushes on top of the silo covers and the underground command and control centers.[61] For a long time the Russian strategic forces seemed anomalous in their operational procedures as they never went on alert. This may have been due in part to the absence of reliable safety devices and procedures similar to those adopted in the United States. The Russians reportedly kept their nuclear warheads as much as fifty miles from their missile sites and reportedly did not order a full missile alert even during the Cuban missile crisis.[62] The Kennedy Administration went to some length to "educate" the Russians in these matters and they now claim that "the missiles are equipped with a reliable blocking system which

---

[59]*Strategic and Foreign Policy Implications of ABM Systems,* Hearings before the Subcommittee on International Organization and Disarmament Affairs of the Committee on Foreign Relations, U.S. Senate. 91st Cong. 1st Sess. Part I, 1969. Testimony by Secretary of Defense Melvin Laird, p. 173. Also *Safeguard Antiballistic Missile System, op. cit.,* pp. 9-10.

[60]Computed from *Jane's Fighting Ships 1967-68,* McGraw-Hill, New York, 1968, pp. 450-51.

[61]Podzemnyi Garnizon, *Ogonyok* (47) November 1967, p. 16, and articles in *Krasnaya Zvezda,* November 18, 1968 and in *Pravda,* January 3, 1968.

[62]Edward Klein and Robert Littell, Shh! Let's Tell the Russians, *Newsweek,* May 5, 1969, p. 47.

can prevent any accident, mistake, or misunderstanding."[63] With the new safety devices the Russians are now stressing alert exercises!

It is impossible to unscramble the motivating considerations behind the Soviet missile programs. It is certainly likely that the large expansion in U.S. missile forces which took place under the Kennedy Administration influenced the Russian choice. (Only 20-40 ICBM's had originally been scheduled for deployment in the U.S. Under the impact of expectations of a possible missile gap in the early sixties, the Eisenhower Administration initiated a program of deploying two hundred ICBM's. The Kennedy Administration greatly expanded this force goal and ended up with a plan for one thousand Minuteman and six hundred fifty six Polaris missiles.) The timing of the Soviet response is, however, somewhat hard to reconcile with a theory of close coupling to the U.S. effort. The American buildup may have set the scale but it seems likely that the Russians made their choice at a time when they had developed the technology required, under the impact of the traumatic experience of the failure at a "quick fix" by deploying missiles in Cuba, and in a context which reflected the bargaining that brought about the coalition which toppled Khrushchev in Moscow. The reactions included are more of the *imitative* than of the *off-set* variety.

It is, furthermore, highly conjectural to suggest that the FOBS tests constituted an anticipatory reaction to U.S. ballistic missile defenses. The incentives may simply derive from the threat inherent in the U.S. strategic bomber force to the extent that they reflect a particular reaction to the American posture at all. Similarly, the Soviet MRV* tests in August 1967 and on subsequent occasions may constitute as much of an *imitative* reaction to the U.S. MIRV program as they were directed towards penetrating future U.S. defenses. They may also reflect a Soviet interest in improved counterforce capabilities, or the Russians have decided to get them simply because they seem to be the newest gadget around.

Some Economic Parameters

A comparison of the official gross defense expenditures of the Soviet Union and the United States since 1955 suggests that

[63]Moscow broadcast in Hungarian, February 24, 1967.

*MRV = multiple reentry vehicle. There is apparently no conclusive evidence that the Soviet multiple warheads are independently targeted, but their triangular footprint reportedly coincides with the way Minuteman silos are deployed.

there may be some correlation between the over-all trends (see Table 1), but the generators of increased expenditures have typically been political crises in the international environment (Berlin, Vietnam). In fact, it is certainly an arguable case that it was such a crisis—the Korean War—which initially produced defense budgets of a magnitude which made the procurement of advanced strategic weapon systems financially feasible.

TABLE I

COMPARISON OF OFFICIAL TOTAL DEFENSE
EXPENDITURES 1955-1970
BY THE U.S. AND THE U.S.S.R.
(U.S. figures in $ billion, Soviet figures in billion rubles, current prices)[64]

	1955	1956	1957	1958	1959	1960	1961	1962
US	37.8	38.4	40.8	41.3	43.6	42.8	44.7	48.2
USSR	10.7	9.7	9.1	9.4	9.4	9.3	11.6	12.7

	1963	1964	1965	1966	1967	1968	1969	1970
US	49.9	51.2	47.4	55.4	68.3	78.2	78.4	77.6*
USSR	13.9	13.3	12.8	13.4	14.5	16.8	17.7	

(The Soviet figures may not always follow the trends in total military expenditures. Thus actual reductions in official defense expenditures may coincide with increases in the hidden categories of spending or vice versa.) *Budget request for FY 1970.

It is not possible on the basis of public information to examine the possible interactions between the Soviet and American expenditures on strategic forces, as there are no data on the detailed structure of the Soviet defense budget and also because prior to 1962 the U.S. defense budget did not contain functional output categories. It is worth noting, however, that the U.S. strategic force budget declined steadily from 1962 to 1966 and that the slight increases in 1968 and 1969 have not brought the budget expenditures up to the level of 1962-64 (see Table II). It should also be noted that even the early years of the Kennedy Administration's missile buildup did not match the fif-

[64]Figures obtained from *Narodnoe Khoziaistvo SSSR v 1964 Godu,* Izd. Statistika, Moscow, 1965; Steven R. Rivkin, *Technology Unbound,* Pergamon, New York, 1968, p. 13; *The New York Times* and the *1969 Posture Statement.*

TABLE II

U.S. STRATEGIC FORCE BUDGETS 1962-1970
(total obligational authority)
(in current $ billions and as % of defense expenditures)

	1962*	1963*	1964*	1965	1966	1967	1968	1969	1970
$	11.3	10.4	9.3	6.8	6.5	6.5	7.6	9.1	8.0
%	23.5	20.8	18.2	14.3	11.7	9.2	9.7	11.6	10.3

*There appears to have been some redefinition of the program elements in 1968. The figures for 1962-64 should probably be somewhat lower, but the adjustments were only given for the period 1965-70.[65]

teen billion dollars annual expenditures on strategic forces during the last part of the 1950's.[66]

According to Secretary of Defense Melvin R. Laird, the Soviet Union is presently outspending the United States in the ratio of three to two converted to dollar equivalents on strategic offensive forces.[67] Of the current U.S. strategic force budget (FY 1969) around two billion dollars goes to strategic defensive forces, so that the current U.S. budget for offensive forces is about $7 billion which again implies that the Russians are spending the equivalent of $10.5 billion. The total strategic force expenditures of the Russians in 1969 (adding $7.5 billion for strategic defensive forces) are thus equivalent to $18 billion.

The announced Soviet defense budget for 1969 was 17.7 billion rubles. The real Soviet defense expenditures differ from the published expenditures by being at a low estimate some twenty-five to fifty per cent above the latter and by the high estimate some seventy to one hundred per cent above (we shall use thirty per cent and eighty per cent respectively). Military research and development and investment in defense industries are e.g. concealed in

[65]*1968 and 1969 Posture Statements,* by Secretaries McNamara and Clifford respectively. The revised FY 1970 figure is $8.031 billion.

[66]Herman Kahn in *Strategy and Science: Toward a National Security Policy for the 1970's.* Hearings before the Subcommittee on National Security Policy and Scientific Developments of the Committee on Foreign Affairs, House of Representatives, 91st Cong. 1st Sess., 1969, p. 142.

[67]Press Conference, February 18, 1969.

other broad budget items.[68] There are also considerable problems
involved in converting the ruble expenditures to dollar
equivalents. The ruble is worth more intrinsically in terms of the
relative costs of a basket of goods and services (the purchasing exchange rate) than the official exchange rate suggests. The Soviet
Union also adheres to a system of subsidizing the raw material in-
puts to heavy military equipment. If we assume that the "real"
exchange rate for military goods and services is on the order of
$2.50 instead of the official $1.10,[69] the total Soviet expenditures
in 1969 will amount to the equivalent of $58 billion at a low
estimate and $80 billion at the high estimate. Thus the 1969
strategic force budget in the Soviet Union is on the order of
twenty-three to thirty-two per cent of the total defense budget
(compared to eleven per cent for the U.S.).

As the current dollar value of the Soviet GNP is less than
fifty per cent of the U.S. level, the Soviet defense effort must be
considered as a major effort. It seems clear that there would be
economic benefits for the Soviet Union associated with an arms
control arrangement with the United States in regard to strategic
forces. But economic incentives are hardly dominant in the Soviet
calculations. The growth rate of the Soviet economy has tapered
off during the sixties (6.4% as an average for the period 1955-61 and
5.4% for the period 1962-67 compared to 2.1% and 5.1% for the
U.S.).[70] However, the declining rate of the increase in capital investment and a rising capital/output ratio may act as further

[68]For analysis and elaboration, see Abraham S. Becker, *Soviet
Military Outlays Since 1955,* RM-3886-PR, The RAND Corp.,
Santa Monica, Cal., 1964; J.A. Godaire, The Claim of the Soviet
Military Establishment, in *Dimensions of Soviet Economic Power,*
Joint Economic Committee, 87th Cong. 2nd Sess., Washington,
D.C., 1962, pp. 33-46; Timothy Sosnovy, The Soviet Military
Budget, *Foreign Affairs,* 42(3) 1964, pp. 487-94; Morris Bornstein,
Economic Factors in Soviet Attitudes Towards Arms Control, in
Emile Benoit (ed.), *Disarmament and World Economic Interde-
pendence,* Columbia University, New York and Universitetsforlaget,
Oslo, 1967, pp. 60-85.

[69]Compare article by William Beecher in *The New York Times,*
December 25, 1966, quoting Washington experts' expectations that
the S.U. would be spending 20 billion rubles on defense in 1967
and that they would have to pay from $50 billion to $60 billion a
year in the American marketplace for the same goods and services.

[70]*Soviet Economic Performance: 1966-67,* Joint Economic Committee, 90th Cong. 2nd Sess., 1968, p. 12.

brakes on the growth of the Soviet economy. It is important to note that while the rates of increase in capital investment, which is the major non-military consumer of machinery and equipment, decreased sharply between 1964 (12.1) and 1966 (4.7),[71] there was a significant increase in the total machinery output which reflects the heavy investments in military hardware. There is considerable evidence of internal difficulties and disputes over allocational policies for the Soviet economy. Thus the postponement of the adoption of the final version of the current five-year plan (1966-70) suggested such conflicts. It now appears that the adopted pattern for resource allocations implies (1) increased expenditures on military and space programs, (2) additions to consumer money incomes, (3) a further deceleration of the growth in capital investments, and (4) a reduction of the planned allocations for agriculture.[72] The Soviet leadership is presently involved in drafting a new five-year plan for the allocation of resources for the period 1971-75 and the outcome of the strategic arms talks with the United States would presumably provide some data and arguments to the various participants in the bargaining process in that connection.

"Assured Destruction" and the Arms Race

The perspective of an arms race interaction spiral which is fueled by *off-set* reactivity seems to be based very largely on the notion that certain "Assured Destruction" potentials constitute a *sine qua non* for the continued viability of deterrence. The concept of "assured destruction" does not seem to have any counterpart in Soviet strategic thinking and even in the United States it was not used until 1965 as a concept differentiating the two missions of American strategic forces, *viz.,* "Assured Destruction" and "damage limitation." Initially it may have constituted a useful concept for purposes of structuring some of the force planning issues. It also permitted some quantification. Thus Mr. McNamara estimated that a second-strike capability to destroy one-fourth to one-third of the Soviet population and two-thirds of the Soviet industrial capability would constitute a sufficient assured destruction potential to deter a deliberate Soviet nuclear

[71]*Ibid.,* p. 13.

[72]*Ibid.,* p. 4.

attack on the United States and its allies.[73] However, by 1968 he had lowered his requirements from one-fifth to one-fourth of the population and one-half of the industrial capacity.[74] The adoption of the assured destruction terminology coincided with a shift in expressed strategic doctrine away from controlled war and counterforce (city avoidance) targeting.

The concept of "assured destruction" may also have served a useful political function at the time in terms of dampening incentives for stepping up the arms race, by providing a barrier against *internal* American pressures for greater offensive weapon arsenals. It provided a standard of nuclear sufficiency which was defendable against pressures for "more." However, in the present predicament the concept may have become dysfunctional by suggesting that the necessary response to the *external* pressures from the active defense measures of the adversary involves *offsetting* improvements in the offensive forces so as to restore the assured destruction capacity which prevailed prior to the introduction of defenses. Hence, in an environment where active defenses are reasonably price-competitive with offensive weapons, there seems to be a good case for reconsidering some of the basic doctrinal assumptions. Surely there is nothing finite about the relationship between American ability to destroy Russian lives and property and deterrence. Is it not feasible, for example, that deterrence requirements be considered in regard to relative expected war outcomes rather than in terms of fixed levels of destruction? The U.S. should be able to deter the Soviet Union by guaranteeing that it would be able to do at least as much damage to the Soviet Union as the Russians could inflict on the United States. Such a shift in outlook might lead in the direction of a Defensive Emphasis posture. It could also lead to renewed interest in controlled response and city avoidance targeting in the event that a war should break out.

While the Russians were not eager to become party to any tacit understanding concerning the limitations to be observed on targeting—particularly on avoiding cities—as the American Administration was clearly aiming for in the period 1962-65, it is worth noting that the Russians have never adhered to the notion

[73]*1965 Posture Statement* (FY 1966-70 Defense Program and 1966 Defense Budget), p. 39.

[74]*1968 Posture Statement* (FY 1969-73 Defense Program and 1969 Defense Budget), p. 50.

that Soviet security rests on an ability to kill a given percentage of the American population. Soviet statements on targeting indicate a combination of a counterforce, a counter-industry and a counter-administration focus: "Nuclear strikes will be launched against targets on the basis of political, economic, and directly military-strategic considerations. The most important targets of military strikes may be the strategic nuclear means of the enemy: the economic base of war, government and military administration, and groupings of enemy troops."[75]

The Russians have consistently been quite unfriendly to Western suggestions that the deployment of BMD should be curtailed for purposes of halting the arms race. Thus Premier Kosygin remarked during a press conference in London, February 10, 1967:

> What weapons should be regarded as a factor making for tension—offensive or defensive? I believe that the defensive systems, which prevent attack, are not the cause of the arms race, but constitute a factor preventing the death of people. Some argue like this: What is cheaper, to have offensive weapons which can destroy towns or whole states, or to have defensive weapons which can prevent this destruction? At present the theory is current somewhere that the system which is cheaper should be developed. Such so-called theoreticians argue as to the cost of killing a man—500,000 dollars or 100,000. Maybe an antimissile system is more expensive than an offensive system, but it is designed not to kill people but to preserve human lives.[76]

It should be emphasized that no currently foreseeable defensive system could prevent large-scale damage to the United States in a central war with the Soviet Union. We are not talking about a potential elimination but rather a potential reduction in damage. The Soviet Union probably wants to retain a capability to inflict some damage on the United States, for purposes of general deterrence. However, as their ability to inflict damage increases, further increases become both less urgent and more costly to attain. The law of diminishing returns above a certain level of potential damage will cause the marginal utility

[75]Maj. Gen. N. Ya. Sushko and Lt. Col. T.R. Kondratkov, *Metodologicheskiye Problemy Voennoy Teorii i Praktiki,* Voenizdat, Moscow, 1967, p. 147.

[76]*Izvestia,* February 11, 1967.

of each increment of potential damage to decrease and the marginal cost will increase. When the two become equal we have conceptually reached an equilibrium point.

The effect of a BMD system is to raise the cost of any level of damage. Raising the marginal cost of potential damage implies that the marginal cost becomes equal to the marginal utility at a lower level of damage, i.e., the equilibrium point will be associated with a smaller potential for damage infliction. Now it can be argued that there is little value in any increment of defensive strength as long as it can be countered at a lower cost by the offense. This objection is valid only if the defense is trying to reduce damage below the level that the offense is intent on being able to do. There is, as noted, no firm indication that the Soviet planners are intent on maintaining a given level of American hostages even if they do it at an incremental cost which is less than the incremental cost to the defense of protecting them. The quotation from Mr. Kosygin does suggest that a government may be more strongly motivated to save its own values than the adversary would be to destroy these same values. Furthermore, the current state-of-the-art of terminal ballistic missile defense is such that the cost-exchange ratio, i.e., the incremental cost which the defense must spend to reduce fatalities a given amount, divided by the cost to the offense to inflict these fatalities, will for the U.S. equal unity at around seventy per cent of the population surviving.[77] (This is the crossover or equilibrium point.) Thus even against attacks from the Soviet Union would the U.S. be able to significantly reduce the level of fatalities (from 120 to 60 million) and this applies even if we adopt the pessimistic expectation that the Russians would react to improvements in U.S. defenses by augmenting their offense up to the level where their incremental costs would equal the American incremental costs on defense.

We should want to emphasize that we have little evidence to support any particular theory of strong Soviet reactivity to U.S. force postures. Any analysis of potential Soviet reactions needs to assess the workings and internal bargaining of the Soviet decision-making system: the attitudes, traditions and vested interests which constitute the filters through which any interaction with the U.S. force posture takes place. We need to understand, for example, the implications of the Soviet Ministry of

[77]Daniel J. Fink, Strategic Warfare, *Science and Technology* (82) October, 1968, pp. 58, 63.

Defense being run essentially by military officers and of the fact that the average age of the top military leadership is around sixty-two, as opposed to fifty-six in the United States. The decisional outcome of any procurement debate is likely to reflect the peculiar workings of the bureaucratic organization that produces them. The outlooks and vested interests are, of course, likely to change as the Soviet force posture develops and new options become available.

It should be clear to the reader that currently available technology is a long way from offering independence in the sense of providing immunity to Soviet power or even to the power of other power centers which may emerge in the years ahead. Thus, there is no suggestion that we may escape the restrictions of interdependence. To a significant degree the acceptance of interdependence is a precondition for the stable functioning of the international system, and our interest in a strategic posture of defensive emphasis ought not to lead us down the blind alley in pursuit of that absolute invulnerability which is neither available nor obviously desirable. It was irretrievably lost with the introduction of nuclear weapons and long-range means of their delivery. In a very real sense, international peace and stability presupposes a general reconciliation with the condition of vulnerability to the power of others, but it does not follow that we ought to structure our forces and actions so as to maximize the "assured vulnerability" and make its perpetuation a central objective of national policy. Moscow is, in any event, unlikely to accept such a scale of priorities.

While the attainment and even pursuit of absolute invulnerability constitutes a dangerous challenge to the moderating influences of the international system on the behavior of the states which make up that system, denying them exemption from injury should they commit "unacceptable" acts, the current or foreseeable BMD options are not such that they can favor the U.S. or the Soviet Union with impunity. They constitute primarily a means of prudential insurance and it remains, we would hope, a primary impact of nuclear weapons to increase prudence in international politics.

The Counterforce Threat

Since the general counterforce effectiveness of a missile force could be described by the quantity $(K) = \sum \text{yield}^{2/3} / \text{CEP}^2$ it has always been clear that the potential vulnerability of a deterrent force would be particularly sensitive to improvements in accuracy.

The estimated accuracy (CEP) of the Minuteman III reentry
vehicles is around one-fourth mile[78] and it seems prudent to assume that the Russians would be able to acquire similar performance of their MIRV'ed missiles in the time period which is relevant
to the installation of the Safeguard system. It has been estimated
that the SS-9 could carry a payload of a single 25-MT weapon or,
for example, a MIRV package of three individually targeted
5-MT warheads. Soviet military officials have emphasized that
recent advances in electronics have resulted in substantial improvements in the reliability of Soviet missiles and that it has made
feasible such tactical choices as retargeting and salvo firings.[79]
Now if we allow a degradation factor based on a .20 failure rate,
it has been estimated that only four hundred twenty SS-9 missiles,
each equipped with three reentry vehicles of 5 MT, would be required to attack one thousand Minuteman silos (currently hardened to withstand an overpressure of 300 psi), if we assume a
retargeting capability, that is, the ability to reprogram missiles to
make up for failures. Such a force would have about a .95 probability of destroying the silos (assuming 1/4-mile CEP),[80] so that
only fifty Minuteman missiles would survive such an attack which
does not even involve any of the SS-11 missiles in the counterforce strike.

In assessing the vulnerabilities of the deterrent force, note
should be taken also of the sensitivity of missile electronics to the
EMP (electromagnetic pulse) effects of nuclear explosions. Thus
"pin-down" attacks aimed at exploiting this vulnerability may also
constitute a problem.[81]

[78]*Aviation Week and Space Technology,* 89(9) 1968, p. 23.

[79]*See e.g. articles* by Col. Gen. Tolubko (then First Deputy Commander of the Strategic Missile Forces) in *Krasnaya Zvezda,* November 18, 1967; by Lt. Gen. N. Leontyev, *Trud,* November 19, 1967;
and by Marshal Krylov (Commander-in-Chief of the Strategic Missile
Forces) in *Nedel'ya,* August 27-September 2, 1967, and *Pravda,*
November 19, 1967.

[80]Address by Dr. John S. Foster, Jr., Director, DDR&E, before the
Aviation/Space Writers' Association, Sheraton-Dayton Hotel, Dayton, Ohio, May 12, 1969, DoD News Release No. 381-69, p. 5.

[81]For a disclosure of the potential importance of EMP effects on
the vulnerability of the strategic forces, see Remarks on Nuclear
Test-Ban Treaty Safeguards, by Senator Henry M. Jackson, September 25, 1968. Floor of U.S. Senate. *Congressional Record* 90th
Cong. 2nd Sess.14 (157): S11351-S11354.

We need not postulate any given Soviet intention of obtaining a first-strike option. The technology may, however, make it available and it could, in the absence of countermeasures such as hard-point defense by ABM's, have a significant impact on the bargaining and behavior in a severe crisis.

It has remained a basic tenet of U.S. defense thinking that deterrence ought to be based on a set of basically different systems which would present qualitatively different challenges to an adversary. Hence, it would seem an imprudent gamble to ignore the emerging threat to the Minuteman force because of the existence of, for example, the Polaris component of the total strategic force. The Polaris system may be found to have unexpected vulnerabilities; advances in anti-submarine warfare (ASW) tactics (e.g. involving satellite reconnaissance and fast, nuclear-powered hunter-killers of the new "V" class, or barrage attacks with nuclear weapons by bombers or missiles) combined with improved ABM systems could conceivably develop as a threat. We do not want to construct paranoid horror scenarios. The basic point is that it requires constant effort to maintain a qualitatively reliable and credible deterrent.

SOVIET-AMERICAN INTERACTIONS: ARMS CONTROL

The Johnson and Nixon Administrations have clearly attempted to put the ABM procurement decisions into an arms control context, and it is likely that the outcome of the prospective strategic arms limitation talks (SALT) between the Soviet Union and the United States will have a significant impact on the further evolution of American and Soviet policies in regard to ballistic missile defense.

The Diplomacy of Arms Control

Provisions for the reduction of strategic delivery vehicles have been incorporated into both the American and Russian plans for "general and complete disarmament" (GCD). As far as the specific Soviet proposals in this area are concerned they have focused on the so-called "nuclear umbrella" concept. It implied that "an agreed and strictly limited number of intercontinental missiles, anti-missile missiles and anti-aircraft missiles in the 'ground-to-air' category" would be retained by the two super-powers "exclusively on their own territory," until the end of the third stage (initially second stage) of the disarmament process.[82] The Soviet Union agreed that there should be control of such remaining missiles directly at their launching sites, but they have been unwilling to quantify their conception of what constitutes a "limited" number, stating only that it should be "minimal."[83] It should be noted that the strategic weapons systems which would make up the umbrella would be confined to land-based (excluding submarine-launched) missiles and to the home territories of the two superpowers. The U.S. draft GCD treaty involves percentage reductions of strategic forces throughout the three stages of the disarmament process (reductions to seventy per cent of initial levels in Stage I, to thirty-five per cent in Stage II, and to zero in Stage III).

The first major attempt to treat strategic delivery vehicles as a separate subject of arms control regulation was the American proposal of January 21, 1964 for a verified freeze on "the number and characteristics of strategic nuclear offensive and defensive vehicles."[84] The American proposal specifically aimed at pre-empting the deployment of ballistic missile defenses. According to Mr. Foster "a freeze on strategic delivery systems without a freeze on anti-missile systems would be destabilizing and there-

[82]See Soviet revised draft GCD Treaty of September 22, 1962, *Documents on Disarmament 1962,* Vol. II, U.S. Arms Control and Disarmament Agency (ACDA), Washington, D.C., 1963, p. 917. The "concession" to have the umbrella extended to the third stage was made by Gromyko in an address to the U.N. General Assembly, September 19, 1963. *Documents on Disarmament 1963,* ACDA, Washington, D.C., 1964, p. 516 and submitted as a formal draft amendment, February 4, 1964, *Documents on Disarmament 1964,* ACDA, Washington, D.C., 1965, p. 22. For the latest version (April 28, 1965) of the Soviet GCD draft treaty proposal incorporating the umbrella concept, see *Documents on Disarmament 1965,* ACDA Washington, D.C., 1966, pp. 77-101.

[83]See, e.g. Statement by Fedorenko to the First Committee of the U.N. General Assembly, October 30, 1963, reprinted in *Documents on Disarmament 1963, op. cit.,* p. 562.

[84]Message from President Johnson to the Eighteen-Nation Disarmament Committee (ENDC), *Documents on Disarmament 1964, op. cit.,* pp. 7-9. The proposal was spelled out in a statement to the ENDC by Mr. Foster on January 31, 1964, *Ibid.,* pp. 17-21; by Mr. Fisher, April 16, 1964, *Ibid.,* pp. 157-62, and by Mr. Timberlake, August 27, 1964, *Ibid.,* pp. 367-73.

fore unacceptable."[85] The proposal did involve a great deal of intrusive inspection[86] and it would have frozen the strategic balance at a time when the Russians were about to carry out a major effort to catch up with the U.S. level. It could also have frustrated such stabilizing developments as the hardening of Soviet missiles.

The Russians rejected the American freeze proposal using a variety of arguments (some of them implicitly) which may be summarized in the following way:

1. It did not cover all nuclear delivery vehicles (e.g. short-range/tactical missiles).
2. It would not prevent the establishment of the NATO multilateral force.
3. It did not imply a reversal of the arms race.
4. It envisaged control over existing armaments without disarmament.
5. It implied the freezing of an American advantage.

In December 1966, Secretary of State Dean Rusk expressed the hope that the two superpowers should be able to prevent a further acceleration of the arms race by agreeing not to deploy BMD systems.[87] President Johnson expressed hopes for a freeze on BMD deployments in his State of the Union message in January 1967. The issue had been discussed with the Soviet Ambassador in Washington, Mr. Dobrynin, and was later resumed by the American Ambassador to Moscow, Mr. Llewellyn Thompson, with Premier Kosygin. Mr. Kosygin expressed his views in favor of ABM during a news conference in London in February. It was, however, rather curious that a commentator in *Pravda* suggested that Kosygin had been more receptive to the idea of discussing the question of preventing a further arms race with offensive and defensive weapons[88] than he had in fact been. Subsequently, this construction was denied by "authoritative sources" in Moscow.[89] However, on March 2, 1967, President Johnson announced that

[85]*Documents on Disarmament 1964, op. cit.,* p. 20.

[86]For a discussion of the verification system involved, see David W. Wainhouse, *Arms Control Agreements: Design for Verification and Organization,* John Hopkins Press, Baltimore, Md., 1968, pp. 62-78.

[87]*The New York Times,* December 22, 1966.

[88]Fedor Burlatskij in *Pravda,* February 15, 1967.

[89]*The New York Times,* February 18, 1967.

Kosygin had agreed to discussions between the two countries on
limiting the arms race in offensive and defensive missiles. Procedural talks were initiated in Moscow. In June of 1967, following
a rather intensive lecture by Mr. McNamara on the dangers of
ballistic missile defenses during the summit meeting at Glass-
boro, Mr. Kosygin had this to say in response to a question about
the Soviet attitude towards an agreement to limit BMD systems:

> We believe that the discussions should center not on merely
> the problem of an anti-missile defense system. Because,
> after all, the anti-missile system is not a weapon of aggres-
> sion, of attack; it is a defensive system. And we feel
> therefore that what should be considered is the entire
> complex of armaments and disarmament questions.
>
> Because, otherwise, if—instead of building and deploy-
> ing an anti-ballistic missile system—the money is used to
> build up offensive missile systems, mankind will not
> stand to gain anything. It will, on the contrary, face a
> still greater menace and will come closer to war. And we
> therefore are in favor of considering the whole range of
> questions relating to arms and disarmament, and we're
> ready to discuss that question—the general question of
> disarmament.[90]

On June 27, 1968, Mr. Andrei Gromyko reaffirmed
Moscow's willingness to participate in missile talks with the U.S.
for purposes of reaching an "understanding on mutual restriction
and subsequent reduction of strategic vehicles for the delivery of
nuclear weapons—offensive and defensive—including anti-missiles."[91] (On June 24th the U.S. Senate had rejected a motion to
eliminate the requested funds for the Sentinel deployment from
the military construction authorization bill.) On July 1, 1968,
President Johnson announced during the ceremony when signing
the nonproliferation treaty (NPT) that the two superpowers had
agreed to proceed with substantive strategic arms discussions.
The Soviet memorandum on arms control of the same day reiterated the Soviet perspectives that "an exchange of opinion" on this
matter should be on "mutual limitation and subsequent reduction
of strategic means of delivery of nuclear weapons."[92] The context of the total Soviet statement on the issue suggested, however,

[90] *Izvestia,* June 27, 1967.

[91] *Pravda,* June 28, 1968.

[92] *The New York Times,* July 2, 1968.

that Soviet thinking was still focused on the "minimum umbrella" concept.

Just as President Johnson was about to announce the imminent opening of the strategic arms talks at the summit level, Soviet tanks moved into Czechoslovakia and the Soviet-American dialogue came to a sudden halt. Following a period of political and strategic reassessments in Washington, the talks will open some time during the summer of 1969.

The Bargaining Ahead

It is not possible on the basis of the available evidence to predict with high confidence what the Russians may be willing to propose and accept in terms of strategic arms limitations. The Soviet decision to talk may be more in the nature of a *tactical* than a substantive decision. We should not be surprised if the initial Russian proposals will reiterate the "minimum umbrella" concept. Such an approach would serve to postpone all important and difficult decisions on the Soviet side until they have had a chance to consider the American position. The Soviet leadership may be under considerable pressures to "normalize" its relations with the United States, particularly in the aftermath of Czechoslovakia, and SALT may look attractive for such purposes. Soviet motivations may be structured also by (1) having achieved strategic parity; (2) wanting to feel out the new American administration; (3) preoccupation with instabilities in Eastern Europe; (4) increasing apprehensions about serious conflicts with China; (5) domestic problems (economic and ideological).

In terms of the modalities, it may be useful to distinguish between *formal* and *informal* arrangements. There may, of course, be a lot of marginal cases along a continuum extending from arms regulation by means of a conversational process to the ratification of a formal treaty. Furthermore, we could make the distinction between *explicit* and *tacit* arrangements and, finally, we may want to consider a strategic arms control arrangement in terms of its *comprehensiveness* both in regard to the details and scope of the understanding.

On the issue of the formality of the agreement to be sought, it is quite likely that it will be necessary to think in terms of a fairly formal arrangement. The Soviet system appears to be better geared to reacting to fairly specific proposals. The idea of an open-ended dialogue would probably constitute the most suspicion-arousing approach as far as the Russian bureaucracy is concerned.

The tradition of political management through reasonable discussion is not a part of the Soviet political culture. The Russian outlook in these matters appears to have a strong legalistic bias.

From a tactical point of view, it may prove difficult and time-consuming to attempt to iron out a very comprehensive agreement. Thus, it would seem useful to focus on the possibility of compartmentalizing some of the issues so that they can be handled by a series of limited package agreements rather than one comrehensive treaty.

An explicit and detailed arrangement has the advantage of leaving less room for ambiguity while on the other hand some residual ambiguity may be desirable from the point of view of giving the agreement sufficient flexibility to keep pace with a volatile technology. In any event the negotiators will be faced with the problem of grinding enough flexibility into whatever arrangements they can agree upon.

For heuristic purposes we could imagine a strategic arms control arrangement to focus on one or more of the following parameters:

1. Number of delivery vehicles.
2. Number of warheads
3. Total megatonnage (or alternatively $NY^{2/3}$ where N is the number of delivery vehicles and Y is the yield of each individual weapon. We focus on the area for a given overpressure as the weapon effect which scales as the cube root of the yield)
4. Total deliverable payload
5. Peacetime operating practices
6. Information exchange
7. Targeting

Here we are, of course, confronted with a series of very complex technical issues in regard to the choice of parameters, in terms of the projected stability which would be associated with the arrangements. (A limitation on number of delivery vehicles only could, for example, lead to the procurement of high-yield weapons which could produce serious first-strike capabilities given current and estimated accuracies of ballistic missiles.) The problem of inspection would also enter into the calculation. The American administration has let it be known that it will no longer insist on intrusive inspection. The verification may be carried out by unilateral means, presumably with high-altitude photography. However, it is not possible for an outsider to estimate the capability of satellite surveillance systems to monitor an agreement which limits, for example, total deliverable payload (this appears to be a desirable parameter to structure the agreement around).[93]

For heuristic purposes we could envisage seven different designs of a strategic force agreement:

1. Offensive force inventories (to be specified) limited to X lbs payload (throw weight) *plus* no limitation on defensive forces.

2. Offensive force inventories (to be specified) limited to Y vehicles—with no vehicles with a payload $> Z$ lbs plus no limitation on defensive forces.

3. All strategic forces (to be specified) to be limited according to (1) or (2).

4. Qualitative restrictions barring certain kinds of weapons and weapon tests (land-mobile ICBM's, MIRV's, ABM's, FOBS, etc.).

5. Some budget limitations combined with (1)-(4) or independent thereof.

6. Some warfighting understandings, including, for example,

    (capital) cities as sanctuaries

    (some) command and control centers as sanctuaries

    no targeting of communication systems

    no first-strike against cities

7. Some institutionalized dialogue about the traffic rules for the arms race.

It is, in my estimate, very unlikely that the Russians will accept any arrangement which would prohibit the deployment of BMD, and our heuristic designs reflect that expectation. We should want to hedge, however, that having bilateral talks with the Soviet Union may tend to bypass the Soviet bureaucracy with its inherited biases and engage the Russians at a high political level where the issues may be viewed more clearly in terms of their foreign policy and economic implications. Thus, it is not unreasonable to expect that just having talks with the Russians will, to some extent, affect who gets what influence over strategic weapons procurement decisions. The available information does suggest, however, that the inherited biases and attitudes in regard to defensive weapons are shared also by the top political leader-

[93]For a very sophisticated discussion of various criteria for the limitation of strategic armaments, see Colonel Glenn A. Kent, On the Interaction of Opposing Forces Under Possible Arms Agreements, Occasional Papers in *International Affairs,* No. 5, Center for International Affairs, Harvard University, Cambridge, Mass., 1963.

ship, as evidenced by Mr. Kosygin's statements which we have quoted earlier in this chapter. Furthermore, the escalation of the Sino-Soviet conflict and the legacy of Soviet fears of German "revanchism" are likely to combine with a general desire to protect the Soviet Union against some possible effects of further nuclear proliferation to make the leadership intent on deploying at least a BMD system which is capable of giving high-confidence protection against small nuclear powers. Here, it would seem that Soviet and American interests do coincide, as indeed they may with the wider interests of international society whose stability might be greatly strained should the two superpowers fail to take precautionary measures so as to deny cheap superpower status to a large number of potential aspirants.

Great uncertainties are certainly involved in any estimates of the political spillovers from the SALT exercise. It will surely never be completely divorced from the normal process of international politics, although it might become somewhat decoupled over time should some kind of permanent institutional framework or tradition evolve. There is a great deal to be said for decoupling strategic arms control issues from specific political issues as the former deal with the long-range framework of the political process. In practical terms, it may never be possible to achieve complete decoupling. It should be emphasized in this context that the Russians are very unlikely to make and adhere to meaningful operational distinctions between technical and political issues in regard to arms control. Previous encounters constitute a pretty good indicator[94] and there is little reason to assume that the Russians have changed their mind. What could, after all, be more of a political issue than the armaments which are acquired to sustain national security and international order? It is, of course, possible to argue, and I tend to favor such a perspective, that it would be useful for the United States, and for the world, if the nuclear powers came to treat nuclear weapons as being somehow beyond the realm of politics and hence not allow them to play any important role in their own politics. Such a tradition may, for example, turn out to be a *sine qua non* for the long-range management of the nuclear proliferation problem. On the other hand, it seems important to avoid creating such vested interest in SALT and similar exercises that the U.S. would become politically inhibited from responding to political and military challenges by the Soviet Union in other areas than the strategic arms race.

[94]See Chapter 12.

Chapter 8

MISSILE DEFENSE:
IMPLICATIONS FOR EUROPE

by Johan J. Holst

SCOPE AND CONTEXT

It seems reasonable to state at the outset that it is quite unlikely that something resembling a single "European" attitude towards the missile defense issues will emerge either within the various European countries or as a concerted reaction from European governments. We should also note that governments do not perceive the implications of major military hardware decisions solely or even primarily in terms of cost-effectiveness analysis or "macro-strategic" calculations. The political reactions to the BMD issues will be structured very largely in terms of how the various governments expect BMD to influence their own aspirations and predicaments. In regard to issues where these implications are ambiguous we should expect the political interpretations to be influenced as much by established images and prejudices—or even various degrees of ignorance—as by the strategic assessments of BMD as military systems. It is worth noting that for many small and middle powers their major foreign policy interests are regionally defined, a state of affairs which may cause them to entertain different priorities and foci than those which structure the global interests of the superpowers. As international politics cannot be understood outside a context of human reactions and calculations, any objective analysis must take account of the subjective considerations that are likely to influence the behavior and interpretations of governments.

The BMD issues have so far received only little attention in Europe and there appears to be a widespread opinion that BMD would have adverse impacts on the stability of the strategic balance, the intensity of the arms race, the level of diplomatic tension, the cohesion of the Atlantic Alliance, the political mobility of the middle- and small powers, etc. Some of the conclusions may be reasonable under a wide range of circumstances. However, the issues are certainly so complex and pervasive that analytical insight rather than axiomatic suppositions should constitute the basis of our assessments. There can be little doubt that the BMD isssues will affect Europe in many ways. The critical question is how. For Europeans it is important to complete their homework in this area in terms of evaluating the implications of BMD and establishing the European interests at stake. This would also seem to constitute one of the prerequisites for being able to influence the decisions and priorities of the United States in regard to BMD.

The present paper is focused on the issues stemming from the possible installation of BMD systems in the Soviet Union and the United States. It will not address itself in any detail to the question of the feasibility or implications of BMD systems deployed for the direct defense of Western Europe or particular countries in that region. This limitation is solely a matter of convenience and should not be construed to reflect any views of the author on BMD in Europe.

HEGEMONY AND POLITICAL MOBILITY

From the point of view of the middle-powers and small powers in Europe, one of the most important considerations might well be the anticipated impact of BMD on the political freedom of action on the international arena enjoyed by the non-superpowers. It is frequently asserted that BMD would tend to reestablish a system of strict bipolarity based on superpower dominance. Sometimes the argument is carried even further in predicting the transformation of a counterpoised hegemony into a Soviet-American condominium aimed at regulating the international system.

Relatively effective hard-point defenses of strategic offensive forces which serve to protect the second-strike capability ought to be appreciated as a contribution to the stabilization of the strategic balance. Such deployments might eventually contribute towards decoupling a wide area of international politics from the influence of the strategic nuclear balance. The fear of inadvertent or pre-emptive escalation to nuclear warfare would tend to diminish in the calculations of the decision-makers. Hence, BMD might in fact corrode the hegemonial position of the superpowers to the extent that that dominance is associated with their nuclear capabilities, although a diminished fear of escalation may tend to remove some of the present constraints on intervention.

Area defenses for populations could, however, serve to make the societies of the superpowers less vulnerable to nuclear attacks than those of the other powers in the international system. This may make it less likely that, for example, the United States would be blackmailed by the threats or execution of exemplary attacks into backing down in a crisis over Europe. It could, however, provide incentives for indirect deterrence (proxy deterrence) whereby the allies of the opposing superpowers are kept as nuclear hostages. There is likely to be a definite asymmetry in this area, since it is hard to imagine the United States pursuing such a strategy of deterrence vis-à-vis the Soviet Union via Eastern Europe. It would be clearly incompatible with the policy of normalizing relations with Eastern Europe and it would most certainly generate political opposition both inside the United States and in Western Europe. The presumed interest in preventing nuclear proliferation might also militate against such developments which seem bound to stimulate the incentives for independent nuclear forces by assigning to nuclear weapons a central role as arbiters of international affairs. It should be noted that BMD as it is presently contemplated would be far from being able to provide absolute immunity against nuclear attacks from a major nuclear power. The damages incurred in a nuclear exchange would continue to be sufficiently disastrous for the decision-makers in the Soviet Union and the United States to assign top priority to avoiding the calamity. We have been discussing marginal trends rather than major shifts in the international system.

The argument about Russo-American condominium begs the question of what consensus on values would uphold the common endeavor. We can easily imagine a variety of fields where a mutuality of interest would cut across the incompatibility of basic world outlooks. Such areas would include the prevention of nuclear war and nuclear proliferation. However, what would constitute a compatible world from the American value perspective is sufficiently incongruent with the Russian outlook to make a Soviet-American global condominium a very unlikely international constellation. The deployment of ballistic missile de-

fenses would certainly not constitute a sufficient or even a necessary prerequisite for the development of a Soviet-American condominium. That issue is, it seems, much more sensitive to the
domestic developments of the two societies as well as the further
process of nuclear proliferation, the behavior of China on the
international arena, etc.

ARMS CONTROL AND THE PROSPECTS OF
A EUROPEAN SETTLEMENT

The whole issue of whether a process leading to a Soviet-
American condominium may evolve as a result of the introduction
of missile defenses will to some extent be determined by the perceived implications of the superpower strategic arms limitation
talks (SALT). In general the European position seems to be favorable to such talks, and the European interests in the talks may even
exceed the enthusiasm of the Americans. Thus, there is some
potential for alliance frictions should the talks fail to produce an
outcome which is consistent with European expectations or
should the United States, for some reason which it would be hard
to communicate convincingly to the European allies, choose to
stop the talks.

It is, on the whole, surprising to note the extent to which
European opinion has been so unanimously unfavorable to any
deployment of ballistic missile defenses. The generally critical
attitude does not differentiate between various alternative U.S.
BMD deployment configurations, particularly between large-
scale defense of population centers and point defense of strategic
forces. The expectation that any BMD deployment is likely to
generate an arms race which, in turn, will increase tensions between the two superpowers and thus produce an environment in
which there will be little movement on the whole issue of the future
of Europe, is based not so much on any detailed analysis of possible interaction patterns as it is on a general attitude which considers any introduction of new armaments as inherently
undesirable. The focus on the arms race dimension of the problem
is in large measure a reflection of the context which the Johnson
Administration structured for a general evaluation of the issues.
Hence, it remains a kind of ironic commentary on the politics of
alliance consultation that the American attempt to structure the
issues so broadly as to make the arms race the central issue—an

issue on which everybody has a legitimate claim to be heard and consulted—tended to narrow the American freedom of action in regard to the deployment of missile defense for purely prudential reasons.

There is a very real sense in which nuclear incredulity has prevailed in Europe. Nuclear weapons, and strategic nuclear weapons in particular, do not look very relevant to the kinds of strains which are likely to challenge the stability of the European order. Having survived more than two decades of the nuclear age, most Europeans have come to learn to "live with the bomb" by largely ignoring it. There have not been too many reminders lately and this, in itself, is a demonstration of the irrelevancy of nuclear weapons to the normal processes of interstate relations. However, having taken the stability of the nuclear balance for granted makes more difficult the confrontation with the prospects of having to worry once more about the survivability of the deterrent and about the general impact of a volatile technology.

There are, of course, some important issues, of a very direct relevance to Europe which would become the subject of negotiations in the SALT context, particularly as concerns the Soviet MRBM/IRBM threat against Western Europe. Given the present build-up of the Soviet ICBM force, Western Europe will, in Soviet calculations, become less of a hostage for American good behavior in a crisis. In this sense European interests may be well served by the establishment of parity in the Soviet-American nuclear balance. The danger remains, however, that the Soviet missile threat against Europe may, under conditions of superpower parity, become more of an operational lever on European politics. A certain percentage of the American strategic force is allocated for targeting the Soviet MRBM/IRBM's and the Europeans would presumably want some assurances that whatever limitations be negotiated between Washington and Moscow did not entail a reduction in U.S. capabilities to target the weapons of greatest concern to European governments. In this perspective one should expect European governments to be concerned about the limitation of American targeting capacities which might be imposed by a Soviet counterforce strike with highly accurate MIRV'ed vechiles. Thus, they may, when the calculations are made, come to support the deployment of hard-point defenses around American missile- and bomber bases as a desirable measure to counter attack ratios favoring the attacker. The alternative to hard-point defense such as multiplying the number of delivery vehicles would hardly seem desirable to a European who is worried about arms races and their generation by potential first-strike postures. Nor would a doctrine which made deterrence dependent on a launch-on-warning (LOW) posture seem particularly attractive to an allied observer who is not only interested in the credibility of the American commitment to the defense of Europe, but also concerned about the possibility of becoming embroiled in a devastating conflict because of American miscalculations.[1]

Raising the issue of the Soviet MRBM's is, of course, likely to make the Russians want to include the British and French nuclear forces in any arrangement made. Thus, the arms talks could potentially exert a very divisive influence on the Western alliance by coupling with the most sensitive issue in NATO, viz., the role of independent nuclear forces. Secondly, the Soviet missile threat to Europe is in a functional sense connected with the 7,000 tactical nuclear weapons in Western Europe. By insisting on this connection, Moscow could potentially obtain a disruptive lever on the whole issue of NATO strategy in an area which is presently being examined quite intensively in the Nuclear Planning Group of the alliance.

The impact of SALT on the continued cohesion of NATO would presumably depend also on the concomitant developments in regard to the U.S. troop levels in Europe. To the extent that the domestic pressures in the United States for some substantial withdrawals from Europe became irresistible within a time frame which would result in a unilateral troop withdrawal at a time when the SALT exercise is still in progress or in its immediate aftermath, such a combination of events would tend to confirm the expectations and perceptions of those who fear a superpower deal over European heads. Such fears have perhaps become more widespread in the aftermath of the invasion of Czechoslovakia and the enunciation of the Brezhnev doctrine.

It would seem to the present author that one of the more effective means of alleviating European fears lest the SALT exercise produce a Soviet-American entente at Europe's expense,

---

[1] We should note a strange *non-sequitur* in the arguments of those who claim that the time available for decisions to launch defensive interceptor missiles is too short, but who also claim, or recommend, that the U.S. should adopt a launch on warning posture which means that they think the President *could* make the decision to strike at the Soviet Union within roughly the same time limitations.

would be for Western Europe to establish its own avenue to the East, particularly on the question of European security. Thus, there would be some institutional insurance against circumvention, particularly with American participation in the endeavor. We need not think in terms of a large European security conference, but rather in terms of a system of working groups devoted to an examination of various means of providing an infrastructure for European security over time. Arms control measures of various kinds would presumably constitute important elements of such a structure wherein the arms control measures will be evaluated not only in terms of such traditional criteria as their ability to provide warning of Soviet preparations for large scale attacks against Western Europe, but also from the wider perspective of providing political obstacles to unilateral alterations in the military status quo (such as Soviet intervention into East European countries) by forging, over time, a system of European security based on an acceptance of the interdependence of its constituent elements. Such a development would also run counter to any trends in the direction of a Soviet-American deal about exclusive spheres of influence on the European continent.

It is probably true that the stabilization of the Soviet-American relationship in the 1960's contributed to the greater freedom of maneuver which is currently enjoyed by the countries in Western and Eastern Europe. It is not at all clear, however, that this condition was necessary and least of all sufficient to provide for a further development of polycentric flexibility. Economic prosperity, industrial revitalization, troubles in other areas of the world, "nuclear incredulity," some *entideologisierung* of Soviet objectives were all contributing factors which were largely independent of the Soviet-American strategic relationship. Recent events in Eastern Europe suggest, furthermore, that Soviet policies in that area are structured by considerations which are clearly outside the framework of strategic force calculations. It could even be argued that uncertainties, deriving from BMD developments and perhaps, even more, from the introduction of accurate MIRV's, regarding the continued stability of that relationship may make the superpowers more intent on working out acceptable solutions in Europe, so as to reduce the chances of a major war being triggered by tensions arising from the present division of Germany.

The Soviet leadership seems intent on obtaining some reasonable assurances against the emergence of a nuclear and hostile

Germany. They may not expect BMD *per se* to slow down the feared process of nuclear proliferation, but they may expect BMD to provide some measure of protection against its consequences should proliferation actually occur. Hence, it is not totally inconceivable that the Russians would be more willing to discuss settlements in Europe—including some forms of German reunification—in an environment in which BMD promised to reduce the vulnerability of the Soviet heartland to possible threats from a major nuclear power in Western Europe. In any case, it is not easy to see how Soviet (and American) BMD acquisition would affect negatively any Soviet interest in accommodation in Europe.

IMPACT ON THE FUTURE OF NATO

Another critical area of inquiry would be the implications of BMD for the future structure of the Atlantic Alliance. Would BMD have an integrating or disintegrating influence, on the alliance or would the influence in this realm be negligible? Here we are not dealing with measurable quantitative relationships but rather with political perceptions and expectations.

Assuming a moderate to large BMD deployment in the United States, including a substantial area defense, those whose preferences are structured by Atlanticist perspectives might expect the American deployment to enhance the credibility and the reliability of the American guarantee to Europe. This perception is based on the calculation that the American willingness to honor the guarantees will increase as the United States is able to limit the damage from Soviet retaliation. Hence, BMD might serve to strengthen the alliance by adding to the potency of the American guarantee. If, however, we assume a similar Russian BMD deployment, the threat the United States could mobilize on part of her allies might look less impressive the more the Soviet BMD promised to reduce the damage of any American retaliation. Hence, a bilateral BMD deployment might on balance also be perceived as reducing the validity of the guarantee. It would seem to be relatively uncontroversial, however, that point defense of the American retaliatory capability would constitute a desirable measure from the point of view of maintaining the credibility and reliability of the American guarantee to Europe.

The introduction of substantial and effective BMD for population protection could serve to differentiate substantially between the security mechanisms of the two superpowers and those of their allies. The security of the United States, for example, might in principle become heavily dependent on direct *defense* while that of Europe rested on dependent (i.e., U.S.) *deterrence*. In such a world the superpowers might develop incentives for deterrence by proxy to the detriment of the countries in Western Europe, which would understandably resent developments assigning to them the roles of client-states constituting hostages at the mercy of American good-will and Soviet good-behavior. (The Soviet Union did, as we have seen,* for a long time structure her strategic forces for a posture of proxy deterrence, emphasizing threats against Western Europe rather than intercontinental threats against the United States.) Such developments might tend to freeze the political confrontation in Europe and, hence, seem to counteract the expectations for European reunification and detente. Alternatively, the European states might perceive pressures for accommodation in such a situation and become willing to make substantial concessions (surrender?) in order to get their cities off the nuclear hook.

Those who question the credibility of the American guarantee today may focus on the differential in the relative vulnerability of the American and European populations to Soviet attacks which BMD might tend to reemphasize. (This argument applies to city defense and not to strategic force defenses.) The United States would be acquiring an option which remained unavailable to her European partners. Hence, it is not inconceivable that BMD to some might look like an expression of American neo-isolationism—a return to Fortress America based on self-defense without entanglements. This perception might be strengthened by the U.S. domestic reactions to the Vietnam war, which may very well escalate in the direction of producing strong pressures for a general isolationist posture. The position of Europe has, of course, always been more vulnerable than the United States to Soviet attacks, but the asymmetry may be more disruptive in a situation where it reflects poverty and fragmentation rather than the technical unavailability of defense systems.

The Europeans have rather consistently held to the view that their national security should emphasize deterrence. Hence they have not been particularly concerned about systems like BMD, which would affect performance in the event that deterrence

*Chapter 7.

should fail. For Europe the success of deterrence is vital given the vulnerability of the European societies to devastation by Soviet nuclear power. The European attitude is a function, I believe, of both the *realization* of the extreme vulnerability of all the states of Europe to the power of other states and a *reconciliation* with that position which, for European states, has been part of their historical predicament for centuries. The nuclear age altered the magnitude of the vulnerability problem for Europeans; it did not introduce it as it did for Americans.

We may note then that there may be a wide variety of interpretations of the implications of BMD for Europe and NATO. The conclusions which will be drawn are probably dependent first of all on the existing images in Europe of the nature and development of the Atlantic Alliance. At this point it would seem relevant, however, to introduce the modifications to this rather stark confrontation of incompatible perspectives. They are both predicated on the assumption that strategic nuclear threats constitute the dominating factor in the security positions of the European states in NATO. That, I would venture, is not an indisputable assumption. Furthermore, the logic of the arguments is expressed in absolute terms which seem to correspond very inaccurately with the probable state of the world. The kinds of area defense systems which the superpowers might deploy within the foreseeable future would be very far from providing absolute invulnerability. The United States and the Soviet Union would still be in a position to inflict upon each other damage of a magnitude that reasonable men may be expected to find unacceptable. There would be no immunity for the superpowers even in a BMD world. We would still be living in a world of some deterrence even though active defenses might play an important role in damage limitation should deterrence fail. Deterrence would presumably remain sufficiently strong to constitute an effective barrier against the use of any nuclear weapons against anybody. Hence, it is certainly arguable that BMD need not significantly affect the European exposure to nuclear threats. The multiplicity of restraining elements in the Soviet-American strategic balance and the mutual interest in excluding the use of nuclear weapons from the realm of international politics are likely to counteract any destabilizing impact of U.S. area defense systems as far as the credibility of the American commitment is concerned.

The introduction of thin BMD systems with area coverage in the United States may have another indirect impact on the deterrent mechanism of the NATO defense posture. The deployment of tactical nuclear weapons in Europe has, in the European view, to a significant degree contributed to the posture of deterrence by constituting a connecting link with the American strategic deterrent through a process of escalation. However, the introduction of controlable strategic nuclear forces and an associated doctrine of flexible and restrained use tended to decouple the tactical nuclear weapons from some of their deterrent value. Thus decoupled, tactical nuclear weapons in Europe may refocus, and I think they, to a considerable extent, already have refocused, European concerns on the possibility of the superpowers' confining an armed conflict to Europe and largely destroying the arena in the process, without having to fear nuclear destruction in their own countries, or having that fear significantly reduced. The area defense systems would introduce an added firebreak which would further decouple the tactical nuclear weapons from the strategic deterrent by largely denying the Soviet Union the option of a nuclear demonstration attack against U.S. territory, because such attacks would only be effective (associated with high confidence of penetration) if the attacks are large. From a European point of view this is not necessarily an undesirable development, although it does beg further questions about the advisability of the strong nuclear emphasis of the NATO ground posture in Europe. European interests might be well served by more efficient efforts at providing a meaningful conventional defense, which will transfer to the Russians the onus of·nuclear initiation.[2]

From the point of view of the actual and potential nuclear powers, BMD might look like a means for the reaffirmation of superpower dominance in the sense that it might be perceived as nullifying the threats from the smaller powers against the superpowers. BMD could, so to speak, raise the entrance fee for great power status and possibly be resented for that reason by certain European countries. Other European states might consider such impacts as a virtue of the system. Let us look at the impact on the French force.

[2]For an extremely interesting and provocative analysis see Alain Enthoven, Methodology for Evaluating Conventional Forces, in *Review of a Systems Analysis Evaluation of NATO vs. Warsaw Pact Conventional Forces.* Report of the Special Subcommittee on National Defense Posture of the Committee on Armed Services, U.S. House of Representatives. 90th Cong. 2nd Sess., 1968, pp. 8-15.

It is not at all clear that the French *force de dissuasion* was designed to elevate France to the level of a superpower. The primary motives behind the force are most likely to be found on the political rather than the military level of considerations. The force may be viewed *inter alia* as a symbol of the restoration of French self-respect, assertiveness, and prestige. As such a symbol, it may have contributed to the reconciliation of a disillusioned army and an embattled political system, *in via* towards a new sense of national purpose and pride. Whether the force be a necessary adjunct of French diplomacy— it is certainly not a sufficient foundation thereof—is not a question which admits of definitive answers. From a policy perspective which emphasizes the ephemeral nature of political alignments, the force may very well be perceived as a necessary hedge against possible transfigurations of the diplomatic arena.

How would a substantial Soviet BMD deployment influence the French calculations concerning the efficacy of the force? The question is not an easy one to answer since it is unclear what the underlying assumptions would be. How effective must the force be in terms of its expected penetration capabilities in order to compete successfully for continued funds in the French decision-making process? The present force consists exclusively of manned bombers (a total of sixty-two Mirage IV-A's have been ordered) which are confronted with a reasonably impressive (as such things go) Soviet air defense system. The French deterrence calculations are probably based on the residual uncertainties in Soviet calculations, i.e., the force is believed to be large enough and sufficiently sophisticated to present to the Russians an unacceptable risk of unacceptable damage. Given the uncertainties about BMD performance, that same calculation may be relevant for the future French missile force confronting a Soviet BMD system. The French force is scheduled to consist of twenty-five to thirty SSBS missiles (Sol-Sol Ballistique Strategique) by 1971 with the addition of forty-eight submarine based MSBS missiles (Mer-Sol Ballistique Strategique) by 1975. It is not unlikely, however, that a Soviet BMD system could deny, with fairly high confidence, such a force access even to urban targets on which it might be concentrated. The French would need to maintain a very sophisticated and expensive penetration aids program to obtain a reasonable confidence of overcoming modern defenses. Whether the residual uncertainty be large enough to deter the Russians would depend *inter alia* on the stakes of the conflict and the political environment in which it is staged. At present it is rather unlikely that the Russians need to be deterred from attacking France and, even if they do, the probability of American intervention is most certainly viewed as unacceptably high in Moscow. The conclusion is much less obvious if we postulate a conflict in which the Soviet Union is confronting France as the protector of Western Europe, for high stakes, and with high confidence in American abstention. To the extent that the perceived utility of the French force derives from its prospective growth into a credible deterrent in such situations, BMD may be expected to interfere significantly with the realism of the prospects.

As we have noted, the kinds of BMD systems which the superpowers might deploy within the foreseeable future would be far from providing absolute invulnerability. The nuclear powers would still be in a position to inflict unacceptable damage upon each other. It is, of course, possible that there might be technological breakthroughs which could make defense ascendant and, perhaps somewhat more likely, that the BMD systems may come to be perceived as much more effective than they actually are. Should the French force thus be widely viewed as impotent vis-a-vis the Soviet Union, it might come to look increasingly as a potentially anti-German force or as an instrument for the assurance of French ascendancy in Europe. We need not belabor the political conclusions which may be caused by such perspectives.

Even in the absence of BMD, the future of independent national nuclear forces is uncertain both on economic and political grounds. The post-De Gaulle Fifth Republic is certainly likely to be much less committed to continued high expenditures on a force which may come to look increasingly like a monument to irrelevant and idiosyncratic aspirations. However, the British experience suggests that it is very difficult to abandon completely a nuclear weapons program which has produced operational capabilities. Thus, it is possible that the alternative of a European nuclear force will receive greater political attention in the years ahead.

It is not unlikely that there will be a psychological and political need to regenerate some kind of conspicuous momentum in European cooperation in the post-De Gaulle Europe. A European nuclear force may be one of the options considered in this connection. The imminent existence of superpower BMD systems will provide an extra incentive for Britain and France (and maybe others) to coalesce in order to benefit from the economies of scale. The creation of a European nuclear force supplanting existing British and French forces would probably, on the whole, be antiproliferatory in its wide impact, not only because it would tend to eliminate the participating European countries as potential proliferators, but also because it would set a standard concerning the requisite size of a nuclear power which would not admit of widespread emulation. Such a force would have to be designed according to some viable doctrine and not constitute the accidental conglomeration of demands and concessions. I have in mind, particularly, a doctrine which emphasizes the difference between escalation and retaliation. In the process of negotiating the political controls over the hardware, the European governments may come to see the virtues of a no-first-use principle as a structuring device for multilateral decision-making.

There remains also the question of whether BMD could be installed in Europe. The question is perhaps somewhat premature, and it is impossible to discuss the many ramifications of the problem within the confines of this chapter. We could think of an American system deployed in Europe, a joint Euro-American system, or an American-built European system. A European-built system does not belong to the realm of near term prospects. The systems of warhead control which might be designed for such a force would raise issues about their compatibility with non-proliferation. Some kind of dual-key system modelled on the Nike Hercules arrangements is conceivable. It is furthermore feasible to design the defensive systems so that the warheads would only explode while the missile was in ascent, above certain altitudes, etc. However, this is not only a design problem but also a political problem in terms of convincing a suspicious audience about the reliability of the design against accidents and abuse.

A BMD system in Europe would also raise the issue of alliance integration. There has been some discussion of using BMD as a substitute MLF (Multilateral Force) for purposes of forging cohesion. It is difficult to foresee how the system could serve purposes of such a political character without entailing the risk of producing dissension and cleavage as equally likely outcomes. Given the multinational texture of Europe, it is easy to see how negotiations about e.g. which cities should be accorded local defenses, could have disruptive rather than integrating effects.

The Russian threat against Western Europe, if measured in numbers of delivery vehicles, is larger than that against North America. Thus, a BMD system in Europe would have to be rather tight in order to prevent easy saturation. The relatively small defense area would, however, generate demands for fewer area-coverage installations than would the areas of the United States and the Soviet Union. There are few hard targets in Europe and BMD in Europe would, therefore, have to be for the defense of population. The technical problem of providing some reasonably effective defense at a meaningful level in Europe is probably surmountable. The warning times would be shorter but MRBM's would constitute easier targets due to their slower reentry speed. The nuclear threat against Western Europe is, however, multi-dimensional in character encompassing e.g. fighter bombers, short range tactical delivery vehicles and submarine-launched missiles as well as intermediate range ballistic missiles and medium bombers. BMD would not close all the gaps. There remains also the issue whether BMD would be the most cost-effective means of damage limitation in Western Europe compared, for example, to civil defense measures and a redesign of the missions and a reduction of the numbers of tactical nuclear weapons in Central Europe.[3]

Furthermore, it will be necessary to assess the political implications in Europe of the possible installation of BMD in its Western regions. What would be the impact on the detente and the process of normalization? There is the danger that a BMD in Western Europe might tend to perpetuate a posture and atmosphere of confrontation.

ATTITUDES TOWARDS CHINA

European and American attitudes and policies towards China have been at considerable variance over a rather long period. The adverse European reactions to the Sentinel decision reflected in large measure a European concern over what is generally considered to be a paranoid streak in the American-China policy. The controversy was compounded by the fact that the decision was announced, without prior consultations in NATO, on the eve of a meeting of the Nuclear Planning Group, although the failure to consult may have been a deliberate choice based on the expectation of unfavorable reactions.

[3]It has been reported that an area defense for Europe (American-built) would cost on the order of $3-12 billion, *The New York Times,* November 28, 1966, and *The Economist,* CCXXI, 1966, 6432, December 3, 1966.

The argument that American BMD deployment might dissuade China from developing nuclear capabilities is unlikely to carry much credence in Europe. There is still a widespread feeling in Europe that China must somehow be reintegrated into the international community, from which she has too long been estranged and in which she is bound to play a major role. It might be argued that the Chinese demand for great-power status is fairly inelastic, so that any increased price would tend primarily to reduce the resources which the Chinese could allocate to other purposes, such as economic growth and consumer-goods production. Such a diversion of resources may not necessarily produce a less belligerent attitude in Peking. The image of unpredictable and extremist hooliganism projected by the events of the Cultural Revolution, and the possibility of disintegration and war-lordism in a country with nuclear weapons, may, however, have caused many to hedge their views about policies towards China.

I suspect that the Americans may find it hard to convince Europeans generally about the necessity and advisability of deploying an anti-Chinese system in order to strengthen the credibility of the American guarantees to the non-nuclear Asian powers. Much will probably depend on the expressed preferences of the Asians themselves. It is quite conceivable that the American deployment will prove counterproductive in the sense that it will magnify, rather than minimize, the importance of the Chinese threat in the eyes of India and Japan. The result could be increased rather than reduced incentives for proliferation. The American insurance against Chinese ICBM's might also cause the Chinese to put greater emphasis on shorter-range missiles covering the major American allies (potential and actual) in Asia.

From the point of view of China, an American BMD system will extend in time the American ability to threaten China with a credible first-strike. The fact that the prospective American BMD deployments were explicitly identified as anti-China measures may tend to reconfirm Chinese assumptions about incompatible hostility and, hence, slow down China's reconciliation with the international community. There is also the danger that emphasizing American nuclear preponderance in Asia may cause other Asian countries to abrogate their responsibilities for building up the requisite conventional forces for local resistance. The latter would seem a vital component in the infrastructure of a stable Asian political system.

While, no doubt, the Europeans would, in principle, favor an American posture which provided credible guarantees for other

Asian countries against Chinese nuclear blackmail and attack, I suspect that the process of spelling out and implementing such guarantees may generate some apprehension in Europe. It could be feared that countries receiving an American guarantee against nuclear blackmail and nuclear attacks would feel freer to commit provocations or indulge in mischief up to this threshold, thereby increasing the chances that the United States and her European allies would become embroiled in a major war. Experiences from NATO would probably suggest to many that the problem of extending credible guarantees is an extremely complex one, even in the context of an organized alliance. The offer of assurances frequently generates demands for spelling out the operational nature of the guarantee in a wide range of circumstances of varying plausibility. The offer of assurances may, indeed, increase the perceived need for protection, and ultimately the very process of spelling out workable arrangements may generate incentives for nuclear autarchy.

It should perhaps be pointed out that Western Europe is closer to China in terms of potential missile trajectories than is the United States or, for that matter, than are the big cities of southern Australia. In a situation in which China had acquired an operational ICBM capability, a recognition of Europe's vulnerability to the Chinese nuclear potential might change the outlook of Europeans. The political conclusion which would be drawn from such a situation would presumably depend rather critically on the extent to which European interests and those of China were at cross-purposes and in active conflict in Asia. In the short run, the majority of European governments will probably argue the case for moderating Chinese objectives and behavior by attempting to integrate her into the international community.

The argument is not, of course, that the potential nuclear threat from China should not be taken seriously. However, it would probably have been better to justify the deployment of a thin area defense system on more general prudential grounds, emphasizing the value of denying cheap nuclear access to the United States to any potential or actual nuclear power. Here there is likely to be coinciding American and Russian interests. These interests would also coincide largely with the interests of international society, whose interests are better served by a limited condominium of the superpowers in nuclear matters than they would be by a more widely diffused capability to challenge and manipulate the basic structure of the international order.

Chapter 9

MISSILE DEFENSE
AND NON-PROLIFERATION:
FRIENDS OR ENEMIES?[1]

by Michael E. Sherman

INTRODUCTION

In recent discussions, certain members of the arms control community have expressed hope that either or both the Safeguard and Galosh decisions could be reversed, and that the age of missile defense might be ended before it had really begun. Admittedly, this could happen, in one of several ways: by executive decision, by legislative obstruction, or by negotiated agreement between the two governments. But although these are still possbilities (leaving aside the question of whether they are desirable possibilities), it is no longer realistic or responsible for arms controllers to count too heavily on them. The cause of missile defense is being advanced in both superpowers by a wide variety of influences, some laudable and some not so laudable. But whether one looks forward to an ABM age, fears it, or really doesn't know what to make of it, it now seems likely that some form of missile defense in both the United States and the Soviet Union is here to stay. This is not to deny that developments in the United States Congress, or elsewhere, may complicate or delay the process of ABM deployment. But, in the long run, I doubt that we shall have a chance to test Secretary of State Rogers' prediction that the U.S. would abandon all forms of ABM if the Russians would do the same. And if the assumption is correct that one form or an-

[1]Portions of this chapter are drawn from the author's Statement to the Canadian House of Commons Standing Committee on External Affairs and National Defense, June 10, 1969.

other of ABM is going to be part of the long-term strategic pattern, then *which* form becomes the crucial issue? In particular, it becomes essential for arms controllers to spend less time inveighing against the concept of missile defense and to turn their efforts to ensuring that such defense can serve rather than undermine the broad goals of arms control. This paper examines one feature of this problem, namely how to keep the opening of the ABM age from frustrating the effort to control nuclear spread.

SOME POSSIBLE EFFECTS OF ABM ON NON-PROLIFERATION

It is a truism that the effect of ABM on nuclear spread will be influenced by the type of systems deployed initially by the superpowers, and by the way those systems are regarded. Equally obviously, there are a great many possible patterns of deployment and perception. Yet, to a surprising degree, participants in the public debate have concentrated on one or another particular alternative, and have proceeded with apparent confidence to draw implications for proliferation from it.[2] The result, in most cases, has been a rather simplistic picture, which may be corrected in part by a brief attempt to distinguish and organize the alternatives. For this purpose it is useful to break down the general issue of the impact of ABM on proliferation into three components: the impact on the central strategic balance, on the place of nuclear weapons in international relations, and on the broad role of the superpowers on the world stage.

The Central Balance: Will ABM Generate Arms Races or Arms Control?

In the first category, the model most popular with opponents of ABM has been one in which the age of missile defense is characterized by volatile, open-ended competition between offensive and defensive forces. Here the central assumption is that defensive deployments by one superpower must provoke the other side to try to regain its earlier strategic position by acquiring more

[2]For two careful exceptions to this criticism, see Oran Young, Active Defense and International Order, *Bulletin of the Atomic Scientists,* Vol. 23, No. 5, pp. 35-42; and Robert Rothstein, The ABM, Proliferation, and International Stability, *Foreign Affairs,* Vol. 46, No. 3, pp. 487-502.

offense. And, from this action-reaction cycle, it is inferred that the competition in strategic arms must increase tensions between the superpowers; that the international environment as a whole must suffer because of this; that failure to control strategic weapons must hurt chances for arms control in other areas—for example, in the area of non-proliferation, either because non-nuclear countries will refuse to adhere to a treaty now revealed as blatantly· discriminatory, or simply because nuclear weapons appear more necessary in a less stable world.

Clearly, there are some controversial linkages in this picture. For example, the leap from resentment against a discriminatory non-proliferation treaty to a "go-nuclear" decision is rather a long one. Some analysts come close to arguing that non-nuclear states will abandon their nuclear restraint out of spite, even though they continue to recognize the destabilizing character of proliferation. To the present writer, it is not obvious that objective nuclear incentives go up as enthusiasm for a particular non-proliferation measure goes down. There may, of course, be ways in which resentment of this sort can weaken the barriers against proliferation. It may provide a plausible excuse for a government that wants to go nuclear but would otherwise have diplomatic difficulties in doing so. Or, it may provide the pro-nuclear faction in a domestic debate with a powerful emotional argument. Thus, as we shall discuss below, it is in the interests of non-proliferation to minimize this kind of resentment even where analysis suggests that it ought not to give Nth countries a greater objective interest in nuclear weapons. But, for present purposes, it is enough to note the main burden of this first model: By generating a divisive offense-defense arms race, the opening of the ABM age will have unpleasant consequences, whether in the long or short run, for the attempt to control nuclear spread.

In the competition for the minds and hearts of strategic analysts, the friends of missile defense have presented an opposing view that regards ABM as a step, not toward an arms race, but toward arms control. The general premise here is that a strategic model that includes some level of ABM can be perfectly consistent with the three main goals of arms control: to prevent war, to limit damage if war occurs, and to reduce the level of arms costs around the world to a level compatible with the first two goals. Beyond this general statement, however, the tree branches rather sharply and one has to be very careful in tracing it. Various members of the "ABM as arms control" school concentrate on different goals or mixes of them. One analyst may feel, for example, that ABM can qualify as an arms control mechanism so long as it promises to save lives. Another contends that missile defenses will make a further contribution by making it easier to arrive at limitations on the offensive forces which are the real threat to international stability, and that such limitations can be honestly presented as a partial fulfillment of the superpowers' obligation under the non-proliferation treaty (NPT) to "pursue negotiations in good faith on effective measures relating to cessation of the nuclear arms race." Moreover, apart from the specific obligation under the NPT, this view holds that if ABM does facilitate such limitations it will help non-proliferation by creating a more stable world in which Nth countries can be more relaxed in their attitudes to national security in general and to nuclear weapons in particular.

Although all analysts in this group share the view that ABM can be made the basis for something they would call arms control, and although all share enthusiasm for some limit on offensive forces, it should not be inferred that all share a common policy on ABM itself. While some have insisted that both offenses and defenses must be subjected to some limits, others have argued for an agreement in which offenses would be frozen but defenses allowed to proceed unchecked, at least at the outset. And an extension of this idea has been to allow the defenses to grow indefinitely in a kind of defense-defense race carried on under a ceiling for the offensive forces.

More detailed formulations of the "ABM as arms control" theory are outlined elsewhere in this volume, and there is no need to dwell on them here. Their present relevance is to provide a basis for a repeated insistence that in assessing the impact of ABM on proliferation, we do not have to accept on faith either the image of ABM as producing an offense-defense arms race or the implications for nuclear spread generally drawn from that model. There is considerable evidence that the governments of the superpowers believe that such a volatile race can be avoided,[3] and while we should not accept that belief on faith either, it does suggest that the issue is more complex and, perhaps, more hopeful than has often been assumed.

[3]See Chapter 7.

*The Role of Nuclear Weapons: Will ABM Raise or Lower
the Importance of Nuclear Weapons in International Politics?*

It is generally accepted that if nuclear weapons appear to
governments to perform a number of useful functions in world
affairs—whether these functions are military, diplomatic, or
domestic—the premium on having them will remain high and
they will continue to spread. For this reason, some analysts
have recommended that the nuclear powers themselves try to
minimize the role of nuclear weapons on the world scene; and
critics of ABM have argued that defensive deployments by the
great powers will undermine this effort. These critics feel that
American and Russian defensive deployments, especially if highly
touted, will enhance the perception of nuclear weapons as a badge
of status, independence, or security—fostering a set of attitudes
that make acquisition of atomic arms seem only natural to governments around the world. It has even been argued that if
ABM's themselves come to be regarded as the new mark of first-
rank national status, those advanced countries that do go nuclear
will seek not only offensive but defensive nuclear weapons as well.
But it could be that the type of nuclear emphasis involved in
American and Russian ABM will be irrelevant to all but the most
ambitious nations. Not all governments seek superpower rank.
The dominant perception might be that just as there are different
fashions in different social strata in domestic society, so the same
applies to international society; and there may be no perceived
reason, at least in terms of status, why Belgium or even Brazil
should be moved to seek either offensive or defensive nuclear
weapons just because the United States or the Soviet Union has
acquired an ABM. More important, probably, than the arms
procurement policies of the superpowers is the nuclear emphasis
or de-emphasis in the way they use their power around the world.

Another faction in this debate maintains that, considered in
a long-term perspective, defensive deployments by the superpowers will reduce, rather than raise, the premium placed on nuclear weapons by most nations of the world. First, they contend
that superpower self-protection, at least against light or unsophisticated nuclear attacks, will make it more credible to provide
security guarantees (whether implicit or explicit) in exchange for
continued nuclear abstention. Guarantees for Asian Nth countries
against China have, of course, been the example usually cited, and
this argument was a principal item in the advocacy of the Sentinel

system by Messrs. McNamara, Warnke and others.[4] By extension, it has also received support from some commentators in
important non-nuclear countries. Consider the following statement by a prominent Australian defense critic:

> If the United States and the Soviet Union are to provide
> China's neighbors with an alternative source of security
> to that represented by national nuclear forces, it is impor-
> tant that they preserve their present military ascendancy
> over China. If disarmament of the great powers is taken
> to the point where the guarantees they issue to the non-
> nuclear states are no longer credible, a more important
> bulwark against the spread of nuclear weapons than the
> treaty itself will have been removed.[5]

A variation of this argument holds that through protection
even against light nuclear attack, it can be demonstrated that the
price of gaining nuclear leverage against a superpower is beyond
all but the richest and most advanced nations. In particular, it is
hoped that by undermining the expected Chinese claim to have
such leverage against the United States (or even against the Soviet
Union), the number of states inclined to emulate China will be
diminished. It may be, however, that this line of argument is either
irrelevant or counterproductive in the effort to check nuclear
spread. It may be irrelevant because it is doubtful that many Nth
countries would regard rudimentary nuclear forces as usable, even
for threats, against one of the superpowers.[6] And it may be
counterproductive because governments will certainly take note
that a relatively backward country such as China could force the
world's strongest nation into a whole new generation of weapons
simply by acquiring a primitive nuclear force. If such a force can
threaten to alter the fundamental strategic relationship between
two such nations, others may see new reasons for having one.
This objection was in fact made by critics of the Johnson Administration's "anti-Chinese" orientation of the Sentinel system,
and the criticism seems to this writer a persuasive one. Rather

[4]See, for example, Mr. Warnke's address before the Advocates
Club, Detroit, October 6, 1967. (News Release, Office of the Assistant
Secretary of Defense, Public Affairs, #950-67.)

[5]Hedley Bull, On Non-Proliferation, *Interplay,* Vol. I, No. 6, p. 10.

[6]More persuasive is the view that this argument would be prominent in some Nth country domestic debates on whether or not to go
nuclear.

than demeaning primitive nuclear capabilities in the eyes of non-nuclear nations, a superpower move to deploy defenses against such forces may do more to dignify them. If this happens, the premium placed even on "oxcart-bombs" will rise, and ABM will have had the effect of fostering rather than restraining nuclear spread.[7]

The Role of the Superpowers: Will ABM Lead to a World of "Fortress Superpowers" or "Superpower Condominium"?

The final pair of alternative models concerns the questions of whether defensive deployments will be read by the rest of the world as a "turning in" or a "turning out" on the part of the U.S. and the U.S.S.R. Both are plausible interpretations, and each has given analysts cause for hope or concern, depending upon their biases. On the one hand, it can be argued that ABM will be construed around the globe as symbolic of, and instrumental to, a weakening of superpower support for distant allies and friends. This line has been especially popular with American critics of ABM, who feel that it will be taken in Europe as a diminution of the United States' commitment to NATO: as the capability for strategic insularity from European conflict increases, runs the argument, the American willingness to intervene will decrease proportionately —or, equally unfortunate, this will be the dominant perception among NATO nations (especially Germany) who will then feel an increased need for national nuclear weapons of their own.

A pessimistic inference, of course, is not the only one that can be drawn from the premise of superpower insularity. A world in which the superpowers made no attempt to extend their power around the globe could conceivably diminish nuclear incentives, either because it bolstered a tradition of defensive foreign policies or because it reduced the broad role of nuclear weapons in international relations. Also, a sense that the superpowers had turned inward might reduce at least one type of nuclear incentive, namely the desire for a modest nuclear capability just big enough to trigger one's superpower ally into the war. It should be noted, however, that the fear that a superpower's protection of its own population will make it insular applies with diminished force to the Safeguard system, which looks primarily (although not exclusively, since it does provide area defense for the whole country

---

[7]It should be stressed that this last point addresses a question more of declaratory policy than of deployment: it was a mistake to *say* that Sentinel was prompted by China, even if that was the case.

against light attacks) to the defense of the strategic forces. But even if one admits the possibility that not all allied observers will make this distinction, a further observation is in order.

Although there are opportunities for compromise in many areas of the ABM debate, here may be a point of genuine irreconcilability: on the one hand, there stand those analysts who believe that America cannot credibly extend nuclear deterrence to others so long as its own population remains hostage to nuclear retaliation. Another group seems to believe that the credibility of American guarantees cannot be maintained *unless* the population of America remains hostage. Thus, a policy judgment must be made here. My own guess, albeit a tentative one, is that the more American friends and allies think about the issue, the more they will come to share the view familiar in Europe since the late fifties. They will come increasingly to feel that a guarantee is incredible if the guarantor risks destruction in implementing it. It is uncertain, of course, how influential such calculations are in governments' decisions to go or not to go nuclear. Some states, for example, may be so skeptical of outside guarantees that nothing could make the assurances credible to them. But to the extent that this issue does play a part, it seems in the interest of the guarantor, the guaranteed, and the cause of non-proliferation in general to reduce the guarantor's vulnerability to retaliation. If that is true, then superpower ABM deployments (especially if they develop as part of an over-all strategic arms control plan) can be regarded not only as consistent with non-proliferation but as a cornerstone of it.

As an alternative to the possibility that ABM might signal superpower insularity to the rest of the world, it could be seen as the basis for a continuation or even extension of Soviet-American dominance in world affairs. Thus, Pierre Gallois wrote of the superpowers' entry into the ABM age that it is hardly surprising that they insist missile defenses are not destabilizing, when those defenses aim only to preserve the duopolistic stability of the past few years.[8] Although such charges bring cries of righteous indignation from the governments of both superpowers, perhaps a citizen of a nation of more modest size may be permitted the observation that there is more than a grain of truth in the charge, and probably more than a grain of truth in the prediction that many

[8]Pierre Gallois, La defense contre missiles (DCM) Americaine et Russe et la 'proliferation', *Revue Militaire Generale,* February 1968, pp. 139-50.

non-nuclear countries will perceive the defensive deployments in this light. It is far from clear, however, what the impact of such a perception would be on the process of proliferation itself. If crucial non-nuclear states come to see the superpower dominance as a threat to national interests that can be protected only by the acquisition of nuclear weapons, that is one thing. But it is not obvious that they will do so; indeed, the arguments made concerning superpower deterrence of China can be generalized to a rather plausible theory that the determination of two well-protected superpowers to stop proliferation might create the most stable framework that could be devised. I am not arguing that this is necessarily the case, or that stability is the only criterion by which we should judge international systems. The point is simply to warn again against analyses that see a clear and straight line from resentment against superpower dominance to extensive nuclear spread.

ORCHESTRATING ABM AND NPT

ABM and "SALT"

The preceding section has attempted to show that the impact of ABM on proliferation is more difficult to assess than is sometimes acknowledged, and also to isolate some of the more unpleasant alternatives in the hope of devising policies to avoid them. Let us turn now to the more specific policy issues, beginning with the relationship between the impending Soviet-American strategic arms limitation talks (SALT) and the non-proliferation treaty. A simple but important point here is that the talks themselves should be cast explicitly as an attempt to meet the superpower obligations incurred under Article VI of the treaty. An explicit linkage between the SALT talks and Article VI would not only demonstrate on the part of the superpowers "a decent respect for the opinion of mankind." It would also symbolize and articulate a recognition that although the link between superpower arms procurement and proliferation may not be as strong as the critics of ABM maintain, nonetheless there is a subtle relationship between them.

An important caveat, however, is that although the treaty does commit the superpowers to pursue strategic arms control negotiations in good faith, it does not presuppose any particular outcome of these negotiations, and it certainly does not presuppose that any initial "cessation of the nuclear arms race" need involve a total ban on missile defenses. The superpowers could hardly have incurred such a commitment when they are still in doubt themselves as to what levels of offense or defense are most conducive to a stable balance. If it turns out, for example, that the SALT talks yield a freeze on offenses and a limitation on defenses at a level low but still higher than zero, there is no necessary inconsistency between this and Article VI. In the short run, careful declaratory diplomacy may suffice to convince others that the initial SALT effort is a satisfactory first step towards a balance of obligations under the NPT. But in the long run further steps will be necessary to keep non-proliferation and strategic arms policies reinforcing rather than conflicting with one another. It seems possible that one such step could be to link ABM tightly with a strengthening of the security guarantees provided in conjuction with NPT.

ABM and Guarantees

The background to this problem is well known. As the draft treaty on non-proliferation developed, it became clear that certain non-nuclear nations might be unwilling to sign without increased confidence that their security against nuclear attack or blackmail would be assured by others. Soon after this danger was dramatized by the Chinese test in 1964, President Johnson announced that "the nations that do not seek national nuclear weapons can be sure that, if they need our strong support against some threat of nuclear blackmail, . . . will have it."[9] There ensued a prolonged international debate, first of all over whether, in principle, security guarantees were more or less effective protection than national nuclear weapons, and, secondly, what form of such guarantees could be made consistent with other requirements such as those of non-aligned nations for continued independence. In June, 1968, the U.N. Security Council passed a resolution which attempted to resolve the guarantee problem in the following way. First, it recognized that aggression with nuclear weapons, or the threat of such aggression, against a non-nuclear state would require the Council, and "above all its nuclear-weapon State permanent members," to act immediately in accordance with their Charter obligations. Secondly, it welcomed the inten-

[9]U.S. Arms Control and Disarmament Agency, *Documents on Disarmament, 1964,* Washington, D.C., 1965, p. 468.

tion expressed by "certain states" (and this intention was declared in parallel statements by the United States, the Soviet Union and Great Britain) that they would provide or support immediate assistance in accordance with the Charter to any non-nuclear state party to the treaty that might be attacked or threatened with nuclear weapons. And, thirdly, it reaffirmed all nations' right to act under Article 51 of the U.N. Charter to provide individual and collective self-defense against attack, pending effective Security Council action. Now, a strict reading of this resolution did not offer much security beyond what non-nuclear states already had under the United Nations Charter. It might have been defended as a first step in a difficult area. But, if anything, subsequent developments weakened rather than strengthened its effect. The U.S. Secretary of State emphasized in Congressional hearings that the Security Council resolution did not extend American commitments beyond the Charter, and some legislators even sought to formalize this point in a reservation to the treaty. Nonetheless, the search for a more solid security basis for NPT should continue, and perhaps the proper formulation of ABM policy can help.

This bears on the danger, noted above, that deployment of missile defense could be interpreted as a superpower attempt to abandon international commitments and to leave smaller states to fend for themselves in the security area. In the event of even low-level ABM deployment by the U.S. and the U.S.S.R., it will not be enough to hope that the right conclusions are drawn by non-nuclear allies. A systematic effort will have to be made to tie ABM into the guarantee framework and to devise some way in which it can reasonably be presented as strengthening rather than weakening these guarantees. A first step might be a stronger statement (perhaps issued jointly by the superpowers) on the circumstances under which the commitment to punish nuclear aggression will be honored; some formulation must be found to allay the fear that obstruction in the U.N. could lead to inaction or be used as an excuse for it. Also, a stronger statement may be required on the nature of the response that the superpowers are willing to make in the event that the guarantee does have to be implemented; among other things, this raises the question of whether Russian and/or American leaders are willing to use nuclear weapons to defend NPT signatories against nuclear attack. I am well aware of the reluctance of governments to pledge specific actions in advance. However, we may have exhausted the potential of oblique and vague declarations. While it is nice to have lots of options open, there comes a time when some must be foreclosed, and in this case there seems to be no escape between the horns of the "commitment or caution" dilemma. And in asking the superpowers to go farther out on a limb, we come to the link to ABM. Along with a real extension by the U.S. and U.S.S.R. of commitment to international stability, it seems reasonable for them to protect their own people against any nuclear aggressor they may confront. In this context, ABM and strengthened guarantees form a sensible package. Ironically, the technological momentum of ABM might in this way force an end to superpower hedging on the guarantee issue. If this happens, ABM wll have helped create a lasting framework for non-proliferation guarantees in place of the present jerry-built structure.

It must be admitted, however, that this argument may have to be carried a step further. Consider this complaint by a Japanese observer:

> It is . . . worthless to argue that America's establishment of an ABM system against China increases confidence in the American atomic deterrent power in Asia and that, by removing to some degree the Asian countries' desire to have their own atomic weapons as defense against Communist China, the existence of such a system assists the realization of a non-proliferation treaty. Such arguments intentionally ignore the contradiction that, if the ABM system of defense against China is as effective as is claimed, then a non-proliferation treaty will merely deny to the non-nuclear countries the system of defense capable of saving the lives of countless millions of people.[10]

If, as seems likely, declaratory diplomacy alone cannot satisfy this concern, a new nuclear sharing scheme may be necessary whereby those non-nuclear countries that want to have ABM's will be allowed to do so under some form of joint control, either with the United States or the Soviet Union or both. Although such a proposal raises the specter of an immense superpower political and economic commitment around the world, this is not necessarily the case. For a variety of good reasons, many governments

[10]Kawata Tadashi, Economic Implications of Nuclear Armament, *Japan Quarterly*, Vol. XV, No. 2, 1968, p. 184. In a similar vein, Edward Teller has written, "The greatest danger in an anti-proliferation treaty might be the circumstance that it could prevent for the next decade a really effective defense of Western Europe." BMD in the Strategy for Peace, in James E. Dougherty and J.F. Lehman, Jr. (eds.), *Arms Control for the Late Sixties*, Princeton, 1967, p. 110.

would not want to share in a jointly controlled ABM. Some would balk at the economic cost, others at the potential political cost in loss of diplomatic independence, others simply at the idea of any kind of nuclear weapons emplaced on their soil.[11] Thus it may be both feasible and desirable for the United States or the Soviet Union or both, perhaps as part of the package which is put together in the SALT talks, to declare their willingness to share defensive nuclear technology and planning with those non-nuclear signatories to the NPT who feel the need for such a share. Independent peacetime control of the defensive systems by the client state would be inconsistent with the NPT as it is presently drawn, but this may not be as serious a drawback for the client as in the case of offensive systems. That is, the junior partner should have little reason to doubt that the major partner would fire the shared weapons in the proper circumstances. Once attacking warheads are on their way, there seems to be scant danger that the donor would refuse to turn his key for fear of escalation; an analogous fear was, of course, a major concern with the shared strike bombers and other nuclear systems in Europe.

The plan proposed here can be attacked from many sides. First, it will not satisfy those nations that seek a nuclear guarantee against conventional attack. This gap in the plan is deliberate, however, for part of the intention is to lead governments, wherever possible, to meet non-nuclear threats with non-nuclear weapons. Secondly, there is the danger that guaranteed states will see more opportunities for non-nuclear mischief under their nuclear umbrella; this seems an unavoidable risk and, on balance, an acceptable one. Finally, although both strengthened guarantees and ABM-sharing should be limited to signatories of the NPT, there remains the danger that participation in shared defenses will create a desire for independent offensive weapons. It can only be hoped that such pressures can be resisted. Even if they cannot, this intermediary step of nuclear defensive sharing may buy us more time in the continuing effort to avoid at least the worst forms of proliferation.

ABM and Nuclear De-Emphasis

We noted above the danger that superpower defensive deployments might be read as a signal that the role of strategic nu-

---

[11]This last is not a fictitious obstacle. In my own country, Canada, it is prominent in all public discussions of both air- and missile-defenses.

clear weapons in international politics had increased, and that this, in turn, could (although not certainly) increase nuclear incentives in other nations. To offset this impression, some new initiative in the attempt to create anti-nuclear fashions might be appropriate at this time. There are many ways of approaching this, and only one of the possibilities can be considered here. I have in mind the suggestion, considered with varying seriousness for some years, that an explicit ban be sought on the legitimate first use of nuclear weapons in a conflict. While this is not the place to attempt a full analysis of the issue, it does seem that such a step would fit well with the attempt to diminish the premium placed by the international system on nuclear weapons. It would deny to the nuclear powers, for example, the ability to threaten the first use of nuclear weapons against a non-nuclear state or even against a nuclear state. In such a context, nuclear sabre-rattling in periods of tension would diminish or even disappear as a "normal" maneuver in foreign affairs. In combination with the structure of ABM-supported guarantees, the business of diplomacy might be conducted for most countries as if nuclear weapons had not been invented.

In considering this proposal, it should be noted that both the Chinese and Russian governments have made statements in the past that are friendly to the concept of no-first-use.[12]. It may be objected that this friendliness stemmed solely from their strategic inferiority to the United States, but the declarations are on the record and could provide a useful point of departure for negotiations. Indeed, it can be argued that some American statements have come close to embracing the principle, for example, in the Posture Statement's specific emphasis on retaliation against nuclear attack as the mission of American strategic forces.[13] This does not guarantee, of course, that the United States would definitely refrain from introducing strategic nuclear weapons to

[12]See *Documents on Disarmament 1964*, U.S. Arms Control and Disarmament Agency, Publication 27, Washington, D.C., p. 450, and *Documents on Disarmament 1966*, U.S. Arms Control and Disarmament Agency, Publication 43, Washington, D.C., p. 11. It should be noted that the Soviet statement referred to here goes beyond the "Kosygin formula" which was limited to nations not having any nuclear weapons on their territory.

[13]Secretary of Defense Clark M. Clifford, *The 1970 Defense Budget and Defense Program for Fiscal Years 1970-74*, prepared January 15, 1969, p. 47.

throw back a conventional attack on an ally. Indeed, it has been objected that such a position—a logical implication of no-first-use—could have the unintended effect of raising rather than lowering nuclear incentives around the world. The most frequently cited example is that of West Germany, whose nuclear appetite (runs the argument) has thus far been checked by confidence in an American willingness to use nuclear weapons, if necessary, to stop even a conventional Soviet attack in Europe. A no-first-use declaration by the United States, in this view, would leave Germany at the mercy of the Russian conventional superiority and create a perceived need in Bonn for a national nuclear force of its own.

In response to this criticism, a variety of positions are open to the analyst who remains friendly to the principle of no-first-use. One is to argue that no policy will be without some adverse effects and that German irritation is an acceptable price to pay for the broad gains. Another is simply to agree to make an exception for Germany in the no-first-use pledge. Finally, it can be argued that the real force in the opposition to no-first-use based on concern for Germany has been largely one of timing. That is, it was reasonable to feel that the last few years constituted an inopportune time for such a declaration. With Bonn-Washington ties already strained by Soviet success in sinking the MLF and in making Germany the villain of the NPT piece, it did seem unwise to add insult to injury by explicitly dashing German hopes for American nuclear assistance against conventional attack. However, in the context of a successful outcome of the SALT talks, a stronger guarantee framework and an ABM-sharing plan in which Germany would probably participate, some progress toward a no-first-use agreement might be possible. And, in general, if the U.S. and U.S.S.R. can be convinced of the need to offset some of the political costs of ABM, missile defense could lead them (ironically) into a coherent policy for control of the arms of both super- and not-so-super powers.

Chapter 10

THE PROBLEM OF CHINA

by Frank E. Armbruster

THE THREAT presented by Communist China's intercontinental and submarine-launched nuclear ballistic missile
force will differ from that presented by the U.S.S.R., and this
condition is likely to apply for a considerable time into the future.
There are indications that, contrary to earlier reports, the nuclear
weapons program of the Chinese People's Republic (CPR) may
have been adversely affected by the turmoil of Mao's "cultural
revolution."[1] The date of the initial installation of Red China's
intercontinental ballistic missile force presumably slipped from
the early to the mid-1970's[2] to some later period because of their
failure to test a long-range missile which, according to Secretary
of Defense McNamara, was due to be tested before the end of
1967.[3]

Of the two nuclear missile submarines reported under construction for the past few years at Dairen, one is now reported

[1]Michael B. Yahuda, China's Nuclear Option, *Bulletin of the
Atomic Scientists,* February 1969, Vol. XXV, No. 2, p. 73; Tillman
Durdin, Nuclear Program Slowed in China, *The New York Times,*
October 28, 1968, p. 10; China Lags in Testing Missiles, U.S.
Reports, *Evening Star,* Washington, D.C., September 3, 1968, p. 3;
The Military Balance 1968-69, The Institute for Strategic Studies,
London, 1968, p. 9.

[2]"McNamara predicted last September that Red China would have
an initial intercontinental ballistic missile capability in the early
1970's." *Evening Star,* Washington, D.C., September 3, 1968, p. 3
and Statement by Secretary Laird, May 22, *Safeguard Antiballistic
Missile System,* Hearings, Subcommittee of the Committee on Appropriations, House of Representatives, 91st Cong. 1st Sess., 1969,
p. 13.

[3]Secretary of Defense Robert S. McNamara in his annual "Posture
Statement" to Congress issued on January 26, 1967; and Yahuda,
op. cit., p. 73.

operational.[4] Each of these submarines (at least the Russian versions) has the capacity to house three intermediate-range (380-600 mile) missiles in its "sail."[5] Whether the Red Chinese have in their arsenal the Soviet-type, solid-fuel missiles to arm these submarines is another question—as is, indeed, the whole issue of whether the Chinese will follow the Western pattern in their weapons development. Even something so far-fetched as considering the use of old-style, liquid-fueled missiles requiring liquid oxygen aboard submarines might possibly not be out of the question in their minds. This would no doubt be an extremely delicate and dangerous operation, and the subs might have to surface to "top off" the missiles with liquid oxygen; but it probably could be done at night off the coast of any country within the range of these vessels (this includes the mainland United States). The point of interest here is that predicting the Chinese missile threat, as in predicting their nuclear program or any other specific portion of their strategic weapons program, can lead one into difficult problems in the areas of delivery dates and quality. Even if one assumes a slippage in the Chinese ICBM and submarine-launched missile systems, the lead time for research and development, procurement and installation of an anti-ballistic missile system to protect United States' cities is so long that, if we start today, the Chinese probably will have missile systems that can reach the United States before we get these defensive systems operable. Predicting the general size of the force is perhaps somewhat simpler and one at least finds, for example, less disagreement on the approximate number of atomic bombs they can build.[6]

There is another element in the CPR nuclear missile equation which, again, could be considered somewhat unique. The reason for it is much more difficult to fathom, however, and has a direct

[4] 2 Red China Subs Get A-Missile Launches, *Evening Star,* Washington, D.C., December 6, 1967, p. A-11; and *The Military Balance 1968-69, op. cit.,* p. 11.

[5] *Evening Star,* Washington, D.C., December 6, 1967, p. A-11, and *Strategic Survy 1968,* The Institute for Strategic Studies, London, 1969, p. 4. On October 27, 1966 China fired a medium-range missile 450 to 600 miles along a test range in Sinkiang Province, *The New York Times,* April 20, 1968, p. 1.

[6] "If they functioned without interruption, Chinese nuclear facilities could probably have produced by now enough fissile material for 70 atomic bombs of 20 KT yield based on uranium and plutonium, and for a small number of hydrogen bombs," *The Military Balance 1968-69, op. cit.,* p. 9.

relation to the validity of the estimates of the production of nuclear weapons and their delivery systems. If the CPR nuclear weapons production has been up to some estimates, a number of these weapons should have been deployed, particularly in areas like Fukien province opposite Taiwan (Formosa). It appears, however, according to some sources, that this has not occurred. Some writers have speculated that the Red Chinese have indeed built a number of nuclear weapons and have IL-28 and even some TU-16 aircraft delivery systems for them, but that they are not deploying them to areas such as Fukien for fear of their falling into the hands of local commanders of doubtful loyalty.[7]

These rather unique problems are by no means the sole examples of their type. At the moment it appears as though Defense Minister Lin Piao will inherit the mantle of Mao; but the nature of totalitarian police states is such that power can shift quickly and in unexpected directions. Furthermore, the secrecy of closed societies seems to work most of the time. No one in the West can predict with any degree of certitude over the next decade who will control the CPR nuclear forces or any given portion of them.

Chinese leaders have made "no-first-use" statements and, at the time of the detonation of their first bomb, urged proposals for no-first-use.[8] It is likely that this indicates a real fear of nuclear destruction, but this appears to be as far as they wish to go on control of nuclear arms. What is more, we cannot be sure that events will not some day cause her attitude to become harder. What we are faced with here is the old problem of deciding whether to use enemy *intent* or *capability* as a guide to measures which should be taken to safeguard our country. Certainly one can think of nuclear powers who would be quite unlikely to be hostile to us—Great Britain, for instance. But what about Red China? One is tempted to point to the fact that General MacArthur's assurance concerning the Chinese intent not to intervene in Korea proved to be illusory, but this may not be a good analogy for the current situation. The one thing that is clear,

[7]Red China Delays Next Atom Step, *The New York Times,* April 20, 1968, p. 1. *Safeguard Antiballistic Missile System,* Hearings, *op. cit.,* p. 12.

[8]Morton H. Halperin, Chinese Nuclear Strategy: The Early Post-Detonation Period, *Adelphi Papers,* No. 18, May 1965, The Institute for Strategic Studies, London, pp. 9-11; Morton H. Halperin, Chinese Attitudes Toward Nuclear Weapons, in Tang Tsou (ed.), *China's Policies in Asia and America's Responses,* Vol. II: *China in Crisis,* University of Chicago Press, Chicago, Ill., 1968.

however, is that there is much more at stake this time than in 1950. Unlike the Soviet intercontinental nuclear force, by any of the current estimates, the Chinese Communist force could under no circumstances be considered to have a *counterforce* capability against our large nuclear delivery systems. In other words, for the next ten years this force probably will present primarily a "city-busting" threat to the United States. No doubt, at least during this period, the Red Chinese intent will be for this force to be a "deterrent" to the United States or other nuclear powers (including the Soviet Union). If something should go wrong, however, a Chinese attack will, of necessity, be constrained by her capability against us: either a small "demonstration" attack (to gain the upper hand in a crisis) or a counter-city strike of anything from a few missiles to a salvo of her whole force. The Chinese leaders who ordered any kind of a nuclear strike against us would, of course, have to be either completely convinced that moral or morale issues would prevent us from retaliating or they would have to be in the extreme stages of insanity.

Since Korea, in the face of a powerful, resolved enemy, the Chinese Communists have shown prudence; and, though always opportunistic, they have been far from foolhardy. In fact, in the conventional warfare area one can only come to the conclusion that to date they have very little offensive capability in most areas outside their borders. There are basic reasons for this. They are inhibited by geographic features like the Himalaya mountains and the Taiwan Straits, among others; they have a marginal economy from which it is difficult to squeeze out enough effort to build large, modern, conventional ground, sea and air forces (as compared to the relatively cheap short-cut to "great" military status—a modest nuclear force)[9]; they are faced in Korea and in the Taiwan Straits by resolute opponents (who have mutual defense pacts with the United States). The Chinese have, because of a heated disagreement over ideology and their freedom of action, cut themselves off from the industrial and scientific potential of the

---

[9]"As a nuclear power and a nation of 750 million citizens . . . China demands a voice in world efforts to deal with arms control and population control, with Asian security and international economic development, with all the great issues of our time." Address by Senator Edward M. Kennedy, Before the National Committee on United States-China Relations, New York City, March 20, 1969, from the *Congressional Record,* March 24, 1969.

Soviet Union. Their aims to date, therefore, match their potential, i.e., they are limited in the face of a resolute opponent.[10]

On the other hand, there is a reason that people do not look on with equanimity as the Chinese acquire a nuclear striking force. The Chinese have, in recent times, occasionally seemed quite brutal and, from our point of view, amoral as, for instance, in dealing with Tibet, U.S. prisoners of war in Korea, etc. Their attitude toward loss of life among their own troops and those of their allies (North Korea and North Vietnam) also seems quite harsh. In Vietnam today, the North Vietnamese also seem to be displaying a "punishment" theory of how to deal with their adversaries—an apparent readiness to see ten of their men die in order to kill one American. Since Korea, the Chinese Communists have not put themselves in such a position (India was "easy" and they do not push the Soviets too far in the Manchurian border disputes). But the problem of handling the Chinese in a crisis in which they could seriously threaten to "punish" the United States (as compared to the present situation in which we have the capability to "punish" their homeland while they can only kill our military men who come within their reach) may prove to be quite taxing on our political system. This may be particularly true if this "punishment" tactic proves successful against us in Vietnam.

Unfortunately, therefore, although any kind of nuclear attack against the United States is highly unlikely, in the case of a crisis with China, for the reasons mentioned above, we may be in a considerable quandary. The Chinese have often talked of the inevitability of a final confrontation with the United States and pointed out their ability to survive a general war while our decadent society could not.[11] There is little doubt that this theory resulted from the rationalization of a non-nuclear power which

[10]For a further discussion of this, see Frank E. Armbruster, China's Conventional Military Capability, in Tang-Tsou (ed.), *China's Policies in Asia and America's Response, op. cit.*

[11]Morton H. Halperin and Dwight H. Perkins, *Communist China and Arms Control,* East Asian Research Center for International Affairs, Harvard University, Cambridge, Mass. 1965, pp. 48-56; Yahuda, *op. cit.,* p. 74; William Chapin, The Asian Balance of Power: An American View, *Adelphi Papers* No. 35, April 1967, The Institute for Strategic Studies, London, p. 2; Halperin, *op. cit., China in Crisis,* Vol. II, *passim.*

assumed it would have to confront a nuclear-armed nation (the
United States) in crises, and that the present Chinese leadership
takes this type of thinking with a grain of salt. But if we show signs
of a lack of resolve or moral doubts about our use of non-nuclear
force, some future (sane or insane) Chinese leader may bring this
theory up in a crisis with the United States. Such a turn of events
could cause grave problems for an American President, for there
is much logic in the reasoning which says that it is not absolutely
certain that under all circumstances we would retaliate in kind
against China.

Let us assume that at the height of a grave crisis between Red
China and the United States, a few Chinese missile-carrying submarines lay off our West Coast (and, depending on the degree of
rationality of the Chinese leadership, the issues which could lead
to such a crisis could vary from things which might appear trivial
to those we hold most dear). The threat to our cities would be
obvious and the Chinese, claiming freedom of the seas, might
(implicitly or explicitly) even let it be known that if we attempted
to destroy these vessels, the submarines might salvo all their missiles. Let us further assume that the United States was in some
turmoil at this time, with very small but very verbal groups con-
demning our defense of the government in country X. Regardless
of the righteousness of our cause, if our cities within range of these
submarine-based missiles were undefended, the President would
be faced with a very difficult decision.[12] His only choice would be
the threat of a retaliatory strike or abandoning our cause. There
are very good, moral reasons for not killing millions of innocent
civilians in Chinese cities or even threatening to do so. Even a
strike against China's other nuclear forces (if she had any) and
against her nuclear production capabilities on the mainland
might cause casualties among the population (through "collateral
damage" due to residual radiation, proximity of weapon systems
to population centers, etc.) which could be morally unacceptable

---

[12]For example, we may be trying to help prevent the violent
oppression of a people by a Chinese-backed communist force (most
likely on the periphery of China). This is not inconceivable and
Chinese support of fanatical groups in both the Arab and Black
African countries (who might well desire the overthrow of the relatively more moderate governments in power today) is already an
established fact. To date such Chinese efforts away from her periphery
have generally been unsuccessful, except perhaps for the guerrillas
they support who over the years have been harassing Israel. But we
are talking about the future—installing ABM requires a long lead
time.

to an American President, particularly if he had another choice. Furthermore, (depending on China's warning system and the size and level of alert of her nuclear weapons systems), a counterforce strike by us might "flush" part of the force we were trying to take out, resulting in a nuclear "exchange" which would make all past wars seem tame by comparison. This would be true even if the Chinese had only a moderate intercontinental capability or even an intermediate-range ballistic missile force—600-1,200 mile range. And millions of Americans, Japanese, Filipinos and Indians might die.[13]

Under these circumstances, one could even imagine the Chinese firing one missile in a "demonstration" attack against the United States mainland (or even taking out a small city) and our forces *still* not going after those threatening submarines and China's intercontinental and intermediate-range ballistic missiles. In light of even the remote possibility of this milieu, a prudent man must have doubts about foreclosing the option to turn to some other means of insuring flexibility of action in a crisis which threatens some relatively helpless victim state or our own vital interests. The ability to press forward toward these limited objectives, with some confidence in the safety of our cities, through means other than threatenting horrendous (and perhaps immoral) escalation seems to me to be something we should not easily dismiss.

China could also cause a threat in the area of "accidental" launch which might be considerably more serious than that presented by the other nuclear powers. In the late 1950's, the Chinese were fascinated by the rocket and nuclear technology of the U.S.S.R. and seemed to feel the Soviets could dominate us in Asia.[14] This somewhat naive fascination is much less likely to overtake them in relation to their own new systems because they now know the realities of nuclear weapons. Nevertheless, the "forced draft" development program which brought them to the hydrogen bomb (much more rapidly than the French) shows a

---

[13]A "theater hostage" technique might be employed by China to neutralize our nuclear striking force. See Alice Langley Hsieh's testimony, Hearings Before the Subcommittee on Military Applications, U.S. Congress Joint Committee on Atomic Energy, *Scope, Magnitude and Implications of the United States Antiballistic Missile Program,* 90th Cong. 1st Sess., 1967, p. 82.

[14]Alice Langley Hsieh, *Communist China's Strategy in the Nuclear Era*, Prentice-Hall, Englewood Cliffs, New Jersey, 1962, pp. 77-94.

high priority and almost frantic effort to get these weapons. The sophisticated command and control systems, however, which keep these weapons under control in the United States may not be so easily attained. The Chinese may settle for something cruder and less safe. In fact, even their present nuclear weapons production and/or testing program may have some flaws in it. There seems to be some evidence that either there was extreme secrecy in the preparation for the testing of one of their nuclear shots or that such preparations were not made. Furthermore, there has been speculation that the 1967 shot of 20 kilotons was a misfire of only the nuclear "trigger" portion of a hydrogen bomb. In any event, something may have gone wrong in their accelerated attempt to get a hydrogen bomb arsenal, but we will probably never know for sure. The Chinese press never even mentioned the shot.[15]

Another danger is that the Chinese nuclear weapons program, and presumably their delivery system program, seem to operate in as "decoupled" a fashion as possible from their economy. This always raises the possibility that some political leader may come to power who has a faulty evaluation of their systems, does not reward people for bringing him "bad news," and/or refuses to believe his briefings.

Considering the nature of the Chinese Communist system, the processes of local and national leadership struggles, their headlong dash into the sophisticated fields of nuclear weaponry and rocketry and the relatively small size of her nuclear ballistic missile force (which presumably means it cannot strike counterforce against us but could be aimed at cities), the danger from a small accidental or intentional strike against United States' cities from this source becomes a subject which cannot be ignored. Short of a completely successful, acceptable (to the United States) first-strike against her nuclear forces,[16] as soon as we feel threat-

[15]Reports of the failure of this detonation by the Chinese on December 24, 1967 appeared in many places: *The New York Times* of December 25, 1967, p. 1, December 26, 1967, p. 9 and January 4, 1968, p. 4; *The Washington Post,* January 4, 1968, p. A-3 and January 5, 1968, p. A-15; the Washington, D.C. *Evening Star,* December 26, 1967, p. 1.

[16]A successful first-strike is taken to mean one which takes out all her nuclear delivery systems capable of threatening us or our allies (which means we probably must catch her submarines on the surface or in port), but does not inflict significant casualties on her population. I have described earlier the inhibitions against such a strike, as well as the complexities and possible dangers involved.

ened,[17] the only other technological solution to the dilemma is defense of our cities. This defense could be passive (evacuation of our cities or effective blast and fallout shelter systems or a combination of these), or active (an anti-ballistic missile system designed to protect our urban areas). The first solution would, of course, not protect above-ground structures, so that the housing and economic capability of the area would be lost, including any complicated industrial plants. Some casualties will also result from an attack on such a passive defense system, even if it worked well. If it worked well, the second solution would presumably prevent any damage to the cities or their population from a light attack of a few unsophisticated warheads.

This posture of active defense, which could possibly negate the Chinese threat while leaving many options open to the United States, is the kind of situation which, since Korea, the Chinese have been reluctant to face. A Chinese "fishing expedition" under the circumstances could not only have too high a probability of their bluff being called, but could—both in the area of the initial confrontation which caused the crisis and in their threatened escalation—be counterproductive.

Their dilemma in regards to Quemoy and Taiwan (Formosa) is perhaps a good case in point. Here the Chinese Communists face the Chinese Nationalist-held island of Quemoy in the harbor of Amoy only two miles off the mainland. Obviously, Mainland China would like to take this island and Taiwan. But there are fifty thousand Chinese Nationalist troops in very well-fortified positions on Quemoy and half a million more on Taiwan; and control of the air over Amoy harbor could be lost to the Nationalists. Furthermore, the Nationalists might strike back at the mainland—which they probably would not recognize as a sanctuary in the event of Communist attack.[18] Here is a case in which Mainland China might not be successful in taking Quemoy and clearly has little chance of crossing the 100 miles of blue water to Taiwan with their tiny surface navy, possibly without control of the air. Furthermore, there is the unknown quantity of the units of the United States Seventh Fleet in the area. The decision by the

[17]This may be very early in a crisis.

[18]For a brief description of the Communist ill-fated attempts in the straits crisis of 1958, in which their air force fared badly at the hands of the Nationalist air force and any attempt at taking Quemoy was finally given up, see Armbruster, *op. cit.,* pp. 173-6.

Communists has been clear (though not explicit): no "fishing expeditions" here. The reasons for the decision also seem clear: strong defenses that put little at risk except to a huge effort, which even then might be unsuccessful, but which would provide time for reaction before a *fait accompli* could be presented to the victim state and its allies. On the other hand, weak defenses on the Indian frontier led to quick and ruthless exploitation by an opportunistic Red China in a crisis situation with India in 1962.[19]

Obviously, both the crises mentioned above are far below anything in the nuclear crisis category, but if any analogies are to be drawn from Chinese Communist behavior in the past, we are forced to choose from a limited number of confrontations.[20] Furthermore, since all crises have a life of their own, one has considerable difficulty writing scenarios which tell one specifically when and how the enemy may react (though the latter is somewhat easier to surmise than the former). What one can do, however, is to indicate with some degree of confidence which options should not be foreclosed in the face of certain potential threats. For example, it was clear to a prudent man in 1938 that theories of why France should not build up her forces against an armed Nazi Germany (and at least one source claimed the rightists in France sincerely believed them)[21] were not as convincing as arguments of why she should gird herself for battle. That option could not be foreclosed even if one believed the fears of the rightists, because, without a strong defense, France would lose the

[19]The Chinese came in along several sectors of the border in a very threatening manner, secured their road through the Aksai Chin, then pulled back from their extended, exposed positions south of the Himalayan barrier in the Northeast Frontier Agency (but kept the road) before India and the Free World could react. *Ibid.,* pp. 181-9.

[20]Though she is pragmatic about the use of force, this limit seems more due to the fact that she has only existed as a communist state for a short period of time (20 years) rather than any reluctance on her part to clash militarily with her neighbors or encourage others to do so. She supported the North Korean attack on South Korea and is supporting the North Vietnamese war effort against South Vietnam. She herself has attacked South Korea (when she failed to stop at the 38th parallel in her offensive of 1951), Quemoy, Tibet, India and (in minor probes) even the U.S.S.R.

[21]Paul W. Blackstock in his book *The Strategy of Treason,* Quadrangle Books, Chicago, 1964, discusses the subversion by the Nazis of the traditional national loyalties of the parties of the

ability to influence events in any direction. This was a life and death matter to France as a nation, but many Frenchmen apparently believed that it would make things worse if they built up their defenses to a level to defeat Germany.

A much more alarming threat, of course, exists today in the minds of men who are not by any means political extremists such as the French rightists, but who, nevertheless, disapprove of the fabrication of any more nuclear warheads, even for antiballistic missiles. They fear an enemy increase in weapons to overcome the ABM's we build, then in turn an increase in our ABM's, and so on—in other words, an acceleration of the arms race and, perhaps, eventually a nuclear holocaust in which civilization is destroyed. Others fear the system of ABM's will not work. These people, as all of us, would prefer an "arms control" agreement limiting nuclear forces. It appears to me, however, that a "unilateral" control situation where we do not build an ABM system and the Russians do,[22] has some inherent contradictions. The arguments that our building such a system will be "provocative" to the Russians and the Chinese seems weak, not only in the face of the traditional Soviet attitude toward these defensive systems,[23] but in the Chinese attitude toward their own offensive nuclear systems vis-à-vis their neighbors. A mere "no-first-use" statement was deemed adequate to quell the fears of India and Japan (and indeed the United States) and show the good intentions of the Chinese. China has a nuclear program for many reasons, some of which may have nothing to do with the United States or even her neighbors. The French nuclear *force de frappe* does not come out well in war games (if one worries about what France looks like after an "exchange"), but the French are building it, possibly for purely political reasons. Nevertheless, it, like the Chinese system, is a real nuclear force and possible target nations must take it into

---

French Right at the time of Munich. He quotes Thierry Maulnier in *Combat,* November 1938: "these parties felt that if war should come . . . Germany's defeat would mean the crumbling away of those authoritarian regimes which are our principal bulwark against Communist revolution and perhaps also the instant Bolshevizing of Europe. In other words . . . a French victory would have less victory for France than for the principles quite rightly regarded as leading straight to France's ruin, and to the ruin of civilization itself." p. 60.

[22]See Chapter 7 for a discussion of the Soviet program.

[23]*Ibid.*

consideration. Furthermore, Peking, at least until recently, has indicated no interest in arms control—even the total destruction of all nuclear weapons—until "imperialism" is defeated and except in the context of "world revolution."[24]

The "unilateral-control" approach of some United States advocates seems to depend on the "good will" we create in the potential enemy if we unilaterally leave ourselves unprotected, which should somehow lead to an end to the arms race. In this approach, the end to the arms race appears to be the overriding issue, even above decreasing United States casualties in the event of attack. Some ABM opponents feel, however, that such an attack should never come since, in it, both sides would be destroyed. In fact, the easier it is to "take out" each other's cities, the less likely the attack (and presumably to some degree vice versa). As pointed out earlier, there are all kinds of political, morale and moral holes in this argument, many of which have been aggravated by the Russians' initial deployment of ABM defenses for *their* cities. As in 1938 in France, the prudent man today, though recognizing the dangers of the arms race, must not foreclose the option to defend himself against the current Soviet force and the potential Chinese force. And threat of nuclear retaliation against the enemy's homeland is not enough. A prudent man must doubt the premise that defending oneself makes things worse, if he wishes flexibility in his dealings even to bring about an end to the arms race, particularly in light of the current "competition" between the communist and non-communist worlds.[25]

One cannot help but recall the logic of Nehru and his Defense Minister, Krishna Mennon, in 1962 which left their Tibetan border inadequately guarded. Mennon and Nehru thought they

[24]Halperin, *op. cit., China in Crisis*, Vol. II, pp. 155-6.

[25]This same theory labeled the current Soviet ICBM program as an attempt on their part to reach "parity" with us, which was supposed to be good. When they reached parity the theory stated they would then feel secure and then we could negotiate an arms reduction agreement with them. We stopped our ICBM program with 1,054 relatively low-payload missiles. They did reach parity with us (except with missiles with huge payloads and large warheads)—but they have kept on going. They are now past us (1,200 missiles) and we don't know how many of these monstrous missiles they intend to deploy—and the arms control talks with them have apparently not altered significantly. Furthermore, they also have a large production program under way for nuclear ballistic-missile-carrying submarines. (See Chapter 7, pp. 167-8.)

"knew" the Chinese; in fact they lectured us *ad nauseam* in the
U.N. and elsewhere about how to get along with them. Their
theory was that if one were "reasonable" with China, if one did
not constantly treat her as an "enemy," if one did not confront her
with troops (i.e., defend one's border), tensions would drop and
the "arms race" with her could cease. Furthermore, the Indians
backed up their theory with action; they let the border defenses
against China deteriorate, and it worked—until China wanted
some territory which belonged to India.

Although the probability of a Chinese nuclear attack against
the United States is extremely low, the probability of a United
States-Chinese crisis is not, and one should probably not look
"uncovered" in crucial dealings with a tough bargaining opponent.
The "Indian-type" of thinking (as compared to the more pragmatic thinking of the Chinese Nationalists and the Russians) seems
somewhat less than prudent in dealing with the opportunistic
Chinese Communists. In fact, one can make the argument that
the United States ballistic missile defense against a Red Chinese
"city-busting" force should lead to stability and, in the event of an
irrational Chinese leader, save lives and essential property of our
citizens.

To sum up, such an ABM system might give the President
options, before and during a crisis, other than threatened or actual
retaliatory strikes against Chinese cities or counterforce strikes,
possibly with considerable collateral damage to civilians. And if
at the moment we do not have ABM systems which are actually
capable of intercepting even a few unsophisticated Chinese warheads,[26] we should pull out all the stops on research, development and deployment in a crash program to get adequate systems.
With our Gross National Product, it is hard to make the argument
that money is the problem, at least not for the successful development of such vital systems.[27] As for domestic political considerations, the polls suggest that few Congressmen need fear to face
their constituents on a record of supporting the active defense of

[26]Though the government presumably seems to think they can
intercept more sophisticated Soviet warheads.

[27]By the time the system is deployed, our GNP should be over a
trillion dollars per year.

our cities.[28] On the contrary, the indicators are that many voters
will find it difficult to understand a Congressman who follows a
reasoning which says we are safer without ABM when the Soviet
Union has one, along with a large intercontinental nuclear missile force. Add to the equation a Red Chinese nuclear missile
force which can reach the United States and the popular American perception of her record in the community of nations and, on
balance, the political climate may be more favorable to Congressional friends of missile defense than to its critics.

[28]The Harris Survey released in the last week of April, 1969 showed overwhelming support (78 to 9) for the proposition that it is "better
to be overprepared militarily than be caught short without proper
defenses." Approval for a "thin" ABM system which "at the beginning
. . . would involve putting the system in at two of our missile bases
in Montana and South Dakota for $7 billion" (the Safeguard system)
won out by less (47% to 26%; 27% of those polled were "not sure").
Although large pluralities agreed that the $7 billion would better be
spent on "housing," etc., that we "should concentrate on peaceful
arms control rather than new missile systems" and that even with
Safeguard "we cannot prevent loss of millions of American lives in
an atomic attack," only 18% felt that installing ABM's would hurt
"chances of reaching arms control agreements with the Russians"
(52% felt it would not, 30% were "not sure").

   Mr. Harris concludes that "While it is clear that powerful arguments have been made on both sides of the issue, the fact remains that
fears over Russian efforts to build an ABM system and the general
belief that it is better to be 'overprepared than underprepared'
elicit support of over 6 in 10 people. In contrast, most of the anti-
ABM arguments have won over only a minority and, in some cases,
are opposed by substantial pluralities." *The Washington Post,*
April 28, 1969, p. A-7.

Chapter 11

CIVIL DEFENSE
AND MISSILE DEFENSE

by Raymond D. Gastil

DISCUSSION of ballistic missile defense raises the question of what other defensive systems may be desirable supplements to Ballistic Missile Defense (BMD). Since civil defense has often been singled out as one area in which additional effort would have to be made if the nation went very strongly in the BMD direction, it is necessary to make some comments on the degree to which civil defense seems to be required by BMD. We will then go on to discuss briefly how BMD might be compared with civil defense and other defensive alternatives.

The argument that there are civil defense requirements for BMD is often based on the persistent linking of the two by Secretary McNamara in the early 1960's. The former Secretary of Defense believed that, before the nation seriously embarked on a BMD deployment program, it should develop a full fallout shelter system. The Department of Defense had developed plans for a system that would provide high-quality fallout protection, but not blast protection, to most of the country with a cost at that time of between five and six billion dollars. If this system's ability to protect against radiation effects were compared with that to be achieved by a very low budget program for developing shelter in existing buildings (such as the current program), it appeared that in a wide range of possible future nuclear wars putting six billion dollars into the fallout shelter program was the most cost-effective available way to spend money to protect people. This linkage was a purely theoretical one based on an examination of what should be done first because it was the best buy. The linkage assumed that Congress should always approve the most cost-

235

effective approach to the solution of any problem. It should be noted that at this time the Defense Department often imagined Soviet attacks primarily against military forces (bomber bases, missile sites, etc.) in which fallout would be the primary counter-civilian effect. Therefore, the fact that missile defense would save buildings or prevent fires, as well as save people directly, was not always taken directly into the calculation of relative system effectiveness.

There was also another closely related but quite different linkage. McNamara and others believed that in the absence of good shelter an opponent could deliberately (as well as inadvertently through attack on military forces) kill the population through fallout effects. To overcome a missile defense an attacker would have only to groundburst[1] one or a few weapons out of BMD range and "upwind" from the city to be attacked. In the absence of good fallout shelter the effects of the BMD could be easily negated by the heavy fallout that would cover the city as a result. This analysis was based on a BMD system that was limited to very short-range, point defense missiles of the Sprint type. Against a sophisticated Soviet attack this may be all we effectively have in the future or it may not. Parenthetically, it should be noted that wind patterns are not so predictable that this would be an inexpensive and high-confidence approach to actually destroying population—it could, of course, be sufficiently threatening.

While the link between fallout shelter and missile defense has often been made, and with some justice, a link between blast shelter and missile defense has not been seriously considered for most BMD systems. The Spartan and Sprint missiles, for example, will detonate at altitudes sufficiently high relative to their size that there will be essentially no effects on the ground, especially for those persons taking any shelter at all. Against these systems an opponent could plan to explode extremely large weapons (such as the U.S. does not have) either by plan or at the moment of ABM intercept. At Sprint intercept altitudes this could produce significant effects on the ground, particularly thermal effects. The blast and thermal protection that good fallout shelter inadvertently gives would be sufficient for this encounter in most cases.

Of course, one could design around blast shelters an ABM that intercepted down to very low altitudes. In this case, blast

[1]When a nuclear weapon is detonated in a manner which causes the fireball to intercept the ground (i.e. "groundburst") the immediate fallout is maximized. When the weapon is "airburst" the fallout is nominal, but blast and thermal effects can be maximized.

shelters and BMD would be linked. However, this is not a likely or desirable way for missile defense to go, in so far as it is a population defense.

Thus, while there is no absolute requirement that BMD, particularly with an effective area defense component, be accompanied by civil defense programs significantly more expensive than the present programs, a defensive system must include some civil defense component. The present shelter system in existing buildings will save millions of lives, especially if plans are made to rapidly upgrade protection in available shelter in the days and hours immediately before an attack. We can do without a full fallout shelter program and obtain good fallout protection, but the rated protection of much of the marked shelter today does not adequately protect against multimegaton upwind ground-bursts close to urban areas. The present program should be greatly improved, or plans to improve it rapidly in crises should be developed.*

As long as there are no blast shelters in the cities, we should have a capability similar to the present Soviet capability to evacuate cities in a very deep crisis. No matter how good a BMD system is, against a sophisticated opponent it will fail in some places, and it would be better not to be in the cities during an attack. Evacuation requires plans for facilitating the movement of people and the rapid preparation of rural fallout shelters. Again, although not highly reliable, evacuation in many scenarios would save millions of lives, and, for attacks directed against cities, evacuation would save more people than any other civil defense alternative other than an extensive blast shelter program.·

The next level of expense is the full fallout shelter program mentioned above. Such a program would probably now cost about one billion dollars annually for eight years. Fallout shelter is actually a misnomer because for essentially the same cost the program would and should be designed to provide some blast and thermal protection. In relation to present CD programs the advantages of this program lie in much higher protection against fallout, which would often be crucial, and in better siting. The latter means that the shelter would be distributed as the population is distributed; it would be less clustered in downtown urban areas. Required warning times would be less both because people would be more likely to be in shelter when weapons went off (less

---

*See Note at the end of the Chapter for a description of the current Civil Defense Program.

important for fallout itself) and because fewer of the shelters would be destroyed by the direct effects of weapons and resulting fires. In spite of these advantages, there is no requirement that such a shelter program be built, even if we procure a large BMD system.

On the next level of expense of programs costing two billion dollars a year or more, we should compare BMD with alternative means of defending the country. Many of the active defenses are partially competitive with BMD for funds. Defenses against manned bombers are likely to continue to compete with BMD in future budgets for defensive systems. There will always be some need for air defenses. Against missile-carrying submarines, antisubmarine warfare may be compared with terminal defense systems such as BMD. However, they are faced with many of the same disadvantages as second-strike counterforce systems in that after a nuclear war has started they would attack launching platforms from which some, perhaps most, weapons may have been already launched. It is likely that BMD can compete favorably with such defensive alternatives. Moreover, the important threat of the immediate future is the ICBM, and BMD is the active defense against this threat.

In strategic terms, it would appear as though we cannot very usefully compare the effectiveness of offensive counterforce weapons with terminal defensive systems such as BMD. Unless we were making a carefully planned surprise attack out of the blue, a U.S. planner would not know at what point we would be in a war when a decision would be made to use our offensive counterforce. To defend ourselves by striking first requires confidence that we will know at some point in a future crisis that nuclear war is unavoidable, and that the President will act on this knowledge in a timely fashion. This we should have a plan for, but not plan on. The prudent American planner must build even our counterforce for second-strikes, although he will recognize a wider range of possible events. However, the Soviet Union might use relatively soft weapons in a first wave and have only hidden weapons and submarines left, or fire so large a fraction of its originally targetable force that U.S. offensive effectiveness would be reduced to a small fraction of its design capability. If there were many weapons left that we could target, these might be on high-alert status, ready to fire on radar warning of attack. Such Soviet weapons might be targeted against cities, or we might fear they were. Even if the Soviet reaction were delayed until after the first U.S. detonations, would our attack in the fog of war be integrated enough to avoid a second attack to be launched against our cities? The only conclusion that can be drawn is that leaders should beware of *relying* on offensive counterforce for damage limitation. BMD, on the other hand, is much less dependent on scenario and command. Against anything more than a single unidentified missile, a BMD system should present few high-level command problems. The unreliabilities would be battle failures common to any system. They would be less likely to be decision failures and across-force integration failures than in the case of our damage-limiting counterforce capability.

In terms of lives saved per dollar, blast shelters and BMD have very comparable costs if we accept the assumptions of effectiveness generally used. However, there are serious problems in comparing the effectiveness of BMD and blast shelters. While the comparison is not as difficult as in the above case, the crucial questions here are also apt to be qualitative and indirect rather than quantitative and direct, assuming that costs are not wildly out of line for one or the other system. Supporters of BMD often maintain that the country could not survive the destruction of the buildings in the largest fifty to one hundred cities. Most studies of economic recuperation potential do not support this position, and a serious effort at pre-attack preparations could go a long way toward solving the remaining problems of city loss. There is no doubt, of course, that recovery would be more rapid with the preservation of some of the larger cities, and that there is some point not too far above two hundred urban targets beyond which economic recovery in the near term becomes very problematical.

BMD could change targeting and weapons in a way that blast shelters would be unlikely to. If we assume that urban centers are the hostages, then attacks may come against cities with blast shelters at about the same levels as without shelters. With U.S. BMD, an opponent might look more to higher levels of attack or new approaches; not knowing the effectiveness of our BMD, the opponent might do more than enough in attempting direct penetration. In Chapter 3 and elsewhere in this volume it has been argued that there is a good probability the Soviets would do none of these things against a BMD system, but surely they are more likely to against BMD than against blast shelters.

If the United States had blast shelters, the opponent's threat would be clear and relatively calculable, whereas BMD would be only one counter in an elaborate game. There are many ways in which an opponent *might* end-run particular BMD systems. There might be high-altitude bursts of giant weapons, or large delivery vehicles might release hundreds of 20-KT warheads. There might be long-range torpedoes with hundred-megaton devices. There might be highly sophisticated aircraft and cruise missiles. Many holes may be plugged, but in a crisis an opponent might announce something else.

In addition, new military systems often perform badly under combat conditions. This might be especially true of an elaborate, complex, untested BMD system that may get only one chance to work or fail. There will not be time for small changes on the basis of war-time experience. U.S. planners would also know more about blast shelters after a war, but doubts here are not nearly as significant as those for BMD. In a crisis, how much reassurance would a twenty billion dollar BMD program really give a President with competent advisors? With blast shelters, he might at least have "periods" of knowing that his people were "relatively" safe.

However, assuming equal reliability and equivalent enemy attacks, BMD has many advantages over blast shelters. BMD could theoretically protect property and people against all effects. No matter how good the civil defense may be against large attacks, only BMD can hope to protect any considerable proportion of our urban productivity even with extensive pre-attack stockpiling or industrial dispersal. Moreover, against the same size attack BMD means many fewer ground zeros of equivalent sized weapons, and thus a much reduced radiation problem after attacks. BMD has less of a warning problem than shelters, although it is better if the population it protects could reach some sort of shelter before a missile battle. While advanced radars should provide sufficient warning for an integrated BMD system to respond, insufficient tactical warning would degrade the effectiveness of blast shelters in many scenarios.

Ballistic missile defense may also have useful flexibility in what it defends as compared with shelter. Area defense systems, and even point defense systems with 25-mile radii, can be used to stop missiles sent against people, industrial targets *and* military force targets. Of course, a system might run out of interceptors defending against one kind of attack and have nothing else for the other. But in so far as individual attacking missiles may achieve multiple damage objectives, BMD should be credited with possible multiple defense achievements in a manner not possible for blast shelters.

The argument that blast shelters would be bad for society should not be taken very seriously, although shelters could be introduced and handled in undesirable ways. Swedish or Swiss shelter programs have not hurt their societies. Today Israel lives under continual threat, and many Israelis, particularly children, sleep in shelters in communities near the border. Without taking sides in the Middle Eastern quarrel, most observers will admit that Israeli society does not seem to be seriously damaged by this situation.

In internal political terms, BMD and blast shelter systems may have different meanings. In the early 1960's Congress was more anxious over the development of a serious shelter program costing five billion dollars than over the development of a BMD system involving military hardware costing up to twenty billion dollars. The articulate minority that now opposes BMD formerly opposed civil defense and would, of course, oppose it again. However, opinion polls suggest that the American people as a whole do not oppose civil defense measures, even blast shelters, to the extent that is often believed. Civil defense might become more acceptable if active defenses were in existence or being developed simultaneously. However, the question seems more budgetary today than previously. Unless there is a deeper sense of need in the nation as a whole than we find today, neither BMD nor blast shelters with significant protection against Soviet attack will be developed.

In terms of international ·reactions, West Germany, Denmark, Sweden or Switzerland have seriously considered or are building blast shelters. Their reaction to blast shelters, compared to BMD, is apt to be much more favorable than the internal U.S. or British reaction, although blast shelters in a large nuclear power raise different questions. France, presently relying on pure finite deterrence, may scoff at both. The Soviet Union, probably judging itself ahead of us in both, is unlikely to be concerned unless (1) it feels that its offensive abilities only barely prevent a U.S. first-strike, or (2) we introduce our programs very rapidly and in concert with the development of further offensive capability. However, if the Soviets think in terms of hostages it is probably cities, not people, that are the more important. In these terms, blast shelters are less likely to enflame an arms competition than BMD. Soviet leaders are liable to make propaganda attacks on a U.S. introduction of either system, although their own claim to BMD capability might lead them to attack U.S. blast shelters more harshly.

In conclusion, BMD does not *require* a larger civil defense program than we have today. However, it would be unwise not to make at least low budget improvements in the present program that would allow protection in crises to be significantly improved. If no blast shelters are built, it might be desirable to develop a full fallout shelter program with or without a BMD system for population protection. Comparison of BMD with equally expensive blast shelter systems suggests a mixed picture. The balance of advantages and disadvantages is such that it is hard to favor one over the other, although advanced BMD systems can be imagined that would clearly be preferable. In the near future the best system for a high budget defense would probably mix BMD, blast shelters, and fallout shelters, but it would not be unreasonable to have a system based primarily on active defenses such as BMD with an improved very low budget civil defense system.

Note on the Current Civil Defense Program

The present civil defense program costs about $100 million a year in federal, state and local funds. A great deal of the effort is placed on warning systems, emergency operations, training, planning and research. The survey, marking and stocking of shelters in existing buildings has, together with associated programs, created a national capability to provide about 200 million fallout shelter spaces. Although this program would save millions of lives in a nuclear war, the shelter spaces are not distributed as the population is, and are often in prime urban target areas. In addition, many of the shelter spaces do not provide sufficiently high protection against large nuclear weapons groundburst upwind within fifty miles or so of the shelter.

Part IV

SOME OTHER PERSPECTIVES

Chapter 12

STRATEGIC ARMS CONTROL AND STABILITY: A RETROSPECTIVE LOOK

by Johan J. Holst

THE ADVENT of reasonably effective ballistic missile defense systems has acted as a strong incentive for an intensification and formalization of the Soviet-American arms control dialogue over the issue of the continued stability of the strategic balance. In a very fundamental sense such a dialogue has become a permanent feature of the international system. There is, of course, a great deal of communication (some of it inadvertent) inherent in the actions and non-actions of the superpowers. During the period of Robert S. McNamara's distinguished stewardship over the American defense establishment a rather vigorous and sophisticated policy of "talking to Moscow at a distance" characterized much of the official discussion of strategic doctrine and force postures. It was, I believe, in large part conceived as an educational exercise aimed at some mutually coordinated tacit management of the gigantic potentials for destruction which had become part of the precarious infrastructure of the international order. The very magnitude of their power to inflict pain and destruction on each other had confined the two most powerful nations in history to a predicament of extreme interdependence.

The prudential management of this state of extreme inter-dependence came to focus on the problem of ensuring the surviv-ability of the strategic forces so as to minimize the incentives for deliberate surprise attack (in the expectation of successfully dis-arming the enemy), the incentives for pre-emptive actions (in anticipation of imminent attacks by the adversary) or the dangers

245

of inadvertent war (due to lack of reliable command and control systems). The Russians assimilated, it now seems, the lesson that unprotected strategic forces constitute a source of tension and insecurity and they have now hardened their systems by means of physical protection and mobility. The American government even went so far as to transfer to the Russians the concepts of a PAL (Permissive Action Link) technology designed to insure control over the release of nuclear weapons and a guarantee against accident.[1] The Russians got the message and have adopted similar measures for their nuclear forces.

While considerable success may be credited to the American policy of educating the adversary about the requirements of a stable deterrent relationship, several issues remained unresolved and certain basic conceptual outlooks have never been reconciled. The latter include the role of active defenses in the strategic postures. Widely discrepant strategic images may constitute a serious obstacle to arms control. However, intensive dialogue may facilitate at least second-order agreement; that is, agreement on where and why there is disagreement. The process of diplomatic interaction may also cause unilateral reexaminations which in turn may enhance the prospects of greater convergence. It is likely that the forthcoming Soviet-American strategic arms talks will demonstrate the importance of a strategic reexamination which may lead to Soviet-American convergence around the concept of Defensive Emphasis. Such a reconstruction would also seem to be consistent with a gradual conversion to a general posture of nuclear de-emphasis so as to minimize both the incentives for nuclear proliferation inherent in the activities of the superpowers and the political benefits which are generally perceived to be associated with the possession of nuclear weaponry.

Advances in weapons technology involving significant improvements in accuracy (CEP $<1/4$ mile) and the introduction of MIRV's threaten once more to raise the possibility of attack ratios in favor of a first-strike. Thus, the forthcoming strategic arms talks will have to focus anew on the instabilities deriving from first-strike incentives. In this context, it seems useful to examine the last intensive Soviet-American encounter over the issue of the instabilities associated with the reciprocal fear of disarming attacks on the deterrent forces, viz. the 1958 experts talks on

[1]Edward Klein and Robert Littell, Shh! Let's Tell The Russians, *Newsweek,* May 5, 1969, pp. 46-7.

surprise attack. These talks took place in the context of considerable apprehension in the U.S. over the instabilities of an environment where a small number of bombers or missiles could eliminate on the ground a large number of vulnerable bombers carrying several weapons each (and also the first-generation liquid-fuel missiles which were deployed in very vulnerable configurations).

DIPLOMATIC PRELUDE

The feasibility of a Soviet first-strike against the American strategic forces had received a great deal of attention in various important studies of the U.S. strategic posture during the 1950's. The issue was first raised seriously in a comprehensive study undertaken by a team of RAND Corporation analysts for purposes of examining the basing of the strategic bombers.[2] The problem of vulnerability was the major focus of the Gaither Committee report in 1957 and the Rockefeller report in 1958.[3] The testing of the first Soviet ICBM in August 1957 and the launching of the first Sputnik in October of that same year lent some ostensible drama to the concerns.

The problem of surprise attack was brought into the arena of disarmament negotiations by President Eisenhower with his "Open Skies" proposal at the 1955 Summit Conference. This envisaged a reciprocal undertaking to exchange blueprints of the existing military establishments and permit aerial inspection of one's territory by the adversary in order to guard against surprise attack.[4] At the same conference Bulganin presented a Soviet plan for the emplacement of ground observers to guard against surprise

[2]A.J. Wohlstetter, F.S. Hoffman, R.J. Lutz and H.S. Rowen, *Selection and Use of Strategic Air Bases,* R-266, The RAND Corp., Santa Monica, Cal., 1954 (second declassified printing 1962). See Bruce L.R. Smith, *The RAND Corporation: Case Study of a Nonprofit Advisory Corporation,* Harvard Univ. Press, Cambridge, Mass., 1966, pp. 195-240 for a discussion of this important study and how it came about. See also A.J. Wohlstetter, F.S. Hoffman and H.S. Rowen, *Protecting U.S. Power to Strike Back in the 1950's and 1960's,* R290, The RAND Corp., Santa Monica, Cal., 1956, for a follow-up study of the vulnerability problem and second-strike requirements.

[3]See Morton H. Halperin, The Gaither Committee and the Policy Process, *World Politics,* (13) April 1961, pp. 360-84, and *International Security: The Military Aspect,* The Rockefeller Report II, Doubleday, New York, 1958.

[4]*Documents on Disarmament 1945-1959, Vol. I,* Department of State, Washington, D.C., 1960, pp. 486-8.

attacks in Europe. The discussion of limited measures during the years 1955-58 concentrated to a large extent on the various plans for aerial surveillance and ground observation posts, in addition to the test ban talks.

The "Open Skies" proposal was elaborated in an outline plan of August 30, 1955. It assumed that the detailed blueprints be verified by on-the-spot observers and that the aerial reconnaissance be conducted on an unrestricted but monitored basis "to augment the efforts of the posted observers."[5] It was essentially a scheme for reassurance by overt intelligence, but it apparently hit the Russians in a sensitive spot by constituting, in their view, control without disarmament. They objected that the plan did not include the United States' allies in Europe and other areas with American overseas bases,[6] and, most important, they insisted that the scheme could provide an aggressor with vital targeting information and thus increase rather than diminish the fears of surprise attack.[7] In terms of policy, the Soviets insisted that the proposal was unacceptable as long as it remained isolated from concrete measures of arms reduction. The United States subsequently declared its willingness to extend the area of inspection to include the territory on which the Soviet Union and the U.S. maintained troops abroad. The Soviets also voiced the fear that knowledge of the real capabilities of the opponent might produce pressures for a further intensification of the arms race. The following excerpts from a letter from Bulganin to Eisenhower are indicative:

> Judge for yourself, Mr. President, what would the military leaders of your country do if it were reported to them that aerophotography showed that your neighbor had more airfields? To be sure they would order an immediate increase in the number of their own airfields. Naturally, our military leaders would do the same in a similar case. It is not difficult to understand that the result would be a further intensification of the armaments race.[8]

[5]*Documents on Disarmament 1945-1959*, Vol. 1, *op. cit.*, pp. 501-3.

[6]See, e.g., Statement by Molotov at the 1955 Foreign Ministers Meeting, November 10, 1955, in *ibid.*, p. 543.

[7]*Ibid.*, p. 544.

[8]Letter from Bulganin to Eisenhower, February 1, 1956, in *ibid.*, p. 590.

The argument overlooks, of course, the incentives for competitive arms increases that may stem from ignorance and the perceived need to prepare for what an opponent *could do* rather than what he *is doing*. It does suggest, however, that in a situation of obvious disparity widespread cognizance of the "real balance of forces" may render the continued acquiescence to an inferior position psychologically and politically untenable. The expressed fear of the aerial inspection is hard to reconcile with another objection which Bulganin made against the "Open Skies" plan, viz. that "aerial photography could not produce the desired results since both our countries cover a vast area in which anything could be hidden."[9]

During the Sub-committee discussions in March 1956, the U.S. offered two proposals designed to facilitate an exploration of inspection systems, including aerial reconnaissance. The proposals suggested a reciprocal establishment of pilot strips of 20,000-30,000 square miles containing prescribed military and industrial installations for the purpose of testing and improving aerial and ground inspection techniques.[10] They also contained a recommendation for an exchange of Technical Exchange Missions among the five members of the Sub-committee for the purpose of studying the technical problems connected with inspection, control and reporting.[11]

In November 1956, the Russians put forward their own proposal for aerial inspection to be carried out in the area of their primary concern to a depth of 800 km in both directions from the demarcation line in Europe.[12] They linked the inspection zone with a commitment of the foreign powers maintaining forces on German territory to put a ceiling on those forces and make Germany into a denuclearized zone.[13]

The Soviet initiative inaugurated a series of proposals for zonal aerial inspection which were made by the two sides during 1957. The Western powers found the Russian proposal unaccept-

[9]From Address by Bulganin to the Supreme Soviet, August 4, 1955, reprinted in *ibid.,* p. 496.

[10]U.S. Working Paper, March 21, 1956, *ibid.,* pp. 600-601.

[11]U.S. Working Paper, March 21, 1956, *ibid.,* pp. 599-600.

[12]Soviet Declaration, November 17, 1956, *ibid.,* p. 727.

[13]*Ibid.,* Vol. II, pp. 756-7.

able as it would tend, in their view, to legitimize and perpetuate the division of Germany. Instead the U.S. advanced the concept of starting aerial inspection by progressively expanding zones. Two such initial zones were discussed informally among the Sub-committee delegates to the London negotiations in April 1957. One of the zones covered Central Europe, as well as Scandinavia and the western parts of Russia, and the other encompassed American and Soviet territory on both sides of the Bering Straits.[14] The Soviet Union in turn responded with a new set of proposals on April 30, 1957. The new European zone was formally designed on the sector principle, but the Soviets insisted that "the line bisecting the aerial photographic sector should run near the demarcation line in Germany." They further objected to the in-clusion of Scandinavia in the sector claiming that it not extend "beyond the parallel passing through the northernmost point of the demarcation line in Germany." This exercise in "geographic gamesmanship" was complete by proposing an expansion of the non-European sector to include the territory of the U.S. west of 90° longitude and the territory of the U.S.S.R. east of longitude 108° E.[15] In terms of the military installations covered this was an obviously unequal bargain, and the probability that the U.S. would accept it cannot have looked very good to the Russians.

The Western response came in August with a proposal com-prising two alternatives. The comprehensive scheme envisaged aerial inspection of all of the continental United States and Canada and the Soviet Union. The alternative proposal covered a zone limited to the area north of the Polar Circle as well as all of Alaska and the Kamchatka peninsula. If any of the two alterna-tives were accepted the West would consent to a wide sector of aerial inspection covering all of Europe from the Atlantic to the Urals. The Western powers left further room for bargaining over the extent of the European sector by stating that a more limited zone could be discussed "but only on the understanding that this would include a significant part of the territory of the Soviet Union, as well as the other countries of Eastern Europe."[16] The Russians rejected the Western proposals, claiming that they could

[14]Bernard G. Bechhoeffer, *Postwar Negotiations for Arms Con-trol,* Brookings Institute, Washington, D.C., 1961, p. 381.

[15]*Documents on Disarmament 1945-59, Vol. II, op. cit.,* p. 785.

[16]*Ibid.,* pp. 872-3.

"only be regarded as a trick designed to distract attention from the pressing problems of disarmament and to win complete freedom of aerial reconnaissance in order to prepare aggression."[17] The Arctic proposal was probably particularly unacceptable because of the great dependence of Soviet bombers on Arctic staging bases in order to be able to deliver nuclear strikes at the U.S. The "negotiations" quickly reached an impasse, and the problem of surprise attack did not reappear in the diplomatic arena until, in the spring of 1958, it became the subject of a Soviet-American dispute in the Security Council over the American system of airborne alert involving SAC bombers making practice runs carrying nuclear bombs. The so-called "fail-safe" system would, however, prevent them from proceeding beyond a certain point without positive orders which could only be given by the American President. The airborne alert constituted part of the operational practices designed to reduce the vulnerability of the American bomber force to missile attacks.[18]

On April 18, 1958 Gromyko, in a statement supporting his request to bring the matter before the Security Council, presented a vivid scenario of how inadvertent war allegedly might result from the U.S. actions:

> And what would happen if the military air forces of the U.S.S.R. began to act in the same way as the United States air forces are now acting? Naturally, meteors and electronic disturbances cause images on Soviet radar screens too. And if in such instances Soviet aircraft loaded with atomic and hydrogen bombs were to take off in the direction of the United States and its bases in other states, then the air formations of the two sides, seeing each other somewhere over the Arctic wastes, would come to the conclusion—very natural in the circumstances—that there was justification for an outright attack on the enemy and mankind would be plunged into the maelstrom of an atomic war.[19]

The scenario may not have been based on an expert knowledge of the U.S. command and control system, but it did suggest an aware-

---

[17] *Ibid.*, p. 863.

[18] Armed airborne alert flights with B-52 bombers were suspended after the B-52 crash on Greenland in January 1968.

[19] *Documents on Disarmament 1945-59, Vol. II, op. cit.*, p. 986.

ness of the interactive processes that might produce inadvertent war in tense situations. The U.S. rejected the charges of provocation and restated its proposal for aerial inspection in the Arctic.[20] In the ensuing bilateral correspondence over the issue the American government gave "categorical assurances" that it had never had the need to launch or, in fact, had ever launched Arctic bomber flights "as a result of a misinterpreted radar blip or other false alert."

In the course of the correspondence which was initiated between Bulganin and Eisenhower in the fall of 1955, Eisenhower, in a letter on January 12, 1958, suggested that the technical aspects of arms control verification be studied by joint expert groups.[21] The proposal was repeated in the correspondence with Khrushchev on the test ban issue in the spring of 1958 and resulted in agreement to hold an expert conference on nuclear test suspension which opened at Geneva on July 1st, 1958. The following day Khrushchev proposed that "the appropriate representatives—including those of the military agencies of both sides, e.g., at the level of experts—designated by the Governments of the U.S.S.R. , the U.S.A., and possibly by the governments of certain other states, meet for a joint study of the *practical aspects* of this (surprise attack) problem and develop within a definite period of time, to be determined in advance, *recommendations* regarding measures for the prevention of the possibility of surprise attack" (emphasis added).[22] The results should be considered at a summit conference. Khruschchev referred also to the Soviet proposals for aerial and ground observation, stating that they might constitute a suitable basis for agreement. On July 31st the U.S. accepted that such a conference be convened and proposed that "qualified persons from each side meet for a study of the *technical aspects* of safeguards against the possibility of surprise attack . . . . . The discussions could bear, if necessary, on the applicability of inspection measures to various areas for *illustrative* purposes only, but without prejudging in any way the boundaries within which such measures should be applied" (emphasis added).[23]

[20]*Ibid.,* pp. 993-4, 1007-12, 1013-20.

[21]*Ibid.,* p. 940.

[22]*Ibid., pp. 1086-7.*

[23]*Ibid.,* p. 1088.

The Soviet reply of September 15th reiterated that the conference should consider the practical aspects of the problem with a view to working out recommendations in a definite period of time. It went on to restate the Soviet proposals for ground observation posts and rejected explicitly the U.S. contention that the discussions should not predetermine the positions of both governments "in connection with the time and the interdependence of the different aspects of disarmament." It was proposed that the conference convene on November 10th, "having in mind that its work should be concluded in the shortest possible time, for example in the course of four to five weeks." It was also suggested that members of NATO and the Warsaw treaty participate in the negotiations on the basis of the "principle" of equal representation.[24] The American reply reemphasized the concept of a purely technical conference to study alternative methods of lessening the danger of surprise attack. It stated that the study "should be undertaken with a view to the preparation of a technical report which could be recommended for consideration by governments." The studies should be made without prejudice to the parties' positions on the delimitation of the areas within which inspection systems might be established or the connection with other disarmament measures. With this understanding, the U.S. accepted that the conference be convened at Geneva on November 10th and proposed that the Western experts would be from the U.S., England, France, Canada and Italy.[25]

On November 1st the Soviet government responded that the time and place could be considered agreed and that representatives of the U.S.S.R., Poland, Czechoslovakia, Rumania and Albania would partake. The Russians confirmed their position that "the work of the forthcoming conference of experts should be directed to *working out practical recommendations on measures for prevention of surprise attack in conjunction with definite steps in the field of disarmament*" (emphasis added).[26]

On November 7th the U.S. submitted the names of the Western experts who would participate in the conference. It stated that the participation should be based on the ability to contribute to the studies of the conference and not "on the basis of 'equal

[24]*Ibid.,* pp. 1129-31.

[25]*Ibid.,* pp. 1145-6.

[26]*Ibid.,* pp. 1213-14.

representation,' which the United States considers to be neither a 'principle' nor a relevant basis for the organization of the conference." The note also took exception to the Soviet statement on the purpose of the conference stating that decisions on measures of disarmament which might accompany measures to prevent surprise attack are *political* in nature and, hence, lie outside the scope of the conference.[27] As late as November 10th the Russians submitted the names of the Warsaw Pact representatives "in accordance with the principle of equal representation of member countries of the Atlantic pact and member countries of the Warsaw treaty" and reiterated the Soviet position on the scope and purpose of the conference scheduled to convene that same day! ". . . practical recommendations should be worked out on the measures concerning the prevention of a sudden attack combined with certain steps in the sphere of disarmament without the implementation of which the consideration of the problem on the prevention of a sudden attack is *useless*" (emphasis added).[28]

Thus the parties went to the conference on short notice and without having reconciled the wide discrepancy between their respective perceptions of the function and nature of the conference. This unresolved conflict was, as it turned out, to characterize the subsequent deliberations.

The difference in viewpoints in regard to the nature and purpose of the conference also carried into the composition of the delegations. The "eastern" delegations amounted to forty-two experts and advisors as compared to one hundred eight "western" advisors and experts. The former included no scientists and consisted entirely of diplomatic personnel and military officers.[29] The U.S. delegation alone consisted of fifty experts and advisors, including top-ranking scientists like G. B. Kistiakowsky (President Eisenhower's science advisor) and Jerome B. Wiesner (who had been a member of the Gaither Committee and later became President Kennedy's science advisor), and several high-ranking military officers. Several experts from The Rand Corporation

[27]*Ibid.,* pp. 1219-20.

[28]*Ibid.,* p. 1222.

[29]Bechhoeffer, *op. cit.,* pp. 469-70. Much of the information about the workings of the conference and the preparations on the Western side was obtained by interviews and must be recorded here without source citation.

were on the delegation, including Albert Wohlstetter, and others had participated in the brief period of intensive planning and briefing that preceded the conference. The chief of the delegation, William C. Foster, was a former Deputy Secretary of Defense who had been co-director of the Gaither Committee. He had, however, no previous experience in disarmament negotiations and was appointed to the position less than thirty days prior to the convening of the conference. (He has been working on disarmament problems ever since and was Director of the U.S. Arms Control and Disarmament Agency until 1969.) In contrast, the chief of the Soviet delegation, V. V. Kuznetsov—a Deputy Foreign Minister—was a diplomat with extensive experience from previous disarmament talks. The joint preparations of the Western experts for the conference took place in the course of two series of meetings, in Washington from October 20 to 25 and in Geneva from November 6 to 9.[30]

THE CONTEXTUAL IMPACT

It is clear that the two sides entered the negotiations with diametrically opposed notions regarding the purpose and character of the conference. The Western representatives came prepared to explore the "technical" problems connected with the implementation of alternative surveillance systems to guard against surprise attack. Their instructions left them little room for maneuver, and the many efforts made to stake out common ground for a productive exchange with their Eastern counterparts led nowhere, except to certain very curious applications of the term "technical question." The Eastern representatives, on the other hand, came prepared, or so it seemed, to enter into diplomatic bargaining about specific schemes which the experts' conference should recommend to the governments concerned for implementation. The conference thus seemed to be dominated by a kind of "Chekhovian state of mind" (Chekhovskoye nastroyenie). The great Russian writer was a master depicter of human isolation and lack of understanding. The following characterization of the dialogue of Chekhov's plays seems to sum up the nature of the dialogue at the surprise attack conference

[30]*Disarmament and Foreign Policy*, Hearings before a Subcommittee of the Committee on Foreign Relations, U.S. Senate, 86th Cong. 1st Sess., Part I, Washington, D.C., 1959, p. 59.

very neatly: "it expresses the mutual unintelligibility and strange-
ness of human beings, who cannot and do not want to understand each other. Each character speaks only of what interests
him or her and pays no attention to what the other people in the
room are saying. Thus the dialogue becomes a patchwork of
disconnected remarks, dominated by a poetic 'atmosphere' but
by no logical unity."[31] The "poetic atmosphere" may have been
lacking but the "logical unity" was clearly absent a good deal of
the time, in spite of frequent exegeses of Hegelian dialecticism
and Cartesian logic, particularly by the Polish and French representatives respectively.

The Conflicting Perspectives

The Western powers had delivered their proposed agenda
for the conference in Moscow two days before the opening of the
conference. The proposal was made on the assumption that the
conference was convened to discuss "technical facts" connected
with the problem of surprise attack in an "objective and scientific
manner." Hence it was proposed that the experts first identify the
objects of control, i.e., the potential instruments of surprise attack,
and subsequently the means of control, i.e., the technology of observation and inspection. On this basis the experts should evaluate
the application of these techniques to the problem at hand and
finally consider the general technical characteristics of systems to
reduce the threat of surprise attack.[32] According to Foster, the
purpose of the meetings would be to assess "the technical facts
which are the warps and woof of the surprise attack problem."[33]
He went on to reveal what was probably a widely held notion in
the West, namely that the previous failure to reach agreement in
the protracted negotiations on disarmament may be due to a
"lack of understanding of the technical facts involved."[34] Thus,
the Western view seemed to imply that the failure to reach agreement was based on a misunderstanding and was not the inevitable
result of opposed and irreconcilable political interests. The Rus-

[31]D.S. Mirsky, *A History of Russian Literature*, Routledge &
Kegan Paul Ltd., London. 1949, p. 365.

[32]GEN/SA/1.

[33]GEN/SA/PV 1, p. 7.

[34]*Ibid.*

sians suffered under no such illusions. According to Kuznetzov "the problem of surprise attack has arisen because certain countries have for many years been pursuing a policy that creates tensions in the relations between countries."[35] He was echoing Khrushchev in counseling the West to "make a realistic appraisal of power relationships in the world."[36] Thus, in the Soviet view, the problem of surprise attack was tied up with political intentions rather than particular military capabilities. But not totally so, for he had some radical solutions up his sleeve which pointed in another direction. Realistic measures for the prevention of surprise attack, the Westerners were told, could be worked out only on the condition of a complete prohibition of atomic and hydrogen weapons, and destruction of their stocks, by a liquidation of military bases on foreign territory, and a substantial reduction of conventional weapons and forces. The problem of surprise attack is, they were told, "inseparable from the problem of disarmament." The alleged connection was axiomatic and not susceptible to technical and scientific verification or disproval. However, in the Soviet view, it had to be accepted at the outset as a "principle" before the parties could address themselves to the substantive "details." This position has been basic to the Soviet approach to arms control; any measure of observation or control, for example, ground observation posts, are only acceptable as a first measure provided they are "coupled or dovetailed with parallel steps in the field of disarmament."[37] Thus, the Soviet agenda included three points. The conference should consider "practical steps" that could be taken immediately with a view to alleviating the danger of surprise attack and the partial disarmament measures to be carried out in conjunction therewith. Secondly, they should consider the tasks of ground observation posts and aerial photography and, thirdly, prepare and submit a report to their respective governments containing recommendations on the measures that should be implemented.[38]

The parties never agreed on an agenda. The lack of such procedural agreement need not have prevented a serious discus-

[35]*Ibid.,* p. 5.

[36]*Ibid.*

[37]GEN/SA/PV 2, p. 17.

[38]GEN/SA/2.

sion *per se.* However, divergent perceptions in regard to the trans-
actions of the conference structured the Chekhovian dialogue
that ensued. The official title of the conference was one of the few
things the parties managed to reach an agreement on following
long talks out of the conference room. The rather inelegant title
was designed so as not to constrain the parties in regard to their
approach to the subject at hand: "Conference of Experts on
Possible Measures Which Might be Helpful in Preventing Surprise Attack and for the Preparation of a Report Thereon to
Governments."

The large number of top American scientists and specialists
in military systems analysis who were assembled at Geneva indicates that the West had some reasonable expectations of being
able to commit the Russians to a scientific investigation of the
problem of surprise attack. The Canadians even brought in some
of their people with experience from truce supervision and control
in Indo-China. It is hard to see how these expectations could be
entertained in view of the diplomatic correspondence that preceded the conference. However, the Western governments may
have hoped that the Russians would come around once they sat
down behind closed doors in private sessions. Another motivating
factor may have been the desire to expose the Russians to the
Western perspectives on a very serious mutual problem produced
by the prevailing arms predicament.

The parties proved unable to reconcile the opposing views on
the approach to the subject of the conference. The Eastern representatives insisted that they could not "envisage this problem
from the restricted point of view of a given degree of military
techniques alone."[39] It was impossible to "escape the realities of
the present military and political situation. Furthermore, whether
we like it or not, the problems confronting us are not governed by
the laws of physics."[40] They insisted that the experts address
themselves to the *practical* measures of preventing surprise attack
and avoid the "academic analysis" implied by the Western
approach. The Western approach was characterized by words
like "abstract," "arbitrary," "divorced from reality," etc. They
found that, in spite of Western assertions to the contrary, the
"technical" approach was "politically motivated." "The centre of

[39]GEN/SA/PV 3, pp. 6-7.

[40]GEN/SA/PV 4, p. 10.

all your efforts, their role and their purpose, is control, and this control does not concern the physical, chemical or technical peculiarities of existing means and possible means of surprise attack, but their possibility of application. . . . You wish to arrive at control, which you have fixed *a priori* as an objective. . . .This *a priori* attitude has been indicated to you by the instructions of the political direction of the NATO countries. . . . It is to those instructions that you refer, and it is those instructions which you apply as experts." The system of observation and control that the Western powers presented for illustrative purposes "would in itself be not a technical measure but a political measure, because it would have to be decided by some agreement, it would have to be based on agreements of states, and therefore be on a political basis." (sic)[41]

The Westerners said they were qualified and authorized only to carry out "technical studies—that is to say, *studies based on physical and scientific data.*" They were "putting forward a *general methodology* for the guidance of our work, consisting of a methodological analysis of the components to be followed by a gradual development of a constructive synthesis"[42] (emphasis added). The Western representatives described their own method as "scientific," "illustrative," "technical" and "concrete," as opposed to the "political" and "unrealistic" approach of the adversary. Foster claimed that in the Western view "a proposal in the field of disarmament does not become concrete until it is possible to make quantitative judgments concerning its requirements,"[43] and he repeatedly invited the Russians to substantiate their contention that the problem of surprise attack is wholly inseparable from disarmament. He suggested that the contention could be analyzed on an objective basis and that the Western experts had not prejudged this question. This is, however, at some variance with the contention of Dr. Wiesner, who was staff director of the American delegation, that "the terms of reference of the United States delegation specifically restricted our discussion to those measures for preventing surprise attack which did not involve any limitations of weapons, i.e., restrictions in their location, numbers, characteristics, etc. Our delegation was required to support the

[41]GEN/SA/PV 20, pp. 12-13.

[42]GEN/SA/PV 16, pp. 3-4.

[43]GEN/SA/PV 30, p. 27.

position that useful measures to reduce the danger of surprise attack could be devised without any limitations on military weapons."[44] The Western negotiators adopted an approach based on the conviction that technical facts have an objective truth which is acceptable to any rational investigator. They tried to separate the technical and political factors for the purpose of creating a "scientific consensus" on which to build subsequent political agreement. The Russians were, it seems, reluctant to contribute to any such scientific consensus for fear of thus committing by implication the Soviet government in political negotiations. In some sense the Western delegates were asking their Eastern counterparts to participate in the kind of systematic quantitative analysis of the effectiveness and implications of arms control systems which should form the basis of any serious proposal in that field. The Russians, however, were evidently extremely sensitive to the political implications of any technical agreement on facts regarding arms control and were, hence, reluctant to consent to any separation of the two components. This reluctance also became very clear during the experts' conference to study the possibility of detecting nuclear explosions.[45]

In their attempt to extricate the "technical" content of the Eastern positions, the Western negotiators at times came close to voicing quite absurd assertions. One such instance was when they suggested that the proposition that large-scale mobilization and concentration of land forces must precede any major surprise attack was an invalid rendering of the facts.[46] It is possible, of course, that the Easterners gave voice to this contention in order to provide a military rationale for their proposal for ground observation posts and limited zones of aerial photography. It is equally conceivable that the contention was a valid rendering of Soviet strategic thinking. Even granted that Soviet strategic thinking on the role of ground forces in a future war had been

[44]Jerome B. Wiesner, *Where Science and Politics Meet*, McGraw Hill, New York, 1965, p. 184.

[45]For an excellent analysis of these negotiations see Ciro E. Zoppo, *Technical and Political Aspects of Arms Control Negotiation: 1958 Experts' Conference*, RM-3286-ARPA, The RAND Corporation, Santa Monica, Cal., 1962, and also Harold Karan Jacobson and Eric Stein, *Diplomats, Scientists, and Politicians: The United States and the Nuclear Test Ban Negotiations*, University of Michigan Press, Ann Arbor, 1966.

[46]GEN/SA/PV 20, p. 6 and GEN/SA/PV 5, pp. 3-6.

shifting, it was by no means settled, and it was probably a fallacy to assume that the powers automatically adjust their arms control and arms politics. (They undoubtedly should, but that is a different point.) In any case, it is difficult to see how the experts could have come up with any meaningful "objective" answer if the strategic outlooks of the two main adversaries were very different (as I believe they were), since they may both be considered equally rational within the frameworks in which they were conceived.

After the first week of the conference it became quite clear to the Western delegates that the discussions were unlikely to lead to joint explorations. From then on the purpose of the exercise changed. The Western powers tabled their documents for the purpose of providing the Russians with material for thought and an appreciation of the Western position. The deliberations changed into *cognitive negotiations* aimed at exploring the position of the adversary on the vital issue of surprise attack and at conveying the Western thoughts and concerns in that connection. Another consideration was to create a favorable image of the Western position in the records of the conference which would be made availabe as U.N. documents.

The Eastern negotiators were obviously somewhat frustrated by the technical approach of the West and frequently attempted to provoke their adversaries into political exchanges. In some instances they were successful, such as when the Westerners found it necessary to refute the allegations about the aggressive nature of NATO, probably for the sake of the record.[47] The Soviet reaction to the Western approach is illustrated well by the following outburst from Kuznetzov concerning one of the "illustrative papers" that the Western experts had introduced: "There is no subject for *discussion* here, no point of possible *approval* or *disapproval* in this document"[48] (emphasis added).

Negotiating Styles
On occasion, the Russians addressed themselves to the audience outside the conference room as much as to their Western colleagues. This much was openly admitted by Kuznetzov, ". . .irrespective of the name of our conference, irrespective of whether

[47]GEN/SA/PV 22, p. 4 and GEN/SA/PV 25, p. 10.

[48]GEN/SA/PV 15, p. 11.

we term it a political or a technical one, peoples throughout the world expect that our conference will achieve a lessening of international tension and will arrive at practical measures to decrease the possibility of the outbreak of a military conflict between states."[49] This approach was in consonance with the official Soviet view of negotiations with non-communist adversaries. It is no accident that (to use a favorite Chinese phrase) most of the Soviet books on the disarmament negotiations refer to the interactive process as the "struggle (bor'ba) for disarmament." The 1961 party program talks of how the peoples will force the imperialists to accept disarmament. Sir William Hayter has observed the Russians consider it useless to convince the Western interlocutor by rational argument, "what you must do is to weaken his position by the threat or the actual mobilization of a hostile public opinion in his rear, so that he has to make concessions willy-nilly."[50] The authoritative Soviet Dictionary of Diplomacy states one of the diplomatic perspectives of Soviet negotiators quite candidly:

> The diplomacy of the socialist states, which is based on the sympathy and support of the broad masses of people throughout the world, exposes with invariable success the aggressive plans of the imperialist governments and their deceptive diplomatic maneuvers by opening the eyes of the peoples to the real state of affairs (deistvitel'noe polozhenie veshchei). It (the socialist diplomacy) does this from the rostrums of the diplomatic conference, in the official diplomatic statements and documents and in the press. The unmasking of the aggressive plans and actions of the imperialists constitutes one of the most important methods of socialist diplomacy, by means of which it mobilizes democratic public opinion and the masses of people throughout the world against the aggressive policies of the imperialist governments.[51]

The Russians quickly perceived that there would be no real negotiations and agreement at the surprise attack conference, and this realization must have structured their approach to the negotiations. In the Soviet perspective they became to a large extent

[49]GEN/SA/PV 9, p. 16.

[50]Sir William Hayter, *The Diplomacy of the Great Powers*, Macmillan, New York, 1961, p. 30.

[51]*Diplomaticheskij Slovar'*, Vol. II, Politizdat, Moscow, 1962, p. 466.

what George Kennan has termed "demonstrative negotiations," i.e., "those which are for outside effect, and usually with a view to embarassing the other fellow rather than reaching agreement."[52]

Since the styles of the negotiators obviously influence the atmosphere in which they convey their own viewpoints and perceive those of the other side, it seems reasonable to assume that they also influence the perceptions of the substantive issues that are being discussed. This must remain an hypothesis as its verification would require a broad comparative analysis of successful and futile negotiations. For the time being we shall assume that it is correct and thus make some observations in regard to the styles of negotiation as they stand out in the verbatim records of the surprise attack conference.

The Eastern negotiators attributed to their Western interlocutors the motive of attempting to acquire a relative advantage by using measures ostensibly designed to prevent surprise attack to outweigh their own technological inferiority. Thus, Kuznetzov asserted: "One can clearly see that in raising the matter of creating a system of control and inspection over ballistic missiles the Western experts strive to cover up, through such a system, a vulnerable position so far as the United States is concerned."[53] The Soviet negotiators exhibited a great amount of repetitiveness in their argumentation and remained ostensibly unaffected by the Western arguments. The Westerners nevertheless frequently voiced the expectation that they should be able to convince the Easterners by logical argument. ("We hope to demonstrate that our methods are more logical than those which you have adopted and so convince you that our proposed plan of work should be accepted."[54]) They also attempted to convince the adversaries that the Western approach was compatible with the Soviet interests and professed goals: "without prejudging the decisions which should be taken . . . I can state that our work would make easier the solution of the disarmament problem. The organization of an inspection system formulated for the purpose of preventing surprise attack could be expanded, *mutatis mutandis,* to the checking of disarmament measures, which , if our Governments so decided, would take place simultaneously. In any case, pro-

[52]*Disarmament and Foreign Policy,* Hearings, *op. cit.,* p. 1015.

[53]GEN/SA/PV 21, p. 11.

[54]GEN/SA/PV 18, p. 6.

gression in this respect would be greatly facilitated."[55] The Westerners showed considerable eagerness to note even the smallest congruence of positions as an encouraging first base of agreement and extracted any "technical" components in the Soviet position so as to get the discussions going, but the Russians did not accept the "invitations." ("So far we have heard little or nothing from the other side on this topic of communications. Let us by all means jointly embark, whenever you wish, on a detailed examination of the type of communications required. . . ."[56])

In response to the Western proposal that they study the feared contingency of surprise attack, Kuznetzov implied that such an approach was structured by a desire to bring it about. The Easterners frequently showed unwillingness or inability to differentiate between *hypothetical contingencies* warranting concern and study and *intentions* to bring the contingencies about: "Mr. Foster stated that the Conference should study the question 'what. . .are the means with which a modern surprise attack can be launched'— It would seem that the experts from the ten countries have met here not to discuss jointly measures directed at the prevention of a surprise attack but in order to devote their energy to the study of the question of how a surprise attack should be undertaken."[57] "The Western delegations propose that we take up matters which are diametrically opposed to the objective of our Conference."[58] The Eastern delegates seemed to put greater emphasis on the manipulation of verbal symbols than the Westerners, and they invariably prefixed their references to NATO, CENTO, etc., with epithets like "aggressive" and "war-mongering." They showed no inclination, in spite of Western prodding, to support their major contentions with analytical arguments or technical facts: "There will always be sufficient signs to indicate a beginning of the preparation by a state for a surprise attack. The measures outlined in our proposals concerning ground control and aerial photography provide sufficient possibilities of an early discovery

[55]GEN/SA/PV 16, p. 8.

[56]GEN/SA/PV 21, p. 20.

[57]GEN/SA/PV 3, p. 19.

[58]GEN/SA/PV 7, p. 7.

of preparations for a surprise attack,"[59] and that is as far as they found it necessary to go to make their point.

The Western delegates claimed that their proposals constituted a novel and hopeful method for breaking the impasse of arms control negotiations. Kuznetzov refuted this contention by referring to the draft of the Preparatory Commission of the League of Nations:

> When Soviet representatives a quarter of a century ago stated that humanity could not wait permanently, endlessly, the drafting of concrete measures for preventing the danger of war, your colleagues in the League of Nations then said that it was necessary first to carry out a scientific study, to create a detailed listing of all arms . . . Thus in claiming that your method is a new, scientific and objective one, you want to force us to accept this rather old and dangerous path for the world, which has been used by your predecessors in the period between the two World Wars.[60]

While the Western delegates, as noted, conceived of scientific facts as somehow speaking for themselves, Kuznetzov asserted that there would always be need for political judgment. He quoted Foster to the effect that obtaining "proof of the fact that the functions of inspection and control can be effectively fulfilled will facilitate the obtaining of an agreement on the reduction of armaments," and went on to argue that: "There arises the question as to who will determine whether a system is effective or not effective. Whoever wishes not to permit the carrying out of practical measures can always claim that from his point of view the system of inspection and control is still not efficient."[61] Kuznetzov undoubtedly had a point here.

By insisting that the conference consider the "concrete political situation" with the focus on Europe, the Eastern delegates were trying hard to build up an unfavorable image of West Germany as dominated by revenge-seeking militants, and memor-

[59]GEN/SA/PV 19, p. 5.

[60]GEN/SA/PV 21, p. 5.

[61]GEN/SA/PV 21, p. 8.

ies of the Second World War were frequently invoked in support
of the contention.[62]

THE SUBSTANTIVE ISSUES

In spite of the fact that the surprise attack conference produced no agreement or even a common undertaking to explore
the relevant problems, it did bring out some rather fundamental
differences in the approaches of the two sides to the problem of
surprise attack. The Western powers aimed at measures that
could produce a marginal stabilization of mutual deterrence by
the introduction of improved capabilities for warning and reassurance. The Easterners rejected the basic assumptions of this
approach, claiming that only systemic transformations in international relations such as would result from disarmament could
produce the desired stability. In the communist perspective the
control systems proposed by the West would constitute instruments of penetration and intelligence collection. The two sides
had incongruent images of the likely course of a future war, and
they were concerned about different contingencies. We shall
presently examine these divergent persepctives in some detail.

Deterrence, Warning and Disarmament

The Western experts perceived the "solutions" to the problem
of surprise attack in terms of establishing new and better systems
of warning about preparation for attack. Modern armaments
tended to give advantages to an aggressor, and the purpose of the
warning systems would consequently be to "reestablish a balance
between attack and defense. . . .In view of the special danger of
the new armaments a system of warning appears to be the only
means of tipping the balance again in favor of defence."[63]
According to Foster a cooperative system of inspection and observation as explored in the Western working papers would merely
reinforce the existing national warning systems and would thus
add to the mechanisms for assuring retaliation against aggression. "A basic assumption. . . is that aggression can be prevented
by the prospects of retaliation and that this contributes to pre-

[62]GEN/SA/PV 22, pp. 16-17.

[63]GEN/SA/PV 26, p. 7.

serving the peace."[64] On that assumption "a system of warning might. . .prevent or make less likely a deliberate attack by an aggressor able to weigh the consequences of his act."[65] The deterrence implications were spelled out quite succinctly in one of the Western working papers:

> A system which increases the likelihood of early detection of a surprise attack reduces the danger of such attacks. It does so because it reduces the probability of success of a surprise attack. Faced with the increased probability of detection, the aggressor must make a choice between achieving surprise and risking that the attack may be too small to be fully effective. Hence, he is less likely to mount an attack and the danger of surprise attack will be reduced.
>
> Moreover, the earlier and more reliable warning provided by an effective observation and inspection system enables the side receiving the warning to react with a more considered response. Thus, the danger of "pre-emptive" attacks arising from a misinterpretation is reduced. The accrued benefits would be shared by both sides.[66]

The Western experts were also emphasizing the destabilizing interaction processes that might be set off by the mutual fear of surprise attack in tense situations. If each side were to neglect the problem of warning it might be possible for either to carry out a devastating first-strike without the fear of retaliation. "Would not this increase enormously existing distrust and tensions?" asked Foster. "Would not each side wonder what it was risking in leaving itself so exposed? Would there not be grave danger that one side might fear that the other might strike if the only way to be sure of survival were to strike first?"[67] The existence of warning systems would have another stabilizing function in providing reassurance in tense situations that preparations for attack are not undertaken and hence dampen the interaction of mutual

---

[64]GEN/SA/PV 19, p. 12.

[65]*Ibid.*, p. 11.

[66]GEN/SA/6 as reproduced in *Documents on Disarmament . . . , op. cit.*, p. 1264.

[67]GEN/SA/PV 19, p. 12.

fears.[68] Such systems could also reduce the probability of war occurring as a result of accident or miscalculation as they would "offer reassurance that an accident or some other ambiguous event remains an isolated incident."[69] Only the superposition of a statistically significant array of signals from the observers and instruments of surveillance would be taken as evidence of surprise attacks. The establishment of a comprehensive warning system, as outlined in the Western working papers, would also reduce the probability of false alerts by providing the means for a correlation of a large number of individual signals. Thus, false alarms could arise only by "the compounding of an accidental superposition of a large number of independent events."[70] They would therefore not only be improbable, but should also be of short duration. Procedures could also be established so that any of the parties to the arrangement could take rapid remedial action should misunderstandings or accidents occur, so as to prove that their intentions were being misinterpreted by the control system. It was readily admitted that cooperative inspection systems as envisaged by the Western experts could only reduce, and not eliminate, the danger of surprise attack. In the Western view they could, however, also constitute an important infrastructure for a subsequent system of controlled disarmament. By reducing tensions resulting from uncertainty, the Western experts argued, comphrehensive cooperative inspection systems would reduce the incentives for an arms race between the two major groupings of states.

This sophisticated analysis of the intricacies of deterrence found no response with the Eastern experts who proclaimed the "deterrent theory" to be a "political principle" which could "only lead to an increase in the arms race, mutual distrust and to a solution which would bring us to the very 'brink of war.' "[71] It was claimed that the theory was "invented" in order to "defend the nuclear arms race, in order to defend various efforts on the parts of NATO in the direction of widening the circle of states possess-

[68]GEN/SA/PV 12, p. 8.

[69]GEN/SA/PV 19, p. 14.

[70]GEN/SA/PV 23, p. 20.

[71]GEN/SA/PV 24, pp. 9-10.

ing atomic and missile weapons."[72] The Russian General Gryzlov did express, however, a "deterrence through residual uncertainty" point of view that was in direct contradistinction to the analysis of the precariousness of the strategic balance presented by the Western experts. In his view, "Whatever the size of the stockpiles of nuclear weapons possessed by the attacking side, the attacker could not, under modern conditions, count on the complete annihilation of the means of retaliation possessed by the attacked and, thus, he could not be sure that retaliation would not follow."[73]

The Easterners objected to the marginalist approach of their Western interlocutors, contrasting it with the more radical solutions they were advocating. In their view, the systems outlined by the West "would not prevent a surprise attack but would, in the best circumstances, give warning of the fact that such an attack was imminent. We, on the other hand, are trying to obtain an agreement, the aim of which would be an ambitious one but still a real one and, of course, a desirable one—namely, the elimination of the threat of surprise attack at its source by the creation of conditions which would make such an attack impossible."[74] They called upon the Western powers to abandon the use of nuclear and missile weapons, "to put a ban on such weapons and to eliminate them from their arsenals."[75] The Western experts referred on many occasions to the technical infeasibility of inspection to assure the elimination of nuclear weapons and pointed out that this fact was conceded by the Soviet Government in its statement of May 10, 1955. Should the Easterners be in possession of scientific factors which were unknown to the Western experts, they were encouraged to put them forward. But the Eastern experts ignored the objection and chose to categorically deny the validity of the Western argument without discussing its merits. They expressed doubts as to whether the Western arguments "were inspired only by technical considerations or also by the political bias which exists in the policy of the United States and its allies

[72]GEN/SA/PV 21, p. 9.

[73]GEN/SA/PV 19, p. 19.

[74]GEN/SA/PV 9, p. 3.

[75]GEN/SA/PV 21, p. 11.

towards the question of banning nuclear weapons."[76] In fact, General Gryzlov asked: "Have we heard any valid argument against our proposal? On the contrary, we have not. . . .We have not received any valid criticism of the. . .suggestions put forward by the Socialist delegations."[77]

The Western documents presented at the conference contained some quite impressive outlines for a systematic technical evaluation of systems designed to reduce the danger of surprise attack. Thus the first document contained a list of the categories of the principal instruments of surprise attack, their characteristics which are most pertinent to the problem of surveillance and observation, as well as the evidence which might indicate their imminent employment in surprise attack.[78] Subsequent papers outlined various alternative surveillance techniques relevant to aerial, ground and sea inspection. It was suggested that due to the delay in converting photographic, radar, electronic and infrared data to useful information the indications obtained from aerial surveillance would normally contribute only to *strategic warning,* i.e., more long-term warning about preparations for attack. Each of the techniques had associated weaknesses so that a combination seemed desirable. Aerial reconnaissance might be combined with systems of ground inspection. The effectiveness of such systems would be a function of the observers' freedom of movement "within or over the area under observation, and of their rights and privileges." Their effectiveness might be improved through the use of vehicles, small craft or low-performance aircraft and the appropriate sensory and/or recording devices. Observers might be located at missile launching sites, airfields, ports and naval bases, rail, land and inland water transportation networks and centers, ground forces, storage points for missiles or other delivery devices, etc. Acoustic, magnetic or pressure techniques might be applied to detect submerged vessels, but none of them would be able to do so under all circumstances.[79] Special explanatory documents were tabled containing "illustrative out-

[76]GEN/SA/PV 24, p. 12.

[77]GEN/SA/PV 10, pp. 10-11.

[78]GEN/SA/4 reproduced in *Documents on Disarmament . . ., op. cit.,* pp. 1230-43.

[79]GEN/SA/5, *ibid.,* pp. 1244-55.

lines" of systems for observation and inspection of long-range aircraft,[80] ballistic missiles[81] and ground forces.[82] It is rather curious that there was no naval paper. Apparently this issue produced some disagreement among the Western experts, but the navy people had their way. We can only speculate that the reason for the absence of such a paper was connected with the general tradition of "freedom of the seas" and, particularly, with concerns for the vulnerability of naval vessels should they be equipped with inspectors. This objection would be particularly pertinent for Polaris submarines which promised to be a most effective second-strike weapon system. The papers stressed that the values of the systems would depend on the time delay in transmitting and processing the data from the surveillance components. For long-range bombers an average message delay of up to thirty minutes was considered acceptable. It was suggested that the only effective means of guarding against missile attacks would be to place all launch sites under direct observation. The advance warning of intent to fire would be obtained from direct observation of simultaneous launch preparations at many sites. The observers would need an ultra-rapid, extremely reliable communication and data-processing capability. Because of the short flight times of the ballistic missiles the signal delay times should not exceed one minute. The emplacement of a small number of radars properly could, it was suggested, provide "a continuous barrier which would deny surprise to a ballistic missile force being launched." The system as outlined would give complete post-launch warning and a significantly improved pre-launch warning capability. The Western experts concluded that "properly applied observation of ground forces can cumulatively provide long-term warning of surprise attack by such forces." In an obvious response to the Soviet proposal for ground observation posts the Western experts argued that observation of transportation centers could not provide adequate warning *per se,* but that it could perform a useful function as a component of an over-all system. We may observe that what constitutes an *adequate system* is in the final analysis a political decision. While the technical and military analyses may indicate how effective any system would be in performing

[80]GEN/SA/6, *ibid.,* pp. 1255-64.

[81]GEN/SA/9, *ibid.,* pp. 1275-84.

[82]GEN/SA/10, *ibid.,* pp. 1284-97.

its functions, the decision of how much is enough and what risks
one is willing to take is a political one. The Western experts conceded that the comprehensive integrated systems, as outlined,
would constitute very complex organizations. They did not speci-
fy the number of personnel needed, although they intimated that
it would involve thousands, "but probably not tens of thousands
of personnel."[83]

The Western delegates suggested that the Russians had indeed accepted the positive benefits from a warning system by
proposing aerial inspection and surface observation posts, though
not under conditions for implementation which were acceptable
to the West.[84] The Russians insisted on their conditions and made
a quite pertinent objection to the comprehensive systems as envisaged in the Western working papers. In their view they would
be used to secure intelligence data by an aggressor. The observers
would constitute particularly valuable sources of targeting information and thus prejudice the relative invulnerability of the relevant weapon systems. They believed "that a detailed knowledge
of the deployment of the defensive forces would permit the aggressor to eliminate with his first blow a sufficient portion of the
defending forces to make it impossible for the defending side to
inflict a blow in return."[85] The Easterners were thus asserting
that the information obtained from the Western proposed systems would enable the parties to develop an effective first-strike
capability. As mentioned above, the Easterners also suggested
that the data which could be obtained from such warning systems
might tend to accelerate the arms race by determining who was
actually behind in the race. The systems, they feared, would be
used for spying in order to obtain the necessary information about
the field of technology in which one of the parties might be ahead,
for example missiles (sic).[86] The demand for a discussion of
missiles and missile control could, so Kuznetzov asserted, "only
be understood as meaning that an attempt is being made in this
way to obtain necessary information on the subject, particularly
if we bear in mind the fact that certain countries do not occupy

[83]GEN/SA/PV 23, p. 25.

[84]GEN/SA/PV 7, p. 6.

[85]GEN/SA/PV 27, p. 6.

[86]GEN/SA/PV 18, p. 23 and GEN/SA/PV 21, p. 6.

leading positions in the field of missile technology."[87] Thus the conference brought out the general Soviet fear of penetration. It also indicated, however, that the Russians considered secrecy as a kind of military asset. Foster, who had several private conferences with Kuznetzov at Geneva, made the following observation after the conference: ". . .We were much impressed by the importance which Soviet representatives attach to secrecy as a military asset. In effect, they seem to believe it enables them to possess a form of 'hardening' of their bases which we do not have. Thus, they regard any encroachment upon this secrecy as a unilateral disarmament step on their part, which must be compensated for by other measures."[88] The concern for "the principle of non-violation of the sovereign territorial rights of states" made its marked imprint on the Soviet proposal for aerial surveillance. Each air group should photograph the territory of its side with control officers from the adversary. The latter would be prohibited, however, from "transmitting information to the other side unless authorized to do so by the party concerned" (sic).[89]

The Western delegates were conspicuously unresponsive on another issue. They emphasized the increments in warning time which information about preparations for an attack would procure. The Easterners tried on a few occasions to reply that under contemporary conditions very little can be done to provide useful warning about attacks with strategic weapons systems, but the Western experts never discussed whether the increments in warning time would indeed permit the reaching and implementation of decisions regarding countermeasures. The systems indicated in the Western illustrative papers would, of course, be worth the associated costs if it could be reasonably demonstrated that they would in fact contribute to a more rational response in a tense situation. An associated question would ask for a consideration of alternative and possibly better ways of approaching the problem. The Western experts acknowledged by implication that an "Open Skies" plan based on aerial reconnaissance could not provide warning of the kind of attack which worried the Americans, viz., a strike at the U.S. with long-range bombers and ballistic missiles. These weapons systems are maintained in a high state of

[87]GEN/SA/PV 5, p. 14.

[88]*Disarmament and Foreign Policy,* Hearings, *op. cit.,* pp. 62-3.

[89]GEN/SA/PV 28, p. 13.

readiness and, in the words of Albert Wohlstetter, "not even the most advanced reconnaissance equipment can disclose an intention from 40,000 feet."[90] It might provide warning of the movement of Soviet bombers to Arctic staging bases, but presumably such activity patterns were also part of the normal pattern of preparedness practice.

The Image of Future War

It became quite clear that the two parties to the conference were concerned about two different contingencies. The Western Powers focused their attention on the possibility of the deliberate or pre-emptive initiation of central war as a strike out of the blue. The Pearl Harbor analogy was perhaps not accidental, but the concern arose out of the realization of the vulnerability of the American strategic force, particularly vis-à-vis a future Russian attack with intercontinental missiles. The Soviets were addressing themselves to the problems associated with the military confrontation in Central Europe and the alleged danger of inadvertent eruption of hostilities and surprise attacks. They denied that the American concern was valid since extensive detectable preparations would have to precede a major attack.

While the Russians conceded that the danger of surprise attack had increased as a result of the development of nuclear weapons and long-range delivery vehicles, they insisted that *experience* (sic) showed that conventional armaments would play an important role. "No attack, whatever its means, is possible without a previous concentration of armed forces, such concentration calling for movements of troops across railroads, highways, harbors, etc., and this cannot be concealed; the recording of such movements of armed forces makes it possible to detect in advance the preparation of a surprise attack."[91] This assessment provided a rationale for the ground observation posts proposal. The strategic weapons were presented as auxiliary instruments without any "individual significance." Their function was to facilitate the advance of large mass armies. "Thus the preparation for a surprise attack cannot be considered without a corresponding preparation

---

[90]Albert Wohlstetter, The Delicate Balance of Terror, *Foreign Affairs*, 37(2), January 1959, p. 232.

[91]GEN/SA/PV 2, p. 17.

of the land forces."[92] The objective in a future war, in the Eastern view, would still be the occupation of specific geographical areas "as the attempt to gain space is one which is tied to important political and economic considerations and forms the sovereign principle of any offensive activities."[93] In the Western view this image of a future war did not "seem to be anything like an accurate statement in the context of the technological possibilities of the present and of the near future."[94] Mr. Foster could find support in an authority like Khrushchev who had said in a speech on November 15th, "Now it suffices to press but one button and not only airfields and the means of communication of various military staffs, but whole towns will be blown sky high, whole countries will be destroyed."[95] At this time Khrushchev's views were not accepted Soviet strategic doctrine and the debate between the Russian "traditionalists" and the "modernists" was only beginning to crystallize. We may surmise also that there was a discrepancy between the verbal announcements of a somewhat impulsive Khrushchev and his action policy as head of the Soviet Government

Attention should, in the Eastern view, be focused on the areas with the largest concentrations of troops, and on Central Europe in particular. Central Europe had, Kuznetzov asserted, an "abnormal" concentration of armed forces in peacetime, so that "a local incident could provide the spark which could lead to a serious and gigantic military conflict. . . ."[96] The image of inadvertent escalation from a local incident was exacerbated by a prediction of automatic explosion: "such a conflict would see, from the very beginning, the use of the latest types of arms and this would lead to the unleashing of an atomic war."[97] General Gryzlov denied emphatically that any one type of arms can have decisive significance and referred to the erroneous theories of Generals

[92]GEN/SA/PV 15, p. 15.

[93]GEN/SA/PV 18, p. 13.

[94]GEN/SA/PV 5, p. 3.

[95]GEN/SA/PV 19, p. 15.

[96]GEN/SA/PV 18, p. 25.

[97]*Ibid.*

Douhet (bombing) and Guderian (armor).[98] The groundlessness
of the Western contentions was allegedly demonstrated by the experience of the Second World War. That traumatic experience of
all the Eastern countries represented at the conference was frequently brought up in the discussions. It evidently constituted a
genuine frame of reference for the East European leaders besides
being a useful analogy for propaganda purposes. The Polish and
Czech delegates emphasized the location of their countries across
the traditional routes of ground invasions in Europe. In the final
analysis, the Easterners would insist, the problem is not one that
is conditioned by a particular military technology: "You will
doubtless admit that the degree of danger represented by this or
that arm, by this or that instrument, depends in very large measure
upon the hands in which that instrument is found."[99] And the
hands they ostensibly feared were those of the "German revan-
chists." In attempting to adjust to the Eastern frame of reference
the Western experts drew attention to the fact that the German
conception of *Blitzkrieg* would not have evolved unless the dive
bomber and the mechanized military units had reached such an
advanced state of development by 1938. Hence, it should be necessary to concentrate attention on the present-day technological
capabilities in order to contain the danger of surprise attacks,[100]
and the Western experts "felt properly compelled to be mainly
concerned with the possibility of a massive initial attack."[101] Because of the range of modern weapons the possible sources of surprise attack were not, in the Western view, confined to any
particular limited area. The implications pointed in another direction, viz., "that nations must be concerned more with areas far to
the rear of where military forces face each other in close proximity.
Indeed, most of the major instruments of surprise attack are usually located away from such areas of contact."[102]

The Russians proposed that the Powers agree on the establishment of ground observation posts at railway junctions, major
ports and on main roads in the United Kingdom, France, the

[98]GEN/SA/PV 19, p. 19.

[99]GEN/SA/PV 20, p. 22.

[100]GEN/SA/PV 5, p. 4.

[101]GEN/SA/PV 23, p. 15.

[102]GEN/SA/PV 14, p. 11.

Benelux countries, Italy, the two parts of Germany, Czechoslo-vakia, Poland, Hungary, Romania, Bulgaria, Albania, Greece, Turkey, Iran, and in the western frontier zone of the Soviet Union and along the east coast of the United States. Twenty-eight posts should be emplaced on Warsaw Pact territory and fifty-four on NATO and CENTO territory. The basis for the selection of these apparently random numbers was not disclosed. The Western ex-perts declared that they were disturbed to find that the Russians had based their estimate "of the ratio of numbers of control posts on either side of the demarcation line on parameters which to us do not appear to be closely related to the problem."[103] The East-ern experts, furthermore, proposed the establishment of an aerial photography zone in Europe extending 800 km to the east and the west of the demarcation line. It would also cover Greece, Turkey and Iran. Another aerial inspection zone was to be established in the Far East and in the U.S. That zone would include Soviet terri-tory to the east of 180° east and a territory of equivalent size in the U.S. to the west of 90° west, as well as all of Japan including Okinawa.[104] The proposals were tied in with a one-third reduc-tion of foreign troops in Europe and an agreement on denucleari-zation of Germany. We have already referred to the particular demands in connection with the manning and control of the air-borne surveillance system, and the problems of observation posts are not directly relevant to our present concerns in this book.[105] The Western experts had no authority to discuss the acceptability of the Soviet proposal. However, they did point out the inade-quacy of aerial photography as a method of detecting preparations for attack due to, for example, the practical restrictions imposed on the frequency of flights by bad weather. It could be effective only in conjunction with ground inspection, and the small number of fixed observation posts proposed by the Soviets could not, in the Western view, "be regarded as the complement of aerial in-spection."[106] The Soviet proposals and strategic views should

[103]GEN/SA/PV 18, p. 8.

[104]GEN/SA/7 in *Documents on Disarmament . . .* , *op. cit.,* pp. 1264-72.

[105]For an extensive discussion of ground observation systems in Europe, see Johan J. Holst, Fixed Control Posts and European Stability, *Disarmament and Arms Control,* **2**(3), Summer 1964, pp. 262-91.

[106]GEN/SA/PV 17, p. 15.

have come as no surprise to the Western experts as they had been outlined in an article in a prominent Soviet journal by Major-General N. Talenskii in August and circulated at The RAND Corporation in English translation in September.[107]

War by Accident?

As it became obvious that there would be no negotiations as envisaged by the Easterners, they invoked the question of the U.S. airborne alert system and introduced a draft recommendation according to which the conference would recommend that the Governments represented at the Conference "undertake not to carry out flights of aircraft with atomic ánd hydrogen weapons over the territories of foreign states and over the open seas."[108]

Kuznetzov designed a hypothetical scenario involving the U.S. flights along the lines of Gromyko's performance in the Security Council. He asserted that it was impossible to ignore that the American actions raised "the danger of unleashing an atomic war as a result of simple chance, without specific intent. . .a technical defect in an aircraft, a bad arrangement of the nuclear bomb, an error by the airmen."[109] He emphasized the danger arising from the psychological tension of the air crews who might also commit navigational errors and accidentally violate Soviet air space. It was the human amplifier who, in the Soviet view, could cause disaster with the modern weapon system. War might arise as a result of miscalculation, wrong interpretation of intentions and technical errors.

The Soviet proposal provided another opportunity for the Westerners to "explain" the nature of the American system. It was pointed out that portions of the long-range bomber force conducted periodic training flights to and from bases in other countries. On these training flights the bombers would operate in strict compliance with international flight traffic rules, including the acquisition of prior clearance and approval by the relevant air traffic authorities. The one-third of SAC which was maintained in alert posture was on the ground ready for instant take-off. After take-

[107]On the Prevention of Surprise Attack, *Mezdunarodnaya Zhizn* (8) 1958, pp. 68-71, translated by Oleg Hoefding for The RAND Corporation in T-95, September 10, 1958.

[108]GEN/SA/3 in *Documents on Disarmament . . .* , *op. cit.,* p. 1227.

[109]GEN/SA/PV 7, p. 14.

off the bombers would remain under positive control and could only be committed to action when positive decisions had been communicated from the responsible authority. In the absence of such an order the force would return and land.[110] The Western experts also described the security mechanisms installed to prevent a nuclear explosion as the result of the accidental dropping of a bomb, an airplane crash or a fire. The exposition was meant to demonstrate that the "probability that a detonation of the conventional high explosive, if indeed any such occurs, would lead to a nuclear explosion is so remote as to be negligible."[111] The Easterners did not contest the technical facts presented but remained ostensibly unconvinced.

SOME CONCLUSIONS

The conference had its last meeting on December 18 when it adjourned *sine diem*. It has not reconvened since. The report submitted to the United Nations stated that the meetings had been helpful "in clarifying for each side the views of the other side."[112] The parties also expressed their hopes that the discussions would be resumed as early as possible. In a note from the Soviet Foreign Ministry of January 10, 1959, it was proposed that the conference resume its work on January 15, but it stressed that the Soviet position on the substance of the problem of surprise attack remained unchanged.[113] The American reply noted that the experts had been operating under two different terms of reference "and that this difference was preventing the type of joint technical analysis that would give real meaning to the discussions." In the American view it would not be useful to resume the discussions until those differences had been resolved.[114] The conference remains adjourned.

It seemed useful to examine the last round of strategic force negotiations for purposes of identifying some of the issues which

[110]GEN/SA/PV 11, pp. 22-3.

[111]GEN/SA/PV 13, p. 12.

[112]GEN/SA/15 in UN DOCA/4078/S/4145, p. 3.

[113]*Documents on Disarmament* . . . , *op. cit.*, pp. 1335-37.

[114]*Ibid.*, p. 1337.

may arise also in the next set of talks. While I believe an examination of this brief encounter has intrinsic interest, the reasons for
including the essay in this volume are predicated on the assumption that the analysis may suggest useful and interesting analogies
for those interested in the forthcoming SALT exercise. We
should, of course, note that the examination of one set of negotiations yields very little predictive insight about the likely course of
future negotiations. However, we may learn about some of the
relevant questions to ask, discover some useful analogies, and beware of some of the pitfalls that should be avoided.

It is clear that the Western experts labored under some very
restrictive terms of reference, being authorized to discuss only
the technical aspects of the surprise attack problem. The issue of
force reductions was specifically ruled out as a matter for negotiation. They tried to make a concession to the Soviet view that
measures to prevent surprise attack could only be considered in
connection with concrete steps of disarmament by including within the third section of their prepared plan of work an evaluation of
the implications of various changes in the force levels for the efficacy of the control systems. The Easterners were, however, not
interested in theoretical examinations which in their view could
only serve as a trap that would prejudice any subsequent political
deliberations. They talked, at least, as if they were not only unwilling but, in a basic sense, also unable to partake in cognitive discussions divorced from any specific target or endpoint in terms of
an agreement. We have suggested earlier that this attitude may be
due to a strong legalistic tradition as well as to unfamiliarity with
the concept of talking at the diplomatic level for the sole purpose
of examining a problem. Soviet statements about SALT suggest
that Moscow will again insist that the negotiations be aimed at
producing an agreement involving force reductions. It is in this
context that the existence of a fairly effective missile defense option may improve the chances of some understanding by making
the uncertainties about compliance more tolerable and by providing a means for restructuring the central war postures of the
superpowers away from sole reliance on assured destruction in
favor of greater defensive emphasis. The idea that active defenses
may serve useful arms control functions is not so novel as the present deterrence theorists often assume. It was, for example, an
important component in the arguments of those who argued in
favor of a substantial U.S. effort on active air defense in the early
fifties. Robert Oppenheimer wrote at the time:

A more effective defense could even be of great relevance should the time come for serious discussion of the regulation of armaments. There will have been by then a vast accumulation of materials for atomic weapons and a troublesome margin of uncertainty with regard to its accounting—very troublesome indeed if we still live with vestiges of the suspicion, hostility, and secretiveness of the world of today. This will call for a very broad and robust regulation of armaments, in which existing forces and weapons are of a wholly different order from those required for the destruction of one great nation by another, in which steps of evasion will be either far too vast to conceal or far too small to have, in view of then existing measures of defense, a decisive strategic effect. Defense and regulation may thus be necessary complements. And here, too, all that we do effectively to contribute to our own immunity will be helpful in giving us some measure of an increased freedom of action.[115]

At the surprise attack conference the parties focused on different contingencies and had dissimilar images of the central war problem. The basic attitudes toward the substantive problem did inevitably influence the perceptions of the relevance and implications of the various technical factors involved. We should note here that, at least until quite recently, Soviet and American perceptions of the impact of missile defenses on deterrence and arms control were as far apart as were the views on how a general war could get started in 1958. Great discrepancies over such a central issue as the value of missile defense are likely to constitute a serious obstacle to concerted efforts at managing the strategic arms race. We have suggested several places in this volume that it may be the Westerners who are in need of some education by the Russians on this issue. Assuming that Moscow will adhere to its view that active defenses are not inconsistent with international stability and a prudent national defense policy, it is possible that SALT may act as an extra incentive for some doctrinal revision in the United States away from stark deterrence and in the direction of greater defensive emphasis. In such a perspective the SALT exercise may turn out to have as important (and, I would argue, as welcome) an impact on American thinking about the strategic

[115]J. Robert Oppenheimer, Atomic Weapons and American Policy, published in the *Bulletin of the Atomic Scientists* in July 1953, and reprinted in Morton Grodzins & Eugene Rabinowitch (eds.), *The Atomic Age: Scientists in National and World Affairs,* Simon and Schuster, New York, 1963. Quote from paperback edition 1965, pp. 195-6.

implications of BMD as did the 1958 talks and, particularly, the preparation for the talks, on the assessment of the implications of ICBM technology and the impact of vulnerable forces on international stability.

For there is a sense in which the 1958 talks were a splendid success. They did serve as a catalyst for much of the serious rethinking of arms control and stabilized deterrence which took place in the U.S. between 1959 and 1961. We do not know what impact the talks had on the Russian assessment of their own predicament, but some of the "improvements" in the Soviet posture are undoubtedly related to the dialogue with the West, and, as far as strategic force postures are concerned, the 1958 conference was a major turning point in that continuous dialogue. While the process of reasonable discussion as a management tool seems alien to the Soviet political culture and diplomatic practice, it is entirely possible that even the occasional formal, and ostensibly "unsuccessful," discussion may have a constructive effect on the continuous dialogue on strategic issues between the two superpowers. It is possible that the process of tacit coordination may be facilitated should the two superpowers agree on an institutionalization of the dialogue. Such a decision also could be important for purposes of decoupling the management of the arms race from oscillations in the political competition between East and West.

It is useful to note that there is a very explicit substantive analogy between the 1958 talks and SALT. The problem of protecting the invulnerability of the deterrent forces so as not to impose upon international society the burden of pre-emptive instability on the strategic nuclear level was dominant in the Western approach to the 1958 talks. Improvements in ICBM accuracies and the concomitant introduction of MIRV's, producing attack ratios which are potentially favorable to the attacker, have now brought us full circle to the concerns of eleven years ago. The deployment of hardpoint BMD for protection of the offensive forces may in this context be viewed as a stabilizing arms control measure. However, redundant BMD systems with both area and point defense capabilities are likely to force a much more basic reconsideration of the role of active defense in general. Hence, the SALT exercise seems unlikely to be confined to the issue of stabilizing offensive deterrents which was the way the Western experts attempted to limit the talks in 1958. The whole structure of the Soviet-American strategic balance may have to be reexamined.

The outlines of comprehensive inspection and control systems during the 1958 conference did challenge the very fundamental role of secrecy in Soviet society and cast an ominous shadow of "imperialist penetration." It would also, in the Russian view, prejudice the relative invulnerability of the Soviet forces. It is generally assumed that any likely agreement on force freeze or force reductions would now be monitored unilaterally by high altitude (satellite) photography and we should note that BMD may constitute a measure of insurance against the uncertainties about compliance.

At the conference in 1958 the Westerners attempted in vain to separate the technical from the political issues. It is a serious methodological question whether the technical components of a problem such as surprise attack can be isolated from the rest and elaborated separately. Certainly the implications of empirical data may be subject to discussion and different evaluations, as the interpretations are likely to be influenced by an array of facts, interests, attitudes, ambitions, prejudices, etc. This is even more true when it comes to deciding on what facts are relevant. There can be no objective yardstick for such selection. The Russians were, as we have noted, unwilling to concede any separation of the political from the other components of the arms control problem. According to George Kennan there is no "question of any importance in international relations which is not viewed by the Soviet leaders as being political in nature, and looked at by them from a political standpoint. So that even if we attempt to treat questions as technical questions, they will treat them as political ones."[116] This insight is clearly relevant to the preparation for the forthcoming SALT exercise between the two superpowers.

Finally, the 1958 talks suggest the importance of thorough preparations for high-level diplomatic consideration of strategic arms control issues. We shall not pass judgment on the speed— often criticized for being too slow—with which the Nixon Administration has moved towards strategic arms talks with Moscow. In the case of the surprise attack talks, the technical staff of the U.S. delegation had only three or four weeks to prepare for the conference, although a small inter-agency group had worked for six weeks before. According to Jerome Wiesner, "It was able to obtain only the meagrest record of work done in previous years

---

[116]*Disarmament and Foreign Policy,* Hearings, *op. cit.,* p. 1024.

and most of it was of little value."[117] One gets the impression that the forthcoming strategic arms talks have undergone more thorough preparations in Washington than possibly any previous arms control negotiations. This is as it should be, for SALT could very well turn out to be the most important of the arms control talks of the nuclear age.

[117]Jerome B. Wiesner, *op. cit.,* p. 184.

Chapter 13

THE MISSILE DEFENSE DEBATE
IN PERSPECTIVE

by Herman Kahn

THE PUBLICATION of the present volume raises an important institutional issue. The Hudson Institute, as an institute,
does not normally take a position on public issues, and it is not
taking one on the ABM debate. Yet it seems likely that despite
this general disclaimer, the mere fact that this book consists of
articles from nine members of the Hudson Institute staff, or
Fellow Members of the Institute, all more or less on the pro-ABM
side of the house, is likely to be taken by many as indicating an
institutional position—a position actually unrepresentative of
our members as a whole. This situation does not arise when an
Institute book is written by one or two staff members (even if one
of the authors is the Director, since we have long taken the position that the Director has the same rights as any other member of
the staff, at least with regard to matters of publication). I should
thus like to reiterate the point that this book does not represent
my concept of a thoroughly balanced discussion, nor does it express a consensus on ABM within the Institute.

I do regard the discussion in this book as a reasonable and
useful attempt to redress what has become a rather one-sided
public discussion. Indeed many who favor ABM would agree that
there is a lack of balance in the present public debate. Thus to the
extent that this book does constitute advocacy, it may supply
a needed balance.

Why has the public debate been so one-sided? I should judge
that about ninety per cent of the scientists who normally speak in
public, or who consult part-time for the government on defense
issues, as well as the vast preponderance of the public literature
on the subject, opposed ABM. So overwhelming a judgment

might be taken as reflecting an intrinsic weakness in the case for
ABM. But I would also argue that the very magnitude of the
phenomena indicates we are dealing with an issue in which fashion, bias, and/or selection is playing a crucial role. I also suspect
that we are dealing with a phenomenon which goes beyond the
public reaction against the Vietnamese War, or a normal swing of
the public pendulum away from a too one-sided reliance on, and
deference to, military and government in recent years.

I list below twelve trends or vogues which seem to me likely
to influence in important ways the political "milieu" in which
government and defense planning and operations will take place
during the next decade or so. (This new milieu seems to me to be
important and I shall refer to it as the "New Political Milieu.")

1. *An eight or nine hundred-year secular trend,* in the
West, towards a sensate culture emphasizing cosmopolitan,
humanistic, anti-militaristic, anti-nationalistic, intellectual, rela-
tivistic, scientific, rationalistic, manipulative, secular, and hedon-
istic values—*and soon the onset of the post-industrial culture.*
(We should also note that in the "secure areas" of the West this
tendency is likely to be overwhelming for at least the intellectuals
and or/the upper and upper-middle classes.)

2. A revival in the West of the *post-World War I reaction*
against nationalism and its symbols and agencies, including government, militarism, military and governmental bureaucracies,
etc.—and of the similar but lesser post-World War II reaction in
much of continental Europe.

3. *A current reaction* (as exemplified by the New Left, but
substantially more general in scope than just this group) against
*modern science: technology, economic and administrative effi-
ciency, and governmental bureaucracies.* (As one graduate student recently put it, "Despite the publicity about the 'Death of
God' it is really Science which is dead—or at least has lost its
central prestige and authority.")

4. *A crisis of liberalism* which is characterized, among
other things, by a reaction against individualism and rationalism,
a rebellion against domination by groups oriented to bourgeois
values, manipulative rationality, economic and material efficien-
cy, and such "classical goals" as economic growth, national
security, and/or the values of various establishment, governmental, business, and other private interest groups.

5. *Increasing role of the intellectual* with a concomitant tendency toward removal of "irrational" taboos and charismas, and toward a questioning of all traditional claims, facts, assumptions, and loyalties, as well as an emphasis on the new and a rejection of the old merely because it is old—in particular, a growing rejection among younger intellectuals of the "conventional wisdom."

6. A continuing and perhaps increasing reaction, both domestic and foreign, *against the United States Government,* which is in part an inevitable result of allies' cutting their post-World War II dependent ties with the United States, but which has been sharply exacerbated by the Bay of Pigs, the U-2 incident, various revelations about the CIA, the Pueblo incident, a general reaction against "Americanization" (whether cultural, economic or political), and, above all, the Vietnam war.

7. *Rising expectations* (internally among the lower income groups and externally the less developed countries) and a *lower tolerance* by intellectuals and upper classes generally of the existence of "irrational," "indefensible," and "unjust" inequities—complicated in many nations by upper and upper-middle class *"guilt complexes" and anti-anti-left ideologies.*

8. *Generation gap*—in part resulting from the affluent classes' tendency to raise their children in an extremely permissive, gratification-oriented, passive, overstimulated, "now!" environment that contrasts markedly with "the Puritan ethic," as well as the depression and World War II milieu in which the current 40 to 50-year old "governing class" was raised.

9. In the United States *a spotlight on*—and start of—the resolution of such *"societal failures"* as Negro aspirations, persistent poverty, pollution, urban difficulties of various sorts, tending to cause an overemphasis on these issues, *unrealistic expectations and subsequent frustration, disillusionment, and/or alienation.*

10. *Alienation of many upper and upper-middle class youth* —in part stimulated by the seeming apathy or callousness of older generations toward various unresolved issues (such as 7-9 above); in part an anarchist-like reaction against bureaucracy and "the system," which often may be simply an extreme version of the first six trends, in part a more or less normal cutting of adult apron-strings—a cutting that now, as always, leads to at least a few dramatic and usually temporary excesses, but that, in the cur-

rent milieu, also seems likely to result in some relatively long-lived and rather eclectic sets of extremist reactions.

11.   *Effects of new news media,* such as television (and of mass media generally), on the reporting of governmental force or violence—both internal and external.

12.   *General decline in reputation and in prestige of armed forces and governing establishments in general*—and of the U.S. Armed Forces and U.S. governing establishment in particular.

It would make a fascinating exercise to discuss and elaborate on the New Political Milieu—from whence it comes, what it means, and what its various effects are likely to be, but I shall only touch on a few of these issues—in particular, some of those which seem to me to have dominated the ABM debate. In doing so, I will have an opportunity to discuss some basic arguments or motives for the anti-ABM school which have not been touched on sufficiently in this book.

Presenting the above list is, of course, a rather unfair debating stratagem—to ignore arguments but look for motives, biases and ideologies instead. And, of course, it is important to emphasize that to some degree it is the actual current situation—political, emotional, and substantive—which determines attitudes and not general trends and vogues. Thus, it is reasonable that in the midst of a cold war (which followed a hot war) that military requests were given the utmost consideration. It seems equally reasonable that in a period of detente and relative international stability—and in the midst of an unpopular war—that there should be a swing of the pendulum—perhaps an excessive swing, and that, as a result, military requests should be much more carefully scrutinized and that this would occur in almost any political milieu. Thus, it can be argued that the present American mood of hostility towards the military reflects the existence of an unpopular war much more than it does any factors of deep or enduring estrangement between the American people and the military forces—or even between the American upper and upper-middle class and the military. Many would argue that the present situation is almost wholly dependent on current conditions and current alternatives, rather than any basic change in the structure of our society or its value systems.

One might also argue that my list above places emphasis on the wrong issues. It is perfectly possible for people in a secular, cosmopolitan, humanistic society to be heroic in the defense of the values which they treasure. I would agree. But I would also point out that people in such a society still tend towards a kind of animosity towards militarism and military values. I would also argue that the current and widespread apprehension that the government (and the military) cannot be trusted, and cannot be relied upon to exercise any discretionary or secret powers they possess with due restraint or with proper regard for humanist, prudential, or liberal values, is as much a product of the New Political Milieu as of the actual record of the immediate past, though specific events of the recent past clearly have contributed greatly.

In any case, arguments about immediate causes aside, I would argue from the above list that the current and recent hostility towards the military will not be transitory, that it feeds on and is supported by a political milieu that will endure, and that there will in the future be substantially growing estrangement between the Pentagon and the "liberal progressive establishment" and, thus, a generally more hostile atmosphere in the United States towards the military and its supporting organizations—perhaps greater than that which existed in this country between 1920 and 1940.

For many Americans, an inward turn, a new focus on the domestic problems of the United States, has come to seem overwhelmingly important. The proposed ABM has come to stand as the symbol of all of the "silly," "stupid," "immoral," "unnecessary," or "impractical" international and defense considerations and projects that have diverted the attention of the United States from urgent and crucial domestic issues. The obvious argument that the proposed ABM would represent about one-fiftieth of our defense budget is judged irrelevant. ABM is what is being proposed at the moment and, therefore, it is where the cutting should start. They feel that even if money could better be saved in some other part of the defense budget, it is not likely to be saved there. ABM is where public and government attention is focused at the moment. And very important to many of these people is the concept of an actual or symbolic political victory over the "forces of reaction" or the "forces of darkness." ABM is a battlefield on which they can rout or weaken important opposition forces and strengthen and rally their own forces of reform, sanity, progress and peace.

I mentioned earlier that the vast majority of the scientists who consult part-time for the government seem to be against ABM. One can, however, also note that the vast majority of full-time defense planners and analysts as well as defense scientists seem generally to favor ABM. One usual explanation for this difference is that the part-time consultants are objective since they come largely from the universities and owe their basic loyalty to the values of Academia, while the full-time staffs have been "bought" —either consciously or unconsciously. Another explanation, and one that is somewhat more attractive to the full-time defense planners, is that the first group really are amateurs or laymen while the second are serious professionals. A third, and I think, more plausible explanation, is that both groups are expressing nothing more complicated than what might be considered to be simple communal biases and attitudes, with fairly little relationship to serious or objective analyses. The first group does owe its loyalties to Academia, and Academia more than anywhere else seems committed to the "New Political Milieu" discussed above. The full-time defense planners are very much apart from this new milieu and at the same time take defense issues quite seriously. Under these circumstances it hardly is surprising that there should be such an extreme difference of opinion between the two groups.

Perhaps the most important motive for opposing ABM— mentioned a number of times in this book, but perhaps not emphasized enough—is the simple but overwhelming desire to call a halt to the arms race. It is often difficult for those who are not deeply concerned about the arms race to understand how deeply concerned with this issue many of us are. I recently published a book, *The Year 2000,* which included the following list describing what the arms race situation might be at the end of the century:

1. As a result of ordinary improvement and development, simple nuclear-armed, long-range vehicles which are very inexpensive and available to even very small powers. Any of the largest powers and many smaller ones should be able to obtain and maintain, say, 500 missiles with, say, current "Minuteman capability" or better for one or two billion dollars procurement cost or less and a few hundred million dollars annual upkeep (1965 dollars).

2. More or less widely available technology:
   New kinds of nuclear weapons
      various kinds of laser or other "death rays"
   A menu of techniques for effective chemical and/or biological warfare in various applications
   New kinds of ballistic missile defense particularly effective against relatively small offense forces or against forces which use unsophisticated technology and/or tactics

Similar developments for air defense against air-borne threats

Well-understood doomsday machines (or near-doomsday machines)

Tsunami (tidal wave) producers

Climate changers, earth scorchers, or others ways to modify or damage the environment on a large scale

New forms of psychological, or even direct mental warfare

The invention of a "nuclear six-gun" technology—or at least the development of inexpensive and widely available versions of the nuclear weapons and other weapons of mass destruction character-istic of the military technologies of the mid- and late twentieth century.

3. Depending on the defenses of the large powers and the superpowers (and other "technical and tactical de-tails"), these weapons systems may prove to be "equali-zers" in the Gallois or "American West" sense, or they may allow for a definite hierarchy of powers. Some of these systems, and certainly much of the technology behind them, might also be relatively available to pri-vate individuals or at least private organizations and extremist political factions.

4. The development of very effective techniques for counterinsurgency warfare—and perhaps for insur-gency and/or terroristic activities as well. The latter could allow even relatively small groups, if not effec-tively opposed, to disrupt, easily and effectively, al-most any society. Yet much of the new technology—with the possible reinforcement of onerous social controls—might also make such insurgency or terror-ism difficult or limit its effectiveness.

I have often used this list in my lectures to make clear to my audience why so many in the United States Government, and so many government advisors and consultants, are preoccupied—al-most to the point of fanaticism—with the need to stop the arms race. If the audience, after examining and discussing this list, does not share this concern, I simply make the list longer and more dreadful until they do. (I have always found it possible to make them concerned.)

If one has the sense that it really is quite impossible for hu-mans to live with this list of horrors, and that it, therefore, is absolutely essential to stop the arms race long before the end of the century, and if one also has an instinctive sense that an automatic and naked balance of terror may be *the optimal arms control arrangement* (perhaps short of total disarmament and/or world government), then it is very easy to bitterly oppose any ABM deployment. In addition, if one does not take seriously certain national security problems—particularly if one feels there is no need to worry about the details of an arms control agreement so long as it is in the direction of disarmament, control, and limitation—then it would seem quite reasonable that the current arms situation is exactly the right place to draw a line—to call a halt—and the sooner the better. Indeed, to many people, "now" and "right here" is almost always exactly the right time and place to stop. Any attempt to add to the American military deployment or to make any kind of qualitative change in the arms situation will then automatically be judged as exactly the wrong thing to do—especially since the individuals who hold this view almost invariably will feel that changes are likely in practice to be used as an argument against current arms control negotiations or have the effect of reducing the public sense of urgency or need for arms control.

From this point of view, and if one simply does not trust the U.S. Government to make reasonable judgments except in the starkest, black and white situations, then only the simplest kinds of solutions can be made feasible and only the simplest types of arguments will be heard. Under these circumstances a stark and naked balance of terror may become, perhaps, the only feasible policy. But even then, from the viewpoint of arms control, it is likely to falter because the Russians may simply be unwilling to accept an unqualified balance of terror. If this is so, it is not likely to be politically feasible for a one-sided ABM deployment in the Soviet Union to be combined with bilateral offensive arms control agreements to make a combination which will pass in the U.S. Congress. Thus, even if one sympathizes with one aspect or another of the arguments against ABM, it does not seem to me reasonable to think that this really makes a practical—much less the only feasible—arms control policy.

Yet for many reasons, analytical and emotional, political and strategic, technological and diplomatic, it seems to many Americans that ABM is the right place at which to stop the arms race. And, in fact, the professional analysis of the current technological and strategic situation can produce a good case for forestalling new innovations—particularly so dramatic an innovation as ABM defense. Even if the present situation were not really perfect for an arms halt, we can certainly argue persuasively that it is not likely, soon, to be so nearly perfect again. Thus, many arms controllers argue that to let this opportunity pass would be a crime.

There certainly is a real value in stopping the arms race at a point where we think we understand the situation well enough to understand the consequences and significance of various agreements. It is then possible to negotiate with relative confidence. Thus, one can argue that even if we were not at a point in the arms race in which the technological, strategic, emotional, political, diplomatic, and other factors were so favorable to a halt, but we did have a real understanding of the situation, then it might be worthwhile to freeze at that point. While a later point might, in theory, be better for one reason or another, it might not be understood early enough that it was better. It seems to take about five to ten years to really understand these situations, and perhaps five, ten, or more years to complete negotiations. From the practical point of view, then, if we do not stop now, when so many factors seem propitious, when will we stop?

The major answer that a proponent of an appropriate ABM deployment can offer to these arguments is that such a deployment can help to achieve almost all of the objectively constructive goals suggested, and that the absence of the suggested ABM deployment would hurt the achievement of these goals. It would greatly and appropriately help the cause of the proponents of ABM if ABM were generally perceived (and presented) as a shield designed to facilitate both current arms control negotiations and, eventually, comprehensive and lasting arms control measures. It is important for the two objectives to be pursued in parallel and jointly. (From this point of view, statements that ABM is dismantlable on a reciprocal basis with the Soviet Union are probably not helpful.)

I should add, in conclusion, that even if the case against ABM is put rather emotionally, this does not itself make it wrong. From the political point of view, having emotional steam behind a point of view is part and parcel of its political practicality. Thus, today's widespread war weariness, all kinds of emotional reactions against defense issues and defense complexities, the growing dismay on the part of academics, of liberals generally, of Congress, and even of relatively conservative Americans with "military solutions" and the so-called "military-industrial complex," provide good reasons for advancing arms control proposals while, so to speak, the iron is hot. By the same token, rational discussion of the issues can cool off the debate and thus weaken "valuable" political pressures. There is a general impression that the military have had things much too much their own way for the last thirty years or so, and that it is time for the pendulum to swing back. Here again the anti-ABM groups argue that even if this pendulum is not on an exactly perfect course, the general impact of even emotional criticism can only be helpful in correcting all kinds of bad habits, attitudes and emphases which have been built up in our national life.

I would certainly concede that those opposed to ABM have the right to take advantage of the current state of public emotions and frustrations. But I would add that this may also be a dangerous and counterproductive option. It seems likely to me that what I think of as illusioned thinking is going to grow in the United States. And I suspect, particularly if the New Political Milieu I have described proves to be as persistent and influential as I fear, that it will be increasingly difficult to maintain rational and useful discourse on national defense issues. Thus, for many of the same reasons that those who believe that they represent the forces of "peace, progress, reform, sanity, and rationality" wish to inflict a stinging defeat to their opponents generally, and to "militarism" specifically, I would argue that a triumph of reasonableness and rational discourse in the ABM debate might have a significance out of all proportion to the issues being considered.

In many ways, the ABM debate has been grossly overemphasized as an issue, but this probably makes it more important rather than less important that it be decided reasonably, and that its decision represent a victory for those in our society who are attempting to apply rational and dispassionate criteria to these issues. The ABM debate by itself and the decision on ABM are not likely to prove the cataclysmic turning points that so much other discussion seems to indicate. But I myself would feel deep concern if the debate grows still more emotional and irrational. These decisions—and the process by which they are made—are important enough so that any improvement in the debate and clarification of the issues (particularly of neglected but important issues) must prove useful. I hope the present book will prove helpful in clarifying the important policy issues involved.

BIBLIOGRAPHY

THE FOLLOWING bibliography lists some of the most important contributions to the debate of the missile defense issue. For the readers of the present volume who are interested in studying the arguments against missile defense we have marked the contributions which oppose the deployment of missile defenses with an asterisk (*). Publications containing contributions by opponents as well as proponents are marked with a dagger (†). We have included also the most important Congressional documents pertaining to the missile defense controversy.

Adams, Benson D., McNamara's ABM Policy, 1961-67, *Orbis,* 12 (1) 1968, 200-25.

American Security Council, *The ABM and the Changed Strategic Military Balance: U.S.S.R. vs. U.S.A.,* Washington, D.C., 1969, 60 pp.

Bergman, Jules, If Zeus Fails, Can Sprint Save U.S.?, *The New York Times Magazine,* March 20, 1966.

*Bethe, Hans, The ABM, China and the Arms Race, *Bulletin of the Atomic Scientists,* 25(5) 1969, 41-4.

*Bethe, Hans, Hard Point vs. City Defense, *Bulletin of the Atomic Scientists,* 25(6) 1969, 25-6.

Boehm, George A., Countdown for Nike-X, *Fortune,* 72 (5) 1965, 133-7, 192-200.

Brennan, Donald G., New Thoughts on Missile Defense, *Bulletin of the Atomic Scientists,* 23 (6) 1967, 10-15.

Brennan, Donald G., Missile Defense and Arms Control, *Disarmament,* #14, 1967, 1-4.

Brennan, Donald G., Post Deployment Policy Issues in Ballistic Missile Defence; D.G. Brennan & Johan J. Holst, Ballistic Missile Defence: Two Views, *Adelphi Papers* #43, 1-23.

†Brennan, Donald G.; Robert Strausz-Hope; Jerome B. Wiesner and Adam Yarmolinsky, The Great Nuclear Debate: Parity vs. Superiority, *War/Peace Report,* 8 (10) 1968, 3-10.

Brennan, Donald G., A Start on Strategic Stabilization, *Bulletin of the Atomic Scientists,* 25 (1) 1969, 35-6.

Brennan, Donald G., The Case for Missile Defense, *Foreign Affairs,* 43 (3) April 1969, 433-48.

Brown, Harold, Security Through Limitations, *Foreign Affairs,* 43 (3) April 1969, 422-32.

†Center for the Study of Democratic Institutions, *Anti-Ballistic Missile: Yes or No?,* Hill & Wang, New York, 1969, 147 pp.

*Chayes, Abram & Jerome B. Wiesner (eds.), *ABM: An Evaluation of the Decision to Deploy an Antiballistic Missile System,* Harper & Row, New York, 1969, 282 pp.

*Coffey, Joseph I., Chinese and Ballistic Missile Defense, *Bulletin of the Atomic Scientists,* 21 (10) 1965, 17-19.

*Coffey, Joseph I., The Anti-Ballistic Missile Debate, *Foreign Affairs,* 45 (3) April 1967, 403-13.

*Coffey, Joseph I., BMD Option: A Critical Appraisal-Arms Control and Ballistic Missile Defenses, in James E. Dougherty and J.F. Lehman, Jr. (eds.), *Arms Control for the Late Sixties,* D. Van Nostrand, Princeton, N.J., 1967, 69-79.

Coffey, Joseph I., Soviet ABM Policy: The Implications for the West, *International Affairs,* 45 (2) 1969, 205-22.

Crane, Robert D., Soviet Military Policy During the Era of Ballistic Missile Defense, in Denis Dirscherl, S.J. (ed.) *The New Russia,* Pflaum Press, Dayton, Ohio, 1968, 157-70.

Davis, Paul C., The Coming Chinese Nuclear Threat and U.S. Sea-Based ABM Options, *Orbis,* 11 (1) 1967, 45-66.

Davis, Paul C., Sentinel and the Future of SABMIS, *Military Review,* 48 (3) 1968, 56-66.

Dyson, Freeman J., Defense Against Ballistic Missiles, *Bulletin of the Atomic Scientists,* 20 (6) 1964, 12-18.

Dyson, Freeman J., A Case for Missile Defense, *Bulletin of the Atomic Scientists,* 25 (4) 1969. 31-4.

Erickson, John, The Fly in Outer Space: The Soviet Union and the Anti-Ballistic Missile, *The World Today,* 23 (3) 1967, 106-14.·

Fink, Daniel J., Strategic Warfare, *Science and Technology,* (82) October 1968, 54-68.

*Forbes, Allen, *ABM: Point of No Return? A Critique of the Nike-X Anti-Ballistic Missile System,* Council for a Livable World, Washington, D.C., 1967, 28 pp.

Foster, Richard B., The Impact of Ballistic Missile Defense on Arms Control Prospects, in Dougherty and Lehman (eds.), *Arms Control for the Late Sixties, op. cit.,* 80-92.

*Foster, William C., Prospects for Arms Control, *Foreign Affairs,* 47 (3) April 1969, 413-21.

Frank, Lewis A., ABM and Non-proliferation: Related Issues, *Orbis,* 11 (1) 1967, 67-9.

*Fulbright, J.W., Foreign Policy Implications of the ABM Debate, *Bulletin of the Atomic Scientists,* 15 (6) 1969, 20-3.

*Garwin, Richard L. and Hans A. Bethe, Anti-Ballistic Missile Systems, *Scientific American,* 218 (3) 1968, 21-31.

*Gilpatrick, Roswell, Are We On The Brink of Another Arms Race?, *The New York Times Magazine,* January 15, 1967.

*Gilpatrick, Roswell, A 'Mad Momentum' May Be Under Way, *The New York Times Magazine,* December 13, 1967.

Hahn, Walter F. and Alvin J. Cottrell, Ballistic Missile Defense and Soviet Strategy, *Orbis* 9 (2) 1965. 316-37.

*Hamilton, Andrew, The Arms Race: Too Much of a Bad Thing, *The New York Times Magazine,* October 6, 1968.

*Hersh, Seymour M., The Great ABM Pork Barrel, *War/Peace Report,* 8 (1) 1968, 3-9, 19.

Herzfeld, Charles M., BMD and National Security, *Survival,* 8 (3) 1966, 70-6.

Herzfeld, Charles M., Ballistic Missile Defense: This Time for Real, *Nature,* 219, September 28, 1968, 1315-17.

Holst, Johan J., BMD and European Perspectives, in D.G. Brennan and Johan J. Holst, Ballistic Missile Defense: Two Views, *Adelphi Papers,* #43, 1967, 24-36.

*Inglis, David R., Missile Defense, Nuclear Spread, and Vietnam, *Bulletin of the Atomic Scientists,* 23 (5) 1967, 49-52.

*Inglis, David R., Conservative Judgment and Missile Madness, *Bulletin of the Atomic Scientists,* 24 (5) 1968, 6-11.

*Inglis, David R., Nuclear Threats, ABM Systems, and Proliferation, *Bulletin of the Atomic Scientists,* 24 (6) 1968, 2-4.

*Inglis, Davis R., The Anti-Ballistic Missile: A Dangerous Folly, *Saturday Review,* 51, September 7, 1968, 26-7, 55-6.

*Inglis, David R., H-Bombs in the Back Yard, *Saturday Review,* 51, December 21, 1968, 11-12, 44.

Kahn, Herman, **Why We Should Go Ahead With ABM,** *Fortune,* 79 (6) June 1969, 120-21, 212, 216.

*Kaysen, Carl, Keeping the Strategic Balance, *Foreign Affairs,* 46 (4) July, 1968, 665-75.

Kent, Glenn A., On the Interaction of Opposing Forces Under Possible Arms Agreements, Occasional Papers in *International Affairs* #5, Center for International Affairs, Harvard University, Cambridge, Mass., 1963, 36 pp.

*Lapp, Ralph E., From Nike to Safeguard: A Biography of the ABM, *The New York Times Magazine,* May 4, 1969.

*Lapp, Ralph E., The Vicious Acronyms, *The New Republic,* 160 (25) June 21, 1969, 15-19.

*Lapp, Ralph E., Fear of a First-Strike, *The New Republic,* 160 (26) June 28, 1969, 21-4.

*Long, Franklin A., Strategic Balance and the ABM, *Bulletin of the Atomic Scientists,* 24 (10) 1968, 2-5.

*McMahan, Richard H., Rationales for Ballistic Missile Defense Policy, *Bulletin of the Atomic Scientists,* 21 (3) 1965, 37-40.

Martin, Laurence W., Ballistic Missile Defense and Europe, *Bulletin of the Atomic Scientists,* 23 (5) 1967, 42-6.

Martin, Laurence W., Into the ABM Age, *Interplay,* 1 (5) 1967, 14-16.

Martin, Laurence W., Ballistic Missile Defense and the Strategic Balance, *The Year Book of World Affairs 1967,* Frederick A. Praeger, New York, 1967, 37-54.

Martin, Laurence W., Strategic Implications of BMD, *Survival,* 9 (7) 1967, 216-19.

Martin, Laurence W., Ballistic Missile Defense and Arms Control, *Arms Control and Disarmament,* 1 (1) 1968, 61-78.

Martin, Laurence W., The Great Missile Defense Debate, *Interplay,* 3 (1) 1969, 39-41.

*Miller, Raphael, The Metaphysical World of Strategic Systems, *Bulletin of the Atomic Scientists,* 24 (10) 1968, 18-22.

*Moldauer, Peter, The ABM Comes To Town, *Bulletin of the Atomic Scientists,* 25 (1) 1969, 4-6, 20.

Morton, Louis, The Anti-Ballistic Missile: Some Political and Strategic Considerations, *Virginia Quarterly Review,* 42 (1) 1966, 28-42.

*Parrent, Allan M., *The Problem of the Anti-Ballistic Missile,* Department of International Affairs, National Council of Churches, New York, 1967, 24 pp.

†Rabinowitch, Eugene and Ruth Adams (eds.), *Debate the Anti-ballistic Missile,* Bulletin of the Atomic Scientists, Chicago, 1967, 172 pp.

*Rathjens, George W., *The Future of the Strategic Arms Race: Options for the 1970's,* Carnegie Endowment for International Peace, New York, 1969, 53 pp.

*Rathjens, George W., The Dynamics of the Arms Race, *Scientific American,* 220 (4) 1969, 15-25.

*Rodberg, Leonard S., ABM—Some Arms Control Issues, *Bulletin of the Atomic Scientists,* 23 (6) 1967, 16-20.

*Rothstein, Robert L., The ABM, Proliferation and International Stability, *Foreign Affairs,* 46 (3) April 1968, 487-502.

*Ruina, J.D., The Nuclear Arms Race: Diagnosis and Treatment, *Bulletin of the Atomic Scientists,* 24 (8) 1968, 19-22.

Russet, Bruce M., The Complexities of Ballistic Missile Defense, *Yale Review,* 56 (3) March 1967, 354-67.

*Stone, Jeremy J., *Containing the Arms Race: Some Specific Proposals,* The M.I.T. Press, Cambridge, Mass., 1966, 252 pp.

*Stone, Jeremy J., ABM—The Next MLF?, *Bulletin of the Atomic Scientists,* 22 (7) 1966, 20-21.

*Stone, Jeremy J., The Anti-Missile Folly, *The New Leader,* January 2, 1967, 13-15.

*Stone, Jeremy J., Beginning of the Next Round?, *Bulletin of the Atomic Scientists,* 23 (10) 1967, 20-25.

*Stone, Jeremy J., Risks, Costs and Alternatives, in Dougherty and Lehman (eds.), *Arms Control for the Late Sixties, op. cit.,* 93-8.

*Stone, Jeremy J., The Case Against Missile Defenses, *Adelphi Papers,* #47, 1968, 15 pp.

Talensky, Nikolaj, Anti-Missile Systems and Disarmament, *International Affairs* (Moscow) (10) 1964, 15-19.

Teller, Edward, BMD in a Strategy for Peace, in Dougherty & Lehman (eds.), *Arms Control for the Late Sixties, op. cit.,* 99-112.

Thomas, John, The Role of Missile Defense in Soviet Strategy, *Military Review,* 44 (5) 1964, 46-58.

Thomas, John, The Role of Missile Defense in Soviet Strategy and Foreign Policy, in John Erickson (ed.), *The Military-Technical Revolution: Its Impact on Strategy and Foreign Policy,* Frederick A. Praeger, New York, 1966, 187-218.

Weinberg, Alvin M., Let Us Prepare for Peace, *Bulletin of the Atomic Scientists,* 24 (7) 1968, 17-20.

*Wiesner, Jerome B., The Cold War is Dead, But the Arms Race Rumbles On, *Bulletin of the Atomic Scientists,* 23 (6) 1967, 6-9.

*Wiesner, Jerome B., The Case Against An Anti-Ballistic Missile System, *Look,* 31 (24) November 28, 1967, 17-25.

*Willrich, Mason, ABM and Arms Control, *International Affairs,* 44 (2) 1968, 228-39.

*Yates, Sidney R., Showdown on the ABM, *Bulletin of the Atomic Scientists*, 25 (3) 1969, 29-32.

*Young, Elizabeth, ABM: No Alternative to Politics, *Bulletin of the Atomic Scientists*, 23 (6) 1967, 47-9.

Young, Oran R., Active Defense and International Order, *Bulletin of the Atomic Scientists*, 23 (5) 1967, 35-42.

Young, Oran R., The Political Consequences of Active Defense, *Bulletin of the Atomic Scientists*, 24 (2) 1968, 16-20.

Congressional Hearings:

United States Armament and Disarmament Problems, Hearings before the Subcommittee on Disarmament of the Committee on Foreign Relations, U.S. Senate, 90th Cong., 1st Sess., 1967.

Scope, Magnitude, and Implications of the United States Antiballistic Missile Program, Hearings before the Subcommittee on Military Applications of the Joint Committee on Atomic Energy, U.S. Congress, 90th Cong., 1st Sess., 1967.

Status of U.S. Strategic Power, Parts I-II, Hearings before the Preparedness Investigating Subcommittee of the Committee on Armed Services, U.S. Senate, 90th Cong., 2nd Sess., 1968.

Nonproliferation Treaty, Hearings before the Committee on Foreign Relations, U.S. Senate, 90th Cong., 2nd Sess., 1968.

Non-Proliferation Treaty, Part II, Hearings before the Committee on Foreign Relations, U.S. Senate, 91st Cong., 1st Sess., 1969.

Military Implications of the Treaty on the Non-proliferation of Nuclear Weapons, Hearings before the Committee on Armed Services, U.S. Senate, 91st Cong., 1st Sess., 1969.

Strategic and Foreign Policy Implications of ABM Systems, I–II, Hearings before the Subcommittee on International Organization and Disarmament Affairs of the Committee on Foreign Relations, U.S. Senate, 91st Cong., 1st Sess., 1969.

Strategy and Science: Toward a National Security Policy for the 1970's, Hearings before the Subcommittee on National Security Policy and Scientific Developments of the Committee on Foreign Affairs, U.S. House of Representatives, 91st Cong., 1st Sess., 1969.

Safeguard Antiballistic Missile System, Hearings before the Subcommittee of the Committee on Appropriations, U.S. House
of Representatives, 91st Cong. 1st Sess., 1969.

See also *Military Procurement Authorizations,* Hearings before the
Committee on Armed Services and the Subcommittee on
Appropriations, U.S. Senate (Annual hearings which con-
tain the "Posture Statements" of the Secretary of Defense).

NOTES ON CONTRIBUTORS

FRANK E. ARMBRUSTER is a specialist in military operations analysis with a strong background in foreign affairs and political analysis. Mr. Armbruster works at Hudson Institute on area studies of a political-military nature on Europe, Southeast Asia and China, as well as on analysis of present and future weapon systems and force postures of the U.S. and U.S.S.R. strategic forces. Mr. Armbruster is the author of "China's Conventional Military Capability," a chapter in Volume II of the book, *China in Crisis,* Tang Tsou (ed.), University of Chicago Press, 1969, and with other members of the Hudson Institute Staff, *Can We Win in Vietnam,* Frederick A. Praeger, 1968. Mr. Armbruster has extensive experience in the analysis and planning activities on military problems, including eight years as a senior intelligence specialist attached to the Directorate for Targets, Air Force Intelligence. Later he was the Chief of Operations Analysis at IT&T on the Strategic Air Command's 465L world-wide Command and Control System. In addition, Mr. Armbruster has worked as a consultant to the Special Studies Group of the Institute for Defense Analyses. Born in 1923, Mr. Armbruster received his A.B. degree in Foreign Affairs from George Washington University and in International Law at American University. He is a member of the Operations Research Society of America, the U.S. Naval Institute, and the Foreign Service Professional Fraternity.

DONALD G. BRENNAN is a mathematician and a student of national security problems with special interests in advanced military policy, alliance relationships, and selected areas of arms control, such as policy issues relating to ballistic missile defense. Prior to joining Hudson Institute, of which he was President from July 1962 until May 1964 and where he now conducts research studies, Dr. Brennan worked for nine years as a research mathematician and communication theorist at Lincoln Laboratory of M.I.T. In addition to technical research there, he devoted substantial time to studies of arms control and national security problems. Dr. Brennan has served as consultant to the Departments of State and Defense, the Arms Control and Disarmament Agency, the Executive Office of the President, and is a member of a Task Force of the Defense Science Board. He is editor of the well-known anthology, *Arms Control, Disarmament, and National Security,* George Braziller, 1961, sponsored by The American Academy of Arts and Sciences. He is editor of the new international journal, *Arms Control and National Security* and has edited studies of future military technology. He has lectured on national security at Harvard, M.I.T., the University of California, and several European defense study centers as well as conducting arms control seminars in Moscow. Born in 1926, Dr. Brennan received his B.S. (1955) and Ph.D. degrees in Mathematics from M.I.T. where he was a Gerard Swope Fellow. He is a Senior member of the Institute of Electrical and Electronic Engineering, the American Mathematical Society, and the Institute for Strategic Studies (London).

RAYMOND D. GASTIL was born in 1931 in San Diego, California. Dr. Gastil received his B.A. degree in Social Relations (1953), M.A. in Middle Eastern Studies (1956), and his Ph.D. degree in Social Science (1958) from Harvard. On a Fulbright Grant (1953-54) he attended the University of the Punjab studying Islam, Persian, and Urdu. In 1956-57 he returned to do field work on Iranian culture in Shiraz, Iran, on a Ford Foundation Fellowship. After a year at the Center for International Affairs (Harvard), Dr. Gastil taught anthropology and social science at the University of Oregon from 1959-62. Dr. Gastil has performed studies for the Office of Economic Opportunity, Department of Health, Education and Welfare, the Arms Control and Disarmament Agency, and the Department of Defense Research and Engineering. His work has included the strategic analysis of nuclear war policy, studies of the U.S. birth rate, guerrilla warfare, and poverty. He has contributed to a number of professional journals, and to *The Year 2000: A Framework for Speculation on the Next Thirty-Three Years,* Herman Kahn and Anthony J.

Wiener, Macmillan Company, 1967. He is a co-author of *Can We Win in Vietnam*, Frederick A. Praeger, 1968.

CHARLES M. HERZFELD, a physicist, is Technical Director of the Defense Space Group of the International Telephone and Telegraph Corporation, and a Fellow Member of Hudson Institute. From 1961 through 1967, he served in the Advanced Research Projects Agency of the Department of Defense. He was Director of Ballistic Missile Defense Research, Deputy Director, and finally Director of the Agency from 1965 through 1967. He was awarded the Meritorious Service Medal of the Department of Defense in 1967. Born in Vienna, Austria in 1925, Dr. Herzfeld came to the U.S. in 1942, and became a naturalized citizen in 1949. He received a B.S. degree in Chemical Engineering from Catholic University in 1945, and a Ph.D. degree in Chemical Physics from the University of Chicago in 1951. Prior to joining the Advanced Research Projects Agency he was Associate Director of the Bureau of Standards and Professor of physics at the University of Maryland.

JOHAN J. HOLST, a member of the professional staff of Hudson Institute, is a graduate of the Norwegian Army Language School (in Russian), received his B.A. in Government (1960) from Columbia College and the Magistergrad in Political Science (1965) from the University of Oslo. In 1962-63 he was research associate at the Center for International Affairs, Harvard University. From 1963 to 1967, he was on the research staff of the systems analysis division of the Norwegian Defense Research Establishment where he directed research on arms control and long-range defense planning. He is the author of *Norsk sikkerhetspolitikk i strategisk perspektiv* (Norwegian Security Policy in Strategic Perspective), Vols I-II, Oslo, 1967, and the first monograph to be published in Europe on ballistic missile defense: *Antirobotvapen - hot eller löfte?* (Antimissile Weapons: Threat or Promise?), Stockholm, 1967. He has contributed to such publications as *Adelphi Papers, Arms Control and Disarmament, Cooperation and Conflict, International Journal* and various Scandinavian journals. He has lectured at the National and Navy War Colleges, as well as at various Universities, research centers and conferences in the United States, Canada and Europe, and is a member of the Harvard-M.I.T. Arms Control Seminar and the Institute for Strategic Studies. He has newly been appointed Director of Research of the Norwegian Institute of International Affairs in Oslo.

HERMAN KAHN, a physicist and specialist in public policy analyses, is Director and Trustee of Hudson Institute and was its principal founder. As Director, he is the senior officer and has principal responsibility for the over-all research program. Among his major interests at Hudson Institute have been studies on Latin American and other development problems, inquiries into alternative world futures and long-run (10 to 35 years) political, economic, technological and cultural changes, and research into strategic warfare and basic national security policies.

Before he left to help found Hudson Institute in 1961, Mr. Kahn was associated for twelve years with The RAND Corporation. There he worked on problems in applied physics and mathematics, operations research and systems analysis, weapon design, particle and radiation diffusion, civil defense, and stategic warfare. During 1959 he was on leave for six months as a Visiting Research Associate at the Princeton Center for International Studies while working on the manuscript of his book, *On Thermonuclear War.*

Mr. Kahn is the author of five books: *On Thermonuclear War,* Princeton University Press, New Jersey, 1960; *Thinking about the Unthinkable* , Horizon Press, New York, 1962; *On Escalation: Metaphors and Scenarios,* Frederick A. Praeger, New York, 1965; in collaboration with Anthony J. Wiener, *The Year 2000: A Framework for Speculation on the Next Thirty-Three Years,* The Macmillan Company, New York, 1967, prepared for the Commission on the Year 2000 of the American Academy of Arts and Sciences; and with members of the Institute Staff, *Can We Win in Vietnam?,* Praeger, New York, 1968. He has written articles for such publications as *The New York Times Magazine, Fortune, Saturday Evening Post, Bulletin of the Atomic Scientists, Daedalus,* and *Commentary,* and has also contributed articles to several books on defense and foreign policies.

Born in 1922, Mr. Kahn holds a B.A. degree in Physics and Mathematics from the University of California at Los Angeles (1945) and M.S. degree in Physics from California Institute of Technology (1948). He is a member of the Council on Foreign Relations (New York), the Center for Inter-American Relations, the American Political Science Association, Phi Beta Kappa, and Phi Mu Epsilon.

WILLIAM SCHNEIDER, JR. is an economist with a background in monetary and international economics, and national security policy issues. At Hudson Institute, Dr. Schneider has been engaged in research on strategic nuclear force exchanges, Soviet budget policy, and the modeling of defense problems. Born in 1941, he received his B.S. degree from Villanova University and his Ph.D. degree from New York University. He is a member of the American Economic Association, the Econometric Society, and the Institute for Strategic Studies (London).

MICHAEL E. SHERMAN is a Canadian political scientist with a primary interest in international affairs. His studies at Hudson have included such subjects as controlling the spread of nuclear weapons, nuclear sharing and NATO strategy, the problem of communication and bargaining in strategic nuclear war, and third party peacekeeping in local conflicts. Dr. Sherman has contributed to the Institute for Strategic Studies' (London) series of *Adelphi Papers,* and to the Canadian periodicals, *International Journal* and *Behind the Headlines.* He is also the author of *Nuclear Proliferation: The Treaty and After,* Canadian Institute of International Affairs, Toronto, 1968, and *Nuclear Sharing: The Canadian Experience* to be published in 1969. Born in 1937, Dr. Sherman received his B.A. from the University of Toronto (Honors Philosophy and History) and his Ph.D. from Harvard (Government.)

PROFESSOR ALBERT WOHLSTETTER, University Professor at the University of Chicago and a Fellow of the Center for Policy Studies, was trained as a mathematical logician and economist. During World War II, he worked on problems of reliability and quality control in electronic and electrical equipment. He has been a member of the RAND Research Council, Professor in Residence at UCLA, Ford Professor at the University of California at Berkeley, and a Fellow Member of Hudson Institute. He was science advisor at the Geneva Arms Control Conference in 1958 on Reducing the Likelihood of Surprise Attack. Professor Wohlstetter received the Distinguished Civilian Service Medal from the Department of Defense in 1964. For the last eighteen years Professor Wohlstetter has done research on problems of arms and arms control and specifically on protecting strategic forces and stabilizing deterrence. He is the author and co-author of numerous articles and several book-length studies. Some of these studies originated the first-strike second-strike distinction, failsafe procedures for reducing the probability of accidental war, programs for hardening strategic vehicles against ballistic missile attacks, and other devices and methods of operation now in use by our strategic forces.

INDEX